PEARSON ALWAYS LEARNING

A Concise Public Speaking Handbook
with APA Update

Custom Edition for
The University of New Mexico

Taken from:
*A Concise Public Speaking
Handbook*, Fourth Edition
by Steven A. Beebe
and Susan J. Beebe

*What Every Student Should Know
About Citing Sources with
APA Documentation: Updated for
APA Sixth Edition*, Second Edition
by Chalon E. Anderson,
Amy T. Carrell,
and Jimmy L. Widdifield Jr.

Cover Art: Courtesy of Photodisc/Getty Images.

Taken from:

A Concise Public Speaking Handbook,
Fourth Edition
by Steven A. Beebe and Susan J. Beebe
Copyright © 2015 by Pearson Education, Inc.
Upper Saddle River, New Jersey 07458

*What Every Student Should Know About Citing
Sources with APA Documentation: Updated for
APA Sixth Edition*, Second Edition
by Chalon E. Anderson, Amy T. Carrell,
and Jimmy L. Widdifield Jr.
Copyright © 2010 by Pearson Education, Inc.
Upper Saddle River, New Jersey 07458

This special edition published in cooperation with
Pearson Learning Solutions.

All trademarks, service marks, registered
trademarks, and registered service marks are the
property of their respective owners and are used
herein for identification purposes only.

Pearson Learning Solutions, 501 Boylston Street,
Suite 900, Boston, MA 02116
A Pearson Education Company
www.pearsoned.com

Printed in the United States of America

6 7 8 9 10 V0ZN 18 17 16 15 14

000200010271910109

LA

ISBN 10: 1-269-91181-3
ISBN 13: 978-1-269-91181-8

Contents

Preface

This fourth edition of *A Concise Public Speaking Handbook* integrates the steps in preparing and delivering a speech with the ongoing process of considering the audience. Although developed and delivered by the speaker, a good speech is centered on the needs, values, and hopes of the audience. Therefore, the audience should be kept in mind during every step of the speech crafting and delivery process. Being "audience-centered" means that, as a speaker, you are constantly aware of and striving to adapt to the cultural, gender, and experiential diversity of the people to whom you are speaking. Adapting to diverse audiences is incorporated into every step of the audience-centered approach.

A Concise Public Speaking Handbook, Fourth Edition, also emphasizes that an effective speaker is an ethical speaker. Ethical speakers articulate truthful messages, formulated so as to give the audience free choice in responding to the message, while also using effective means of ensuring message clarity and credibility. In addition to emphasizing ethics throughout the book, and in Chapter 4, "Ethics and Free Speech," we provide an Ethics Assessment question at the end of each chapter to spark thought and discussion on ethical issues in public speaking.

New to the Fourth Edition

> New **learning objectives** at the beginning of every chapter provide a preview of chapter content and help students focus their study.

> New and **expanded examples** throughout the text ensure that the examples are contemporary and useful for students.

> New **How To** boxes provide clear instructions for applying textbook concepts to real-life public speaking.

> Additional information on the sources of public-speaking anxiety in Chapter 2 helps students build confidence by understanding that most people are nervous.

> Updated discussion of listening styles in Chapter 5 helps students use the strengths and overcome the challenges of their particular style.

> Updated discussion of sex, gender, and sexual orientation in Chapter 6 emphasizes the importance of considering variations in listeners' gender and sexual identities, and an expanded table helps guide students as they analyze their speaking situations.

> Updated section on evaluating Internet resources in Chapter 9 adds new discussions of Wikipedia and domains, as it guides students to think critically about information they find on the Internet. Suggestions for research strategy are updated to reflect the technology many students use today.

> Revised discussion of signposting in Chapter 11 helps students understand how these organizational clues help communicate their message to listeners.

> Added discussion of using tablet computers or other technology to hold speaking notes updates Chapter 14.

> Chapter 17 offers new tips for effective eye contact, gestures, and facial expressions in speeches delivered via videoconferencing or similar technology.

> Updated and streamlined discussion in Chapter 19 helps students understand how to adapt their delivery to diverse audiences.

> A broader discussion of computer-generated presentation aids in Chapter 20 includes popular new alternatives to PowerPoint^{TM}.

> Streamlined discussion in Chapter 22 clarifies how to paint word pictures to help listeners understand information.

> New section on reasoning by sign in Chapter 24 expands the repertoire of reasoning techniques students can use in their persuasive speeches.

> New section on using evidence effectively in persuasive speaking helps students to organize and craft successful persuasive talks (Chapter 24).

Every chapter contains a number of effective, pedagogical features, including:

> **Learning Objectives** listed at the beginning of every chapter.
> **Quick Checks**—Lists of items that can be checked off as each step in the process of preparing a speech is completed.
> **How To** boxes—Clear instructions for applying textbook concepts to real-life public speaking.
> **Study Guides**—At the end of each chapter, a summary of chapter content that reinforces the learning objectives from the beginning of the chapter. Each end-of-chapter Study Guide also includes (1) Self Assessment questions to help readers evaluate how prepared they are to apply the chapter material in their own speeches; (2) Ethics Assessment questions designed to encourage consideration of ethical issues; and (3) Critical Assessment questions, a variety of speechmaking scenarios to help students think critically and further apply chapter concepts.

Strategies to Improve Speaker Confidence

To help students manage the anxiety they may experience when they think about speaking to an audience, an entire chapter (Chapter 2) is devoted to improving speaker confidence. Techniques for managing speaker apprehension, such as how to look for positive listener support when delivering a message, are also included throughout the book.

Critical Listening Skills

Besides learning how to speak in public, one of the most valued benefits of studying public speaking is becoming a more discriminating listener. A section on listening, critical thinking, and analyzing and evaluating speeches helps students better understand their roles as speakers and listeners, and Critical Assessment questions at the ends of chapters offer further critical thinking, listening, and analysis opportunities.

Instructor and Student Resources

Key instructor resources include an Instructor's Manual (ISBN 020598259X) and Test Bank (ISBN 0205996973), available at www.pearsonhighered.com (instructor login required). Also available is Pearson's MySearchLab™, a valuable tool to help students conduct online research. Access to MySearchLab is available in an optional package with new copies of this text or for purchase at **www.mysearchlab.com** (access code required).

For a complete list of the instructor and student resources available with the text, please visit the Pearson Communication catalog, at www.pearsonhighered.com/communication.

Acknowledgments

Thanks to Sheralee Connors, our development editor, for spearheading this revision and working so closely with us. We are extremely grateful to all of the instructors who provided us with invaluable feedback that helped shape the features and content within this new edition. We'd like to extend our sincere appreciation to the following instructors who shared their expertise and insight: Martin Arnold, University of Connecticut; Merry Buchanan, University of Central Oklahoma; Jethro DeLisle, Tacoma Community College; Richard Falvo, El Paso Community College; Tina McDermott, Antelope Valley College; Amy Smith, Salem State University; Jason Stone, Oklahoma State University – Oklahoma City; Thomas Wright, Temple University.

STEVEN A. BEEBE
SUSAN J. BEEBE

1 Speaking in Public

OBJECTIVES

1. Explain why it is important to study public speaking.
2. Discuss in brief the history of public speaking.
3. Sketch and explain a model that illustrates the components and the process of communication.

Why Study Public Speaking?

As you study public speaking, you will learn and practice strategies for effective delivery and critical listening. You will discover new applications for skills you may already have, such as focusing and organizing ideas and gathering information from print and electronic sources. In addition to learning and applying these fundamental skills, you will gain long-term advantages related to *empowerment* and *employment*.

The ability to speak with competence and confidence will provide **empowerment**. It will give you an edge that less skilled communicators lack—even those who may have superior ideas, training, and/or experience.

Perhaps an even more compelling reason to study public speaking is that the skills you develop may someday help you get a job. In a nationwide survey, prospective employers of college graduates said they seek candidates with "public speaking and presentation ability."[1] Surveys of personnel managers, both in the United States and internationally, have confirmed that they consider communication skills the top factor in helping college graduates obtain employment. (See Table 1.1.) Furthermore, billionaire investor Warren Buffet suggests that strong communication skills can help you earn more throughout your career.[2]

TABLE 1.1 Top Skills Valued by Employers

Rank	Results of Survey of Personnel Directors[3]	Results of Survey by College Career Department[4]	Results of Survey of Prospective Employers[5]	Results Compiled from Several Research Studies[6]
1	Spoken communication skills	Communication and interpersonal skills	Communication skills	Communication skills
2	Written communication skills	Intelligence	Honesty and integrity	Analytical/ Research skills
3	Listening ability	Enthusiasm	Teamwork	Technical skills
4	Enthusiasm	Flexibility	Interpersonal skills	Flexibility/ Adaptability
5	Technical competence	Leadership	Motivation/ Initiative	Interpersonal skills

The Rich Heritage of Public Speaking

When you study public speaking, you are also joining a long history with many traditions, including the following:

> **Fourth to first centuries** BCE. During this golden age of public speaking, the Greek philosopher Aristotle formulated, and Roman orators refined, guidelines for speakers that we still follow today.
> **Nineteenth century.** Students of public speaking practiced the arts of **declamation**—the delivery of an already famous address—and **elocution**—the expression of emotion through posture, movement, gestures, facial expression, and voice.
> **Twentieth and twenty-first centuries.** Audio, video, computer, and mobile technologies let speakers reach worldwide audiences and expand the parameters of public speaking, as they draw on age-old public-speaking traditions to address some of the most difficult challenges in history.

The Communication Process

Even the earliest communication theorists recognized that communication is a process. The models they formulated were linear, suggesting a simple transfer of meaning from sender to receiver. Later researchers began to consider more elements in the process.

Communication as Action

> A public speaker is a **source** of information and ideas for an audience.
> The job of the source or speaker is to **encode**, or translate, the ideas and images in his or her mind into a **code**, made up of verbal or nonverbal symbols, that an audience can recognize. The speaker may encode into words (for example, "The fabric should be two inches square") or into gestures (showing the size with his or her hands).
> The **message** in public speaking is the speech itself—both what is said and how it is said.
> If a speaker has trouble finding words to convey his or her ideas or sends contradictory nonverbal symbols, listeners may not be able to **decode** the speaker's verbal and nonverbal symbols back into a message.
> A message is usually transmitted from sender to receiver via two **channels**: *visual* and *auditory*. Audience members see the speaker and decode his or her nonverbal symbols—eye contact (or lack of it), facial expressions, posture, gestures, and dress. If the speaker uses any visual aids, such as PowerPoint™ slides or models, these too are transmitted along the visual channel. The auditory channel opens as the speaker speaks. Then the audience members hear words and such vocal cues as inflection, rate, and voice quality.
> The **receiver** of the message is the individual audience member, whose decoding of the message will depend on his or her own particular blend of past experiences, attitudes, beliefs, and values. An effective public speaker should be receiver- or audience-centered.

> Anything that interferes with the communication of a message is called *noise*. **External noise** is physical, such as the roar of a lawn mower or a noisy air conditioner. **Internal noise** may stem from either physiological or psychological causes and may directly affect either the source or the receiver. A bad cold (physiological noise) may cloud a speaker's memory or subdue his or her delivery. An audience member who is worried about an upcoming exam (psychological noise) is unlikely to remember much of what the speaker says. Noise interferes with the transmission of a message.

Communication as Interaction

One way that public speaking differs from casual conversation is that the public speaker does most or all of the talking. But public speaking is still interactive. See Figure 1.1 for an interactive model of communication. Without an audience to hear and provide **feedback**, public speaking serves little purpose.

The **context** of a public-speaking experience is the environment or situation in which the speech occurs. It

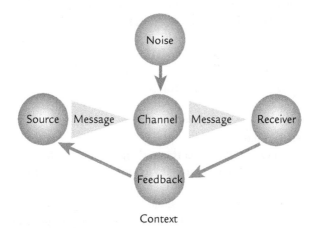

FIGURE 1.1 | An interactive model of communication. Visit this chapter of MySearchLab (**www.mysearchlab.com**) to see more models of communication.

includes such elements as the time, the place, and both the speaker's and the audience's cultural traditions and expectations. For example, if the room is hot, crowded, or poorly lit, these conditions affect both speaker and audience. A speaker who fought rush-hour traffic for 90 minutes to arrive at his or her destination may find it difficult to muster much enthusiasm for delivering the speech.

Communication as Transaction

The most recent communication models focus on communication as a simultaneous process. For example, in a two-person communication transaction, both individuals are sending and receiving at the same time. In public speaking, listeners nonverbally express their thoughts and feelings at the same time the speaker is talking.

Public Speaking and Conversation

Models of communication suggest that public speaking has much in common with conversation. Public speaking also differs from conversation in the following key ways.

Public Speaking Is More Planned Public speaking is more planned than conversation. A public speaker may spend hours or even days planning and practicing his or her speech.

HOW TO

Respond to Audience Messages

When you have a conversation, you have to make decisions "on your feet." For example, if your friends look puzzled or interrupt with questions, you reexplain your idea. You can use the same audience-centered skills to help you become an effective and confident speaker. Pay attention to the nods, facial expressions, and murmurings of the audience. Respond to those messages by adjusting your rate of speaking, volume, vocabulary, or other variables. As a bonus, focusing on the needs of your audience can keep you from focusing on any nervousness you might be feeling.

Public Speaking Is More Formal   Public speaking is also more formal than conversation. The slang or casual language you often use in conversation is not appropriate for most public speaking. Audiences expect speakers to use standard English grammar and vocabulary.

The nonverbal communication of public speakers is also more formal than nonverbal behavior in ordinary conversation. People engaged in conversation often sit or stand close together, gesture spontaneously, and move about restlessly. The physical distance between public speakers and their audiences is usually greater than that between people in conversation. And public speakers often plan and rehearse some gestures and movements to emphasize especially important parts of their speeches.

Roles of Speakers and Audiences Are More Clearly Defined   Public speaking is less fluid and interactive than conversation. People in conversation may alternately talk and listen and perhaps even interrupt one another, but in public speaking, the roles of speaker and audience are more clearly defined and remain stable. Rarely do audience members interrupt or even talk to speakers.

QUICK CHECK

Become an Effective Public Speaker

- Plan your speech.
- Focus and vocalize your thoughts.
- Adapt your speaking to your listeners.
- Use standard English vocabulary and grammar.
- Use more formal nonverbal communication.

STUDY GUIDE

MEET YOUR OBJECTIVES

1. **Explain why it is important to study public speaking.** Public speaking can empower you and help you secure employment or advance your career.

2. **Discuss in brief the history of public speaking.** Speakers today use many technologies to deliver speeches, but rely on guidelines formulated more than 2,000 years ago in ancient Greece and Rome.

3. **Sketch and explain a model that illustrates the components and the process of communication.** Public speaking is an example of the communication process, by which a source transmits a message through a channel to a receiver within a particular context. Senders and receivers simultaneously exchange messages and feedback to build a shared meaning. Public speaking is more formal and planned, with clearly defined roles, than conversation.

THINK ABOUT THESE QUESTIONS

1. **Self Assessment** Review Table 1.1 on page 2. Rate yourself, using a scale of 1 to 5 (1 = poor; 5 = excellent), on the skills listed in the table. How do your spoken communication skills compare with your ratings on the other skills listed in the table?

2. **Ethics Assessment** *Declamation* is defined as "the delivery of an already famous address." Is it ethical to deliver a speech that was written and/or already delivered by someone else? Explain your answer.

3. **Critical Assessment** Reflect on the most recent public-speaking situation in which you were an audience member. Identify the specific elements in the communication model presented in Figure 1.1. Which elements of the model explain the speaker's effectiveness? (For example, the message was interesting and there was little noise.) If the speaker was ineffective, which elements in the model explain why the speaker was ineffective?

2

Improving Your Confidence

OBJECTIVES

1. Explain the reasons for and processes involved in nervousness about public speaking.
2. Describe effective strategies for building public-speaking confidence.

Understand Your Nervousness

It's normal to be nervous about giving a speech. Most people are nervous.[1] More than 80 percent of people report feeling anxious about public speaking,[2] and one in five college students feels "highly apprehensive" about speaking in front of others.[3] In one classic survey, respondents said that they were more afraid of public speaking than of death![4]

Given these facts, it is unrealistic to try to eliminate speech anxiety. Your goal is to understand and manage your nervousness so that it does not keep you from speaking effectively.

Know Your Reasons for Anxiety

Understanding why you are nervous is the first step to making nervousness work *for* you instead of against you.[5] As you read the following list, you'll probably find a reason that resonates with you.

> One study found several reasons people feel anxious about public speaking: fear of humiliation, concern about not being prepared, worry about their appearance, pressure to perform, personal insecurity, concern that the audience won't be interested in them or the speech, lack of experience, fear of making mistakes, and an overall fear of failure.[6]

> Another study found that men are likely to experience more anxiety than women when speaking to people from a culture different from their own.[7]
> There is also evidence that being a perfectionist may be linked to increased apprehension.[8]

In addition to the reasons we've listed, some people may have inherited a trait, or genetic tendency, to feel more anxiety than others would in any speechmaking situation.[9] Even if you have a biological tendency to feel nervous, you can still use strategies to help you manage your apprehension.[10]

Use Your Anxiety

Begin by realizing that you are going to feel more nervous than you look. Your audience cannot see evidence of everything you feel. If you worry that you are going to appear nervous to others, you may, in fact, increase your own internal symptoms of anxiety:

> extra adrenaline
> increased blood flow
> pupil dilation
> increased endorphins to block pain
> increased heart rate

Realize Your Body Is Helping You   Even if you do experience these symptoms, they are not all bad. Believe it or not, your body is actually trying to help your brain deal with the difficult task of public speaking.[11] Physical changes caused by anxiety improve your energy level and help you function better than you might otherwise. Your heightened state of readiness can actually help you speak better, especially if you are able to relabel your feelings. Speakers who label their feelings as "excitement" or "enthusiasm" feel less anxious than do people who experience the same physical changes but call them "nervousness," "fear," or "anxiety."[12]

Know Your Apprehension Style   Do you fit into one of the following four apprehension styles? Knowing your style can help you choose the most effective confidence-building strategies for *you* and predict the point in the speechmaking process when you will need them most.

> **Confrontational** speakers have the most anxiety and highest heart rates as they begin speaking, then taper off to average levels as they continue. Most people are in this group, and they can make good use of strategies that help them prepare and calm themselves *before* they begin speaking.

> **Inflexible** speakers feel high levels of anxiety and show the highest heart rates all the way through their speeches. These speakers may need to use many strategies, *before, during,* and *after* their speeches.

> **Average** speakers generally approach public speaking positively and show average heart rate increases while speaking. The most helpful strategies for them may vary speech by speech.

> **Insensitive** speakers are usually experienced speakers. They feel little apprehension and have the lowest heart rates while speaking. They may already be using many strategies.

How to Build Your Confidence

There are several more things you can do to help manage your nervousness and anxiety.

Know Your Audience

Learn as much about your audience as you can. The more you can anticipate their reactions to your speech, the more comfortable you will be in delivering your message.

Don't Procrastinate

Fear of speaking often leads speakers to delay preparing their speeches until the last minute. The lack of thorough preparation often results in a poorer speech performance, which reinforces a speaker's perception that public speaking is difficult. Don't let fear freeze you into inaction. Take charge by preparing early.

Select an Appropriate Topic

You will feel less nervous if you talk about something with which you are familiar or in which you have a lot of interest. Your focus on the subject of your speech will be reflected in your delivery.

Be Prepared

Being prepared means that you have researched your topic, developed a logically coherent outline, and practiced your speech several times before you deliver it.

Be Organized

Most speeches should have a beginning, a middle, and an end and should follow a logical outline pattern. Anxiety about a speech assignment decreases and confidence increases when you closely follow the directions and rules for developing a speech.

Know Your Introduction and Conclusion

Actor and famed public speaker George Jessel once quipped, "The human brain starts working the moment you are born and never stops until you stand up to speak in public." As we noted earlier, the opening moments of your speech are when you are likely to feel the most anxious. Being familiar with your introduction will help you feel more comfortable about the entire speech.

If you also know how you will end your speech, you will have a safe harbor in case you lose your place. If you need to end your speech prematurely, a well-delivered conclusion can permit you to make a graceful exit.

Make Practice Real

Practice aloud. Stand up. Vividly imagine the room where you will give your speech, or consider rehearsing in the actual room. Picture what you will be wearing and what the audience will look like.

Breathe

Nervous speakers tend to take short, shallow breaths. Break that pattern: Take a few slow, deep breaths before you rise to speak. Besides breathing deeply, try to relax your entire body.

Channel Your Nervous Energy

An adrenaline boost before speaking can make you jittery. Channel the energy, using tips from the How To box.

Dissipate Nervous Energy

- Take a slow walk before you arrive at your speech location.
- While seated and waiting to speak, keep both feet on the floor and wiggle your toes.
- Gently (and without calling attention to yourself) grab the edge of your chair and squeeze it.
- Unobtrusively, lightly tense and release the muscles in your legs and arms.
- As you wait to be introduced, think and act calm to feel calm.
- Walk to the front of the room as though you were calm.
- Take a moment to look for a friendly, supportive face before you begin.

Visualize Your Success

Imagine yourself giving your speech. Picture yourself walking confidently to the front and delivering your well-prepared opening remarks. Visualize yourself giving the entire speech as a controlled, confident speaker. Imagine yourself calm and in command.

Give Yourself a Mental Pep Talk

Replace any negative, anxious thoughts with positive messages, such as the following:

Negative Thought	Positive Self-Talk
I'm going to forget what I'm supposed to say.	I've practiced this speech many times. I've got notes to prompt me. If I lose my

| | place, no one will know I'm not following my outline. |
| So many people are looking at me. | I can do this! My listeners want me to do a good job. I'll seek out friendly faces when I feel nervous. |

Focus on Your Message, Not on Your Fear

The more you think about being anxious about speaking, the more you will increase your level of anxiety. Instead, in the few minutes before you speak, mentally review your major ideas, your introduction, and your conclusion. Focus on your ideas rather than on your fear.

Look for Positive Listener Support

When you are aware of positive audience support, you will feel more confident and less nervous. Although there may be some audiences that won't respond positively to you or your message, the overwhelming majority of listeners will be positive. It may help to prepare speeches with a group of classmates who will offer one another support.[13] And when you are listening, be sure to support other speakers with your full attention.

Seek Speaking Opportunities

The more experience you gain as a public speaker, the less nervous you will feel. Consider joining organizations and clubs that provide opportunities for you to participate in public presentations, such as Toastmasters, an organization dedicated to improving public-speaking skills.

Focus on What You Have Accomplished, Not on Your Fear

When you finish your speech, tell yourself something positive to celebrate your accomplishment. Say to yourself, "I did it! I spoke and people listened." Don't replay your mental image of yourself as nervous and fearful. Instead, mentally replay your success in communicating with your listeners.

QUICK CHECK

Build Your Confidence

- Prepare your speech early.
- Know your audience and select an appropriate topic.
- Be prepared and well organized. Know your introduction and conclusion.
- Re-create the speech environment when you practice.
- Use deep-breathing techniques.
- Channel your nervous energy.
- Visualize your success.
- Give yourself a mental pep talk.
- Focus on your message, not on your fear.
- Look for positive listener support.
- Seek additional speaking opportunities.
- After your speech, focus on your accomplishment, not on your anxiety.

STUDY GUIDE

MEET YOUR OBJECTIVES

1. **Explain the reasons for and processes involved in nervousness about public speaking.**
   Genetic traits, as well as several specific reasons, can cause anxiety. Physical symptoms, such as a racing heart, are signs your body is trying to support you. Speakers can also experience different types of anxiety.

2. **Describe effective strategies for building public-speaking confidence.**
   Manage your apprehension by being prepared and knowing your audience, imagining the speech environment when you rehearse, and using relaxation techniques, such as visualization, deep breathing, and focusing thoughts away from your fears.

THINK ABOUT THESE QUESTIONS

1. **Self Assessment** Visit MySearchLab (www.mysearchlab.com) for tests to measure your general level of public-speaking apprehension.

2. **Ethics Assessment** Should a speaker reveal to the audience that he or she is nervous?

3. **Critical Assessment** Mike Roberts, president of his fraternity, is nervous about his first report to the university academic council. What advice would you give him?

Presenting Your First Speech

3

OBJECTIVES

1. Explain why it is important to be audience-centered during each step of the speechmaking process.
2. Select and narrow an appropriate topic for a speech.
3. Differentiate between a general speech purpose and a specific speech purpose.
4. Develop a sentence that captures the central idea of a speech.
5. Identify three strategies for generating the main ideas for a speech.
6. Describe several types of supporting material that could be used to support speech ideas.
7. Develop a speech with three main organizational parts—an introduction, a body, and a conclusion.
8. Identify successful strategies for rehearsing a speech.
9. Describe the essential elements of effective speech delivery.

Consider Your Audience

Although you have heard countless speeches in your life, you may still have questions about how a speaker prepares and presents a speech. To help you begin, this chapter gives a step-by-step overview of the steps and skills you need for your first speech. Those steps are diagrammed in Figure 3.1.

Considering your audience is at the center of the model, because your audience influences the topic you choose and every later step of the speechmaking process. Considering the audience is a continuous process rather than a step in preparing a speech.

16

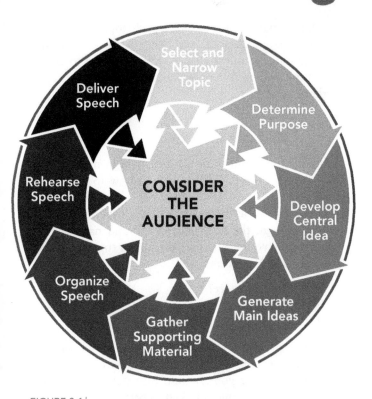

FIGURE 3.1 | This model of the speechmaking process emphasizes the importance of considering your audience as you work on each task in the process of designing and presenting a speech.

Being audience-centered involves making decisions about the content and style of your speech *before* you speak, based on knowledge of your audience's attitudes, values, and beliefs. If you learn new information about your audience at any point during the process of preparing your speech, you may need to revise your thinking or your material. It also means being sensitive to your audience's responses *during* the speech so that you can make appropriate adjustments.

To be effective, an audience-centered speaker also needs to understand, affirm, and adapt to diverse audiences. Such factors as the gender, ethnicity, and culture of audience members influence their expectations for appropriate and effective speech topics, argument structure, language style, and delivery. To adapt to the expectations of your audience, you may need to adjust your topic and pattern of organization, delivery style, or perhaps your attire.

Select and Narrow Your Topic

While keeping your audience foremost in mind, determine what you will talk about and how to limit your topic to fit the constraints of your speaking assignment.

You might be asked to speak about a specific subject. Often, though, the task of selecting and narrowing a topic will be yours. You may discover a topic by asking three standard questions:

1. Who is the audience?
2. What is the occasion?
3. What are my interests, talents, and experiences?

Once you choose your topic, narrow it to fit the time limit for your talk. Allow plenty of time to choose your topic and prepare your speech. Research suggests that more preparation time is linked to better grades.[1]

Determine Your Purpose

Decide on both a general purpose and a specific purpose before you start the research process. There are three **general purposes** for giving speeches:

1. **To inform.** The primary objective of class lectures, seminars, and workshops is to inform. When you inform, you teach, define, illustrate, clarify, or elaborate on a topic.
2. **To persuade.** Ads on TV and radio, sermons, political speeches, and sales presentations are designed to persuade. When you persuade, you seek to change or reinforce attitudes, beliefs, values, or behavior.
3. **To entertain.** After-dinner speeches and comic monologues are intended mainly as entertainment.

The key to an effective, entertaining speech lies in your choice of stories, examples, and illustrations, as well as in your delivery.

After you are sure you understand your general purpose, formulate a **specific purpose**: a concise statement indicating what you want your listeners to be able to do when you finish your speech. For example, "At the end of my speech, the class will be able to describe how to get assigned to a counselor from the campus counseling service."

Create and Use a Specific-Purpose Statement

- Always consider your audience.
- Start with the phrase *By the end of my speech the audience will [be able to]...*
- Add your goal. State the response you desire, in precise, measurable terms.
- Write down the entire specific purpose, and keep it before you as you gather ideas for your talk.
- Use your specific purpose to guide your research and help you choose supporting materials.
- Modify your purpose, if necessary, while you prepare your speech.

Develop Your Central Idea

You should now be able to write the **central idea** of your speech, sometimes called your *thesis statement*. Your central idea identifies the essence of your message. Think of it as a one-sentence summary of your speech. If you met someone in the elevator after your speech, and this person asked you to summarize the speech as you traveled between floors, you would be stating your central idea. Here is an example:

Topic: The Wheat Belly diet

General Purpose: To inform

Specific Purpose: At the end of my speech, the audience will be able to identify the three key elements in the Wheat Belly diet.

Central Idea: The Wheat Belly diet is based on reducing the amount of processed foods that you eat, avoiding all processed flour, and increasing the amount of exercise you get.

Generate the Main Ideas

Effective speakers are good thinkers; they say something. They know how to play with words and thoughts to develop their **main ideas**. The ancient Romans called this skill *invention*—the ability to develop or discover ideas that result in new insights or new approaches to old problems.

Once you have an appropriate topic, a specific purpose, and a well-worded central idea, identify the major divisions of your speech, or key points that you wish to develop. To determine how to subdivide your central idea into key points, ask yourself these three questions:

1. *Does the central idea have logical divisions?* For example, are there three ways to read an annual report? Can your talk about putting on stage makeup be divided according to areas of the face? Looking for logical divisions in your speech topic is the simplest way to determine key points.
2. *Are there several reasons the central idea is true?* If your central idea is a statement that something is good or bad, you should focus on the reasons your central idea is true. Use these reasons as the main ideas of the speech.
3. *Can the central idea be supported with a series of steps?*

Your time limit, topic, and information gleaned from your research will determine how many major ideas will be in your speech. A 3- to 5-minute speech might have only two major ideas. In a very short speech, you might develop only one major idea with examples, illustrations, and other forms of support. Don't spend time trying to divide a topic that does not need dividing.

Gather Verbal and Visual Supporting Material

With your main ideas in mind, gather material to support them—facts, examples, definitions, and quotations from others that illustrate, amplify, clarify, and provide evidence. As you gather and prepare your supporting material, think about how you can connect stories, descriptions, facts, or statistics to the lives of your audience:

> Tell stories based on your own experiences, and help the audience see how the stories relate to them.
> Provide vivid descriptions of scenes, people, and objects so that the audience can visualize them. Appeal to the senses of touch, hearing, taste, and smell when appropriate, too. The more senses you trigger with words, the more interesting your talk will be.
> Relate abstract statistics to something tangible. It is easier for an audience to understand that a company sells 2.6 billion pounds of snack food each year if you also tell them that 2.6 billion pounds is triple the weight of the Empire State Building.[2]

You can find interesting and relevant supporting material by developing good research skills. Although it is important to have good ideas, it is equally important to know how to build on existing knowledge. In order to speak intelligently about a topic to an audience, you will probably need to do some research.

> Polish your skills with search engines and directories to help you find and evaluate information on the Internet.
> Learn to use electronic databases, as well as the online and on-site resources of your local library.

> Be on the lookout as you read, watch TV, and listen to the radio for ideas, examples, illustrations, and quotations that you can use in a speech.

> Learn how to gather information through interviews and written requests for information on various topics.

> Seek visual supporting material. For many people, seeing is believing. You can enhance almost any presentation by reinforcing key ideas with visual aids. It's easy to make computer-generated aids using software such as PowerPoint™, Prezi™, or Keynote™. Often, however, the most effective visual aids are the simplest: an object, a chart, a graph, a poster, a model, a map, or a person—perhaps you—to demonstrate a process or skill.

QUICK CHECK

Gather Effective Supporting Material

- Learn to research Internet, library, and human sources.
- Look for materials throughout your daily life.
- Relate materials to your audience.
- Tell stories and give vivid descriptions.
- Make statistics understandable.
- Use visual materials.

Organize Your Speech

A clearly and logically structured speech helps your audience remember what you say. A logical structure also helps you feel more in control of your speech, and greater control helps you feel more comfortable while delivering your message.

Divide Your Speech

Every well-prepared speech has three major divisions:

1. The introduction helps capture attention, serves as an overview of the speech, and provides the audience with reasons to listen to you.

2. The body presents the main content of your speech.
3. The conclusion summarizes your key ideas.

Because your introduction previews the body of your speech and your conclusion summarizes it, prepare your introduction and conclusion after you have carefully organized the body of your talk.

Outline Your Speech

If you have already generated your major ideas on the basis of logical divisions, reasons, or steps, you are well on your way to developing an outline.

Use Roman numerals to indicate your major ideas. Use capital letters for your supporting points. Use Arabic numerals if you need to subdivide your ideas further. To see examples of speech outlines, visit this chapter of MySearchLab (**www.mysearchlab.com**).

Do not write your speech word for word. If you do, you will sound stilted and unnatural. It may be useful, however, to use brief notes or written cues instead of a complete manuscript. Many students use a laptop or tablet computer to display their speaking notes during their presentations.

Rehearse Your Speech

The best way to practice is to rehearse your speech aloud, standing just as you will when you deliver it to your audience. As you rehearse, try to find a comfortable way to phrase your ideas, but don't try to memorize your talk. In fact, if you have rehearsed your speech so many times that you are using exactly the same words every time, you have rehearsed long enough. Rehearse just enough so that you can discuss your ideas and supporting material without leaving out major parts of your speech. It is all right to use notes, but limit the number of notes you use.

Here are a few points to remember as you rehearse:

> Practice making eye contact with your imaginary audience as often as you can. For speeches

delivered on video, practice looking into the camera lens.

> Be aware of the volume of your voice; practice speaking loudly enough for all in the room to hear.

> If you are not sure what to do with your hands when you rehearse, just keep them at your side. Focus on your message, rather than worrying about how to gesture.

> Avoid jingling change with your hand in your pocket or using other gestures that could distract your audience.

The words you choose and your arrangement of those words make up the style of your speech. Some audiences respond to a style that is simple and informal. Others prefer a grand and highly poetic style. To be a good speaker, you must become familiar with the language your listeners are used to hearing, and you must know how to select the right word or phrase to communicate an idea. Work to develop an ear for how words will sound to your audience.

Deliver Your Speech

Delivery is the final step in the preparation process. Before you walk to the front of the room, look at your listeners to see whether the audience assembled is what you were expecting. Are the people out there of the age, race, and gender that you had predicted? Or do you need to make last-minute changes in your message to adjust to a different mix of audience members?

> When you are introduced, walk calmly and confidently to the front of the room.

> Establish eye contact with your audience.

> Smile naturally.

> Deliver your attention-catching opening sentence.

> Concentrate on your message and your audience.

> Deliver your speech in a conversational style.

> Try to establish rapport with your listeners.

> Deliver your speech just as you rehearsed it before your imaginary audience:
> - Maintain eye contact.
> - Speak loudly enough to be heard.
> - Use some natural variation in pitch.

> Remember the advice of President Franklin D. Roosevelt: "Be sincere, be brief, and be seated."

○ STUDY GUIDE

MEET YOUR OBJECTIVES

1. **Explain why it is important to be audience-centered during each step of the speechmaking process.**
   Your audience influences your topic selection and every aspect of presenting a speech.

2. **Select and narrow an appropriate topic for a speech.**
   Answers to three questions can help you select and narrow your speech topic: Who is the audience? What are my interests, talents, and experiences? And what is the occasion?

3. **Differentiate between a general speech purpose and a specific speech purpose.**
   Your general purpose is the overarching goal of your speech (to inform, persuade, entertain, or some combination of these purposes). Your specific purpose is a concise statement of what you want your listeners to be able to do when you finish your speech.

4. **Develop a sentence that captures the central idea of a speech.**
   A central idea states the essence of your speech in a one-sentence summary.

5. **Identify three strategies for generating the main ideas for a speech.**
   Virtually any speech can be organized by answering the following three questions: Does the central idea have logical divisions? What are the reasons the central idea is true? Can you support the central idea with a series of steps?

Continued

6. **Describe several types of supporting material that can be used to support speech ideas.**
   Supporting material consists of the facts, examples, definitions, statistics, analogies, quotations, stories, and visual material that illustrate, amplify, and clarify your speech. You can find supporting material through the Internet, library resources, other people, or your daily life.

7. **Develop a speech with three main organizational parts—an introduction, a body, and a conclusion.**
   Your introduction provides an overview of your main points, the body of your speech presents the key points, and the conclusion summarizes what you have said.

8. **Identify successful strategies for rehearsing a speech.**
   Rehearse your speech several times in a way that re-creates the actual speech presentation experience.

9. **Describe the essential elements of effective speech delivery.**
   The essential aspects of effective delivery include good eye contact with your listeners, a voice that can be heard by all, and appropriate gestures and posture that seem natural.

THINK ABOUT THESE QUESTIONS

1. **Self Assessment** Explain how you think your culture influences your expectations of a public speaker.

2. **Ethics Assessment** One of your friends took public speaking last year and still has a file of speech outlines. Since you will give the speech yourself, is it ethical to use one of your friend's outlines as the basis for your speech? Explain your answer.

3. **Critical Assessment** Shara is preparing to address the city council in an effort to tell its members about the Food for Friendship program she has organized in her neighborhood. What steps should she follow to prepare and deliver an effective speech?

Ethics and Free Speech

OBJECTIVES

1. Describe the relationships among ethics, free speech, and credibility.
2. Explain how free speech has been both challenged and defended throughout U.S. history.
3. List and explain five criteria for ethical public speaking.

Ethics

Ethics are the beliefs, values, and moral principles by which people determine what is right or wrong. Ethics serve as criteria for many of the decisions we make in our personal and professional lives and also for our judgments of others' behavior.

Ethics and Free Speech

Although you are probably familiar with ethical issues, you may have given less thought to those that arise in public speaking. These issues center on one main concern: In a country in which **free speech** is protected by law, the right to speak freely must be balanced by the responsibility to speak ethically.

Ethical considerations should guide every step of the public-speaking process. The National Communication Association's Credo for Communication Ethics emphasizes the essential role of ethics: "Ethical communication is fundamental to responsible thinking, decision making, and the development of relationships and communities."[1]

Ethics and Speaker Credibility

Aristotle used the term *ethos*—the root word of *ethics* and *ethical*—to refer to a speaker's **credibility**, or believability. He thought that to be credible, a public speaker should be ethical, possess good character, have common sense, and be concerned for the well-being of the audience. You can enhance your credibility among your listeners by ethically considering their beliefs, values, and morals, as well as your own, when you select your topic, determine the goal of your speech, outline your arguments, and choose your evidence.

The History of Free and Ethical Speech

The history of the United States reflects our evolving thought on the ethical limitations to free speech:

1791   **First Amendment** to the U.S. Constitution guaranteed that "Congress shall make no law abridging the freedom of speech."

1919   U.S. Supreme Court ruled that it was lawful to restrict speech that presented "a clear and present danger" to the nation. This led to the founding of the American Civil Liberties Union, the first organization formed to protect free speech.

1940   Congress declared it illegal to urge the violent overthrow of the federal government. However, for most of the last half of the twentieth century, the U.S. Supreme Court continued to protect rather than limit free speech, upholding it as "the core aspect of democracy."[2]

1964   U.S. Supreme Court narrowed the definition of *slander* and ruled that before a public official can recover damages for slander, he or she must prove that the slanderous statement was made with "actual malice."[3]

1989   U.S. Supreme Court defended the burning of the U.S. flag as a **"speech act"** protected by the First Amendment.

1997   U.S. Supreme Court struck down the federal Communications Decency Act of 1996 and ruled that "the interest in encouraging freedom of expression in a democratic society outweighs any theoretical but unproven benefit of censorship."[4]

2001   The September 11 terrorist attacks sparked passage of the Patriot Act and new debate over the balance between national security and free speech.[5]

2010s   In a digital era, free speech, especially via the Internet and cell phones, has become a global issue.[6]

Speaking Ethically

Each person's ethical decisions reflect his or her individual values and beliefs, as well as cultural norms. Any discussion of **ethical speech** is complicated by the fact that ethics are not hard-and-fast objective rules. However, many agree that ethical speakers have a clear, responsible goal; use sound evidence and reasoning; are sensitive to, and tolerant of, differences; are honest; and avoid plagiarism.

Have a Clear, Responsible Goal

The goal of a public speech should be clear to the audience. For example, if you want listeners to buy something, do not suggest that you are speaking to entertain them. If you keep your true agenda hidden, you violate your listeners' rights. In addition, an ethical goal should be socially responsible. A socially responsible goal is one that gives the listener choices, whereas an irresponsible, unethical goal is psychologically coercive. Politicians, managers, teachers, and others in positions of power must be especially careful to avoid coercive speech that holds a hidden agenda or gives audience members no real choices.

If your overall objective is to inform or persuade, it is probably ethical; if your goal is to coerce or corrupt, it is unethical.

Use Sound Evidence and Reasoning

Ethical speakers use such critical-thinking skills as analysis and evaluation to draw conclusions and formulate arguments. Unethical speakers manipulate emotions and substitute false claims for evidence and logical arguments. It is sometimes tempting to resort to false claims to gain power over others, but it is always unethical to do so.

One important requirement for the ethical use of evidence and reasoning is to share with an audience all information that might help them reach a sound decision, including information that may be potentially damaging to your case. Even if you proceed to refute the opposing evidence and arguments, you have fulfilled your ethical responsibility by presenting the perspective of the other side.

Be Sensitive to, and Tolerant of, Differences

Being audience-centered requires that you become as aware as possible of others' feelings, needs, interests, and backgrounds. Sometimes called **accommodation**, sensitivity to differences does not mean that you must abandon your own convictions. It does mean that you should demonstrate a willingness to listen to opposing viewpoints and learn about different beliefs and values. Such willingness not only communicates respect but can also help you to select a topic, formulate a purpose, and design strategies to motivate an audience.

A speaker who is sensitive to differences also avoids language that might be interpreted as biased or offensive. Learn more about avoiding biased language in Chapter 15.

Be Honest

Knowingly offering false or misleading information to an audience is an ethical violation. However, many speakers rely on hypothetical illustrations—stories that never actually occurred, but that *might* happen. To use hypothetical illustrations ethically, make clear to the audience that the story is indeed hypothetical. For example, begin with a phrase such as, "Imagine that . . . ."

Avoid Plagiarism

Honesty also requires that you give credit for ideas and information that are not your own. Presenting the words and ideas of others without crediting them is called **plagiarism.**

Even those who would never think of stealing money or shoplifting may be tempted to plagiarize—to steal ideas. Perhaps you can remember copying a grade-school report directly from an online or paper encyclopedia, or maybe you've even purchased or "borrowed" a paper to submit for an assignment. These are obvious forms of plagiarism. A less obvious, but still serious, form is **patchwriting**—lacing a speech with compelling phrases that you find in a source but do not credit.[7] A speaker whose sentences were very similar to those used in a news article would be patchwriting if he or she did not acknowledge that the phrasing came from the article.

Do Your Own Work   You will be doing yourself a disservice if you do not learn how to compose a speech on your own. The most flagrant cases of plagiarism result from speakers not doing their work. A more subtle form of plagiarism is asking another person to edit a speech so extensively that it becomes more the other person's work than the speaker's own.

Acknowledge Your Sources   An ethical speaker is responsible for doing his or her own research and then sharing the results of that research with audience members. Some information is so widely known that you do not have to acknowledge a source for it. For example, you need not credit a source if you say that a person must be infected with the HIV virus in order to develop AIDS. This information is widely available in a variety of reference sources. However, if you decide to use any of the following in your speech, then you must give credit to the source:

> direct quotations, even if they are only brief phrases
> opinions, assertions, or ideas of others, even if you paraphrase them rather than quote them verbatim
> statistics
> any non-original visual materials, including graphs, tables, and pictures

Take Careful Notes To be able to acknowledge your sources, you must first practice careful and systematic note-taking. Indicate with quotation marks any phrases or sentences that you photocopy or copy by hand verbatim from a source, and be sure to record the author, title, publisher or Web site, publication date, and page numbers for all sources from which you take quotations, ideas, statistics, or visual materials.

Cite Sources Correctly In addition to keeping careful records of your sources, you must also know how to cite your sources for your audience, both orally and in writing. The How To box offers advice for integrating **oral citation** smoothly into a speech.

You can also provide a **written citation** for a source. Style guides, such as those published by the MLA (Modern Language Association) or the APA (American Psychological Association), are now available online as

Present an Oral Citation

- **Name the source.** For example, "At its 2013 Web page 'Bed Bugs,' the Centers for Disease Control and Prevention outlines three problems caused by bed bug infestations."
- **Pause briefly.** The pause signals listeners that you are about to begin quoting.
- **State the quote.** "Property loss, expense, and inconvenience."[8]
- **Provide enough information.** Tell listeners the author, the title, the year, and the fact that the information is available online.

well as in traditional print format. Visit this chapter of MySearchLab (**www.mysearchlab.com**) to learn more about oral and written citations.

What about those times when you are not certain whether information or ideas are common knowledge? A good rule is this: When in doubt, document. You would never be guilty of plagiarism if you documented something you didn't need to, but you could be committing plagiarism if you did not document something you really should have.

QUICK CHECK

Deliver an Ethical Speech

- Have a clear, responsible goal.
- Provide your listeners with choices, and use sound evidence and reasoning.
- Share all evidence that will help your audience reach a sound decision.
- Be sensitive to, and tolerant of, differences, and avoid language that is biased or offensive.
- Be honest and do your own work.
- Avoid plagiarism, and give credit for any ideas and information that are not your own.
- Acknowledge your sources accurately and completely.

STUDY GUIDE

MEET YOUR OBJECTIVES

1. **Describe the relationships among ethics, free speech, and credibility.**

   In the United States, citizens have the right to speak freely, but that right comes with the responsibility to speak ethically. Speaking ethically allows your audience to trust you. Being trustworthy is an important part of being credible, or believable.

Continued

2. **Explain how free speech has been both challenged and defended throughout U.S. history.**
Although the U.S. Congress and courts have occasionally limited the constitutional right to free speech, more often they have protected and broadened its application. Social media offer a new context for twenty-first-century challenges to free speech.

3. **List and explain five criteria for ethical public speaking.**
An ethical public speaker should have a clear, responsible goal; use sound evidence and reasoning; be sensitive to, and tolerant of, differences; be honest; and take appropriate steps to avoid plagiarism. Avoid plagiarizing by doing your own work and acknowledging—orally, in writing, or both—the sources for any quotations, ideas, statistics, or visual materials you use in a speech.

THINK ABOUT THESE QUESTIONS

1. **Self Assessment** You have found the perfect pie chart for your talk in *USA Today*. It shows U.S. Census figures for population trends. If you tell the audience that the source of the visual is *USA Today*, do you also need to cite the U.S. Bureau of the Census?

2. **Ethics Assessment** Speechwriters have written many of the best speeches made by U.S. presidents. Is such use of speechwriters ethical? Is it ethical for presidents to get the credit for the speeches?

3. **Critical Assessment** As you listen to classmates' speeches, try to identify specific ways in which they try to gain your trust.

5   Listening

OBJECTIVES

1. List and describe five barriers to effective listening.
2. Identify and implement strategies for becoming a better listener.
3. Identify and implement strategies for improving your critical listening and critical thinking skills.
4. Use criteria to effectively and appropriately evaluate speeches.

Overcoming Barriers to Effective Listening

You hear more than 1 billion words each year. Yet how much information do you retain? Improving your listening skills will make you not only a better listener but also a better speaker. Listening requires you to do all of the following:

> **Select** or single out a message from several competing messages. Your job as a speaker is to motivate listeners to select *your* message.
> **Attend** to, or focus on, the message.
> **Understand,** or assign meaning to the message.
> **Remember** ideas and information.
> **Respond,** or react with behavior that demonstrates you listened to the message.

Listening barriers are created when you fail to perform any of these activities effectively.

Information Overload

According to the **working memory theory** of listening, as listeners, we find it harder to concentrate on and remember messages when our working memory is full.[1]

As a public speaker, you can keep your audience from tuning out by:

> delivering a message that is clear and easy to understand.
> using interesting and vivid supporting material to keep your listeners listening.
> building redundancy into your message so that if listeners miss an idea the first time you present it, perhaps they will catch it during your concluding remarks.

Personal Concerns

Are you thinking about the weekend while your instructor speaks? As a listener, recognize when your own agenda keeps you from listening, and then force yourself to focus on the speaker's message. As a speaker, focus on maintaining your audience's attention and use occasional "wake-up" messages such as "Now listen carefully, because. . . ."

Outside Distractions

As a listener, do your best to control the listening situation.

> Move to another seat.
> Close the blinds.
> Turn up the heat.
> Turn off the lights.
> Close the door.
> Do whatever is necessary to minimize distractions.

When you are a speaker, use the tips in the How To box.

Minimize Listeners' Distractions

• Arrive early at the speaking space so you can assess the physical arrangements before you speak.
• Sit where your audience will be seated.
• Listen and look around you for any possible distractions.
• Fix any problems before listeners need to do it themselves.

Prejudice

Are you convinced speakers from another political party have nothing useful to say? As a listener, guard against becoming so critical of a message that you don't listen to it or, doing the opposite, becoming so impressed that you decide too quickly that the speaker is trustworthy.

To counteract **prejudice** when you are the speaker, use your opening statements to grab the audience's attention so they will listen to your message. If you think audience members are likely to disagree with you, use careful language, sound reasoning, and convincing evidence that your listeners will find credible.

Differences between Speech Rate and Thought Rate

Most people talk at a rate of 125 words a minute[2] but are able to listen to up to 700 words a minute. The difference gives listeners time to ignore a speaker periodically. Eventually, you stop listening. Listen more effectively by mentally summarizing what the speaker is saying from time to time.

As a speaker, be aware of your listeners' tendency to stop paying attention. Build in message redundancy, be well organized, and make your major ideas clear.

QUICK CHECK

Overcoming Your Listening Barriers

- Decide what is important in a speech and focus on that.
- Force yourself to focus on the speaker's message.
- Try to minimize outside distractions.
- Don't prejudge a message or speaker.
- Use the time lag created by the difference between speech rate and thought rate to summarize what the speaker is saying.

How to Become a Better Listener

Good listeners focus on a speaker's message, not on delivery style. Although poor speakers are a challenge to good listening, you also need to be wary of glib, well-polished speakers.

Listen with Your Eyes as Well as Your Ears

Nonverbal clues play a major role in communicating a speaker's emotions and messages. Interpret the speaker's expressions, posture, and gestures in the context of the speaker's words; look for clusters of cues that occur together; and look for cues that show the speaker's level of power, attitude toward listeners, and responsiveness to listeners.

If you have trouble understanding a speaker's words, get close enough so that you can see the speaker's mouth. A good view can increase your level of attention and improve your understanding.

Stay on Task

Good listeners are open-minded. They put their own thoughts aside so they can be present mentally as well as physically. They invest time in listening and make a conscious, mindful effort to listen. If you get off task and find that you're not doing these things, periodically remind yourself why the message can be helpful or important to you.[3]

Monitor Your Emotional Reaction to a Message

If you become angry or emotional in response to something a speaker says, your listening comprehension decreases. Don't let a speaker's language close down your mind.

Be a Selfish Listener

If you find your attention waning, ask yourself questions such as, "What's in this for me?" Find ways to benefit from the information you are listening to, and try to connect it with your own experiences and needs.

Listen for Major Ideas

Listen for major ideas and principles. In speeches, facts as well as examples are used primarily to support major ideas. Facts are useful only when you can connect them to a principle or concept. Try to mentally summarize the major idea that the specific facts support.

Identify Your Listening Goal

There are at least four major listening goals. Being conscious of your listening goal can help you listen more effectively.

> **Listen for pleasure.** When listening for pleasure, just enjoy what you hear. You can, however, observe how effective speakers gain and maintain your attention and keep you interested in their messages.

> **Listen to empathize.** Listening to try to share the speaker's feelings requires these essential steps:
> * **Stop.** Stop what you are doing and give your complete attention to the speaker.
> * **Look.** Make eye contact and pay attention to nonverbal cues that reveal emotions.
> * **Listen.** Pay attention to both the details of the message and the major ideas.
> * **Imagine.** Visualize how you would feel if you had experienced what the speaker experienced.
> * **Check.** Check your understanding by asking questions to clarify what you heard and by summarizing what you think you heard.

> **Listen to evaluate.** When you evaluate a message, you make a judgment about its content. The challenge is to not become so critical that you miss a key point the speaker is making.

> **Listen for information.** Listen for the details of a message, and make certain you link the details to major ideas. Mentally summarize the information you hear to increase your ability to remember messages. Also, compare unfamiliar information to ideas and concepts with which you are familiar.

Practice Listening

Listening skills do not develop automatically. Skill develops as you practice listening to speeches, music, and programs with demanding content.

Understand Your Listening Style

There are at least four different listening styles. Understanding your listening style can help you become a better and more flexible listener.[4]

> **Relational-oriented listeners** are comfortable listening to others express feelings and emotions.
> **Task-oriented listeners** listen for actions that need to be taken. Task-oriented listeners tend to be skeptical and prefer being given evidence to support recommendations for action.
> **Analytical-oriented listeners** prefer to listen to complex information laced with facts and details. They reject messages that don't have adequate support.
> **Critical-oriented listeners** spend time evaluating messages. They are likely to catch inconsistencies and errors in the reasoning and evidence used to reach a conclusion.

Become an Active Listener

An active listener is one who remains alert and mentally re-sorts, rephrases, and repeats key information when listening to a speech. To be a more active speaker:

> **Re-sort disorganized or disjointed ideas.** Figure out ways to rearrange them into a new, more logical pattern. Put a series of examples into chronological order, for example.
> **Rephrase or summarize what the speaker is saying.** Listen for main ideas, and then put them into your own words.
> **Repeat key points you want to remember.** Go back to essential ideas and restate them to yourself.
> **Look for "information handles" provided by the speaker,** in the form of previews, transitions, signposts, and summary statements.

QUICK CHECK

Become a Better Listener

- Adapt to the speaker's delivery.
- Listen with your eyes as well as your ears.
- Monitor your emotional reaction to a message.
- Stay on task and be a selfish listener.
- Listen for major ideas.
- Identify your listening goal, practice listening, and become an active listener.

Listen Ethically

Audience members share responsibility with speakers for ethical communication. The following guidelines for ethical listening incorporate what Harold Barrett calls "attributes of the good audience."[5]

Communicate Your Expectations and Feedback

As an audience member, you have the right—even the responsibility—to enter into a communication situation with expectations about the message and how the speaker will deliver it.

> Know what information and ideas you want to get out of the communication transaction.
> Expect a coherent, organized, and competently delivered presentation.
> Communicate your objectives, and react to the speaker's message and delivery through appropriate nonverbal and verbal feedback.
> If a question-and-answer period follows the speech, ask any questions you still have about the speaker's topic or point of view.

Demonstrate Sensitivity to and Tolerance of Differences

As a member of an audience, it is important for you to exercise social and cultural awareness and tolerance.

> Be attentive and courteous.
> Remember that different cultures have different styles of speaking. If a speaker uses an approach different from the one you prefer, the speaker's approach is not necessarily wrong, just different.
> Try to understand the needs, goals, and interests of both the speaker and other audience members so that you can judge how to react appropriately and ethically as a listener.

Improve Listening and Critical Thinking Skills

Critical listening is the process of listening to evaluate the quality, appropriateness, value, and importance of the information you hear. Related to being a critical listener is being a critical thinker. **Critical thinking** is a mental process of making judgments about the conclusions presented in what you see, hear, and read. Your goal as a critical listener is to assess the quality of the information and the validity of the conclusions presented.

Separate Facts from Inferences

Facts are information that has been proven true by direct observation. An **inference** is a conclusion based on partial information or an evaluation that has not been directly observed. The ability to separate facts from inferences is a basic skill in critical thinking and listening.

Evaluate the Quality of Evidence

Evidence consists of the facts, examples, opinions, and statistics that a speaker uses to support a conclusion. Without credible supporting evidence, it would not be wise to agree with a speaker's conclusion.

Some speakers support a conclusion with **examples**. But if the examples aren't typical, or only one or two examples are offered, or other known examples differ from the one the speaker is using, then you should question the conclusion.

An **opinion** is a quoted comment from someone. To be a credible source, the person quoted must have the credentials, experience, and skill to make an observation about the topic at hand.

A **statistic** is a number that summarizes a collection of examples. Are the statistics reliable, unbiased, recent, representative, and valid?

Evaluate the Underlying Logic and Reasoning

Logic is a formal system of rules applied to reach a conclusion. A speaker is logical if he or she offers appropriate evidence to reach a valid, well-reasoned conclusion. For example, the fact that a product sells well is not necessarily logical evidence that the product is made well.

Reasoning is the process of drawing a conclusion from evidence within the logical framework of the arguments. As a critical listener, review the logic and reasoning used to reach a conclusion. If a speaker wants to change your behavior, listen especially carefully to the logic or structure of the arguments presented.

Analyze and Evaluate Speeches

When you evaluate something, you judge its value and appropriateness. In making a judgment about the value of something, such as a speech, it's important to use criteria for what is and is not effective or appropriate. **Rhetorical criticism** is the process of using a method or standards to evaluate the effectiveness and appropriateness of messages.

Understand Criteria for Evaluating Speeches

What makes a speech good? Underlying any list of what a good speaker does are two fundamental goals: creating a speech that is both effective and ethical. The mission of the National Communication Association—to promote effective and ethical communication—mirrors these two goals.

The Message Should Be Effective To be effective, the message should be understandable to listeners and should achieve its intended purpose.[6] If listeners fail to comprehend the speaker's ideas, the speech fails. It can be challenging to determine the speaker's true intent. You might be able to discern whether the *general purpose* is to inform, persuade, or entertain, but decoding the *specific purpose* may be tricky unless the speaker explicitly states his or her objective. Often the best you can do is try to determine the purpose by being a careful listener.

The Message Should Be Ethical　If the audience clearly understands the message and the speaker gets the reaction he or she desires but uses unethical means to do so, the message may be *effective*, but it is not *appropriate*. A good speaker is an ethical speaker.

An ethical public speaker tells the truth, gives credit for ideas and words where credit is due, and doesn't plagiarize. As a listener, you can hold a speaker accountable for presenting ethical messages by noticing whether or not he or she presents both sides of an issue, discloses all the information you know is available about a topic, and is honest about his or her purpose for the speech. You can signal your disapproval of ethically questionable messages through your nonverbal feedback during a speech. After the speech, you can also question the speaker, read more on the topic, or seek appropriate other forums to express your disagreement.

Identify and Analyze Rhetorical Strategies

Rhetoric involves the use of symbols to achieve goals. **Symbols** are words, images (a flag, a cross, a six-pointed star), and behaviors that create meaning for others.

One way to enhance your listening skills and become more mindful of how messages influence your behavior is to analyze the rhetorical strategies a speaker uses. **Rhetorical strategies** are methods and techniques that speakers employ to achieve their speaking goals. Speakers sometimes use unethical rhetorical strategies to achieve their goals, such as misusing evidence, relying too heavily on emotion to persuade, or fabricating information.

Rhetorician Robert Rowland offers a simple but comprehensive framework for describing and analyzing rhetorical messages: Be conscious of the goal of the message, its organization, the speaker's role, the overall tone of the message, the intended audience, and the techniques the speaker uses to achieve the goal.[7] The more clearly you can identify and analyze the speaker's methods, the more effectively you can assess whether the message and the messenger are worthy of your support.

Give Feedback to Others

When you have an opportunity to critique a speech, follow these guidelines to give feedback.

1. **Be descriptive.** In a neutral way, describe what you saw the speaker doing. For example, say, "You made eye contact during about half of your speech" rather than, "Not enough eye contact."
2. **Be specific.** Make sure your descriptions are precise enough. Instead of saying, "Great visuals," say, "The graph and picture in your slides really helped me visualize the growth in the annual Midwest corn harvest."
3. **Be positive.** Begin and end your feedback with positive comments. Beginning with negative comments immediately puts the speaker on the defensive and can create so much internal noise that she or he stops listening.
4. **Be constructive.** Give the speaker some suggestions or alternatives for improvement.
5. **Be sensitive.** Use *I-statements* as a way of phrasing your feedback so that your comments reflect your personal point of view ("I found my attention drifting during your speech"). A *you-statement* is less sensitive because it implies that the other person did something wrong ("You didn't summarize very well").
6. **Be realistic.** Provide usable information. Provide feedback about things over which the speaker has control.

Give Feedback to Yourself

Consider the following suggestions for enhancing your own self-critiquing skills.

1. **Look for and reinforce your skills and speaking abilities.** Take mental note of how your audience analysis, organization, and delivery were effective in achieving your objectives.
2. **Evaluate your effectiveness based on your specific speaking situation and audience.** Give yourself permission to adapt principles and practices to specific speech situations.
3. **Identify one or two areas for improvement.** Identify what you did right; then give yourself a suggestion or two for ways to improve. Concentrate on one or two key skills you would like to develop.

STUDY GUIDE

MEET YOUR OBJECTIVES

1. **List and describe five barriers to effective listening.**
   Barriers to listening include information overload, personal concerns, outside distractions, and prejudice.
2. **Identify and implement strategies for becoming a better listener.**
   "Listen" to nonverbal messages with your eyes. Understand your listening style. Listen mindfully, monitoring your emotional reactions to messages, and avoid jumping to conclusions. Identify your listening goal and listen for major ideas. Re-sort, restate, or repeat key messages. Be an ethical listener.
3. **Identify and implement strategies for improving your critical listening and critical thinking skills.**
   Evaluate the speaker's use of facts, examples, opinions, and statistics as evidence. Examine the logic and reasoning leading to the speaker's conclusions.

Continued

4. Use criteria to effectively and appropriately evaluate speeches.
   A good speech is understandable to the audience and achieves its intended effect. When offering feedback to yourself or others, be descriptive, specific, positive, constructive, sensitive, and realistic.

THINK ABOUT THESE QUESTIONS

1. **Self Assessment** One of your professors does nothing during lectures but read in a monotone voice from old notes. What are some strategies you can use to increase your listening effectiveness in this challenging situation?

2. **Ethics Assessment** Janice thought her classmate's speech was pretty good, but she gave the speaker low marks because she strongly disagreed with what the speaker was saying. Was this an ethical evaluation?

3. **Critical Assessment** For some reason, when Alberto hears the president speak, he just tunes out. What are some of the barriers that may keep Alberto from focusing on the message he is hearing?

6 Analyzing Your Audience

OBJECTIVES

1. Describe informal and formal methods of gathering information about your audience.
2. Explain how to analyze and use information to adapt to your audience.
3. List important demographic characteristics of audience members.
4. Discuss audience attitudes that can affect your speech.
5. Analyze key aspects of the speaking situation.
6. Identify methods of assessing audience reactions after your speech.

Gather Information about Your Audience

As an audience-centered speaker, try to find out as much as you can about the audience before planning the speech. There are two approaches you can take: informal and formal.

Gathering Information Informally

Observe your audience informally and ask questions of people who know something about the audience you will be addressing. What is the audience's average age? What are their political affiliations? What are their attitudes toward your topic?

Gathering Information Formally

If time and resources permit, you may want to conduct a more formal survey of your listeners. Your topic and the speaking occasion can help you determine what you want to know about your audience that you don't already know. You may want to ask questions about audience members' age, sex, occupation, and memberships in professional organizations. Whenever possible, you should also ask specific questions about their attitudes. You can ask two basic types of questions:

1. **Open-ended questions** allow for unrestricted answers, rather than limiting answers to choices or alternatives. An open-ended question asks, "What do you believe is the best way to lower our district's high-school drop-out rate?" rather than a yes/no question, such as, "Do you believe that a longer school year will lower the drop-out rate?" Use open-ended questions when you want more detailed information from your audience.

2. **Closed-ended questions** offer alternatives from which to choose. Multiple-choice, true/false, and agree/disagree questions are examples of closed-ended questions.

Visit MySearchLab (**www.mysearchlab.com**) to see examples of open-ended and close-ended questions. After you develop your own questions, test them on a small group of people to make sure they are clear and will encourage meaningful answers.

Analyze Audience Information

Once you have gathered information, you can begin the processes of **audience analysis**, examining information about your listeners, and **audience adaptation**, ethically using your information to customize your speech to the audience.

Use the results of your audience analysis to tailor your message so that listeners will understand it and you will achieve your speaking goal. Ethically adapt your topic, speech goal, content—including organization, information, examples, and visual aids—as well as your delivery.[1] For example, use popular culture references your listeners are likely to know. *Adapting ethically means you do not tell your listeners only what they want to hear or fabricate information simply to please your audience or achieve your goal.*

Analyze Audience Information

As you examine your data, look for these three things:

- **Audience member similarities,** whether in demographics or in beliefs and attitudes, can help you craft a message that resonates in the same way with many of your listeners.
- **Audience member differences** will alert you to the range of people you must reach with your message.
- **Common ground** with your audience refers to the ways you and your listeners are alike. The more you have in common with your audience, the easier it will be to establish a **relationship** with them that helps them understand your message and helps you achieve your purpose.

Demographic Audience Analysis

Demographics are statistics on audience characteristics, such as age, sexual orientation, race, gender, educational level, and religious views. Demographic information can help you develop a clear and effective message by providing clues about your listeners. Use caution in making inferences based on general information, however, as they may lead to faulty conclusions.

Age

The audience's age can suggest topics, as well as the kinds of examples, humor, illustrations, and other types of supporting material you use in your speech. Be careful, however, about generalizing from only one factor.

Gender and Sexual Orientations

Gender is the perception of one's self as feminine or masculine. Gender is based on cultural upbringing as well as genetics. Listeners' gender identities can fall anywhere along a continuum from female to male and may or may not reflect their biological **sex**. Your listeners may also have a range of sexual orientations. As an audience-centered speaker, avoid assumptions about gender identity, as well as sexist language or remarks. Take time to educate yourself about what words, phrases, or perspectives are likely to offend or create psychological noise and distract your audience from listening. Make your language, and your message, as inclusive of all gender identities and sexual orientations as possible.

Culture, Ethnicity, and Race

Culture is a learned system of knowledge, behavior, attitudes, beliefs, values, and norms shared by a group of people. **Ethnicity** is that portion of a person's cultural background that relates to a national or religious heritage. A person's **race** is his or her biological heritage—for example, Caucasian or Asian. To be an effective speaker, adapt to differences in culture, race, and ethnicity.

Ethnocentrism is an assumption that your own cultural approaches are superior to those of other cultures. Be sensitive to cultural differences and avoid remarks that disparage the cultural background of the audience.

Group Membership

Know what political, social, service, professional, or religious groups your listeners belong to so that you can make inferences about their likes, dislikes, beliefs, and values. Making references to the activities that your audience members may participate in can help you tailor your speech to your specific audience. Use great care, however, when touching on religious beliefs or an audience's values.

Socioeconomic Status

Socioeconomic status is a person's perceived importance and influence based on such factors as income, occupation, and educational level. The amount of disposable income of your listeners can influence your topic and your approach to the topic. Knowing what people do for a living can give you useful information about how

---

QUICK CHECK

Analyze Audience Demographics

- Know the age of your audience.
- Avoid making sweeping judgments based on gender stereotypes.
- Consider your audience's sexual orientations.
- Avoid an ethnocentric mind-set, and use great care when touching on religious beliefs.
- Learn what groups, clubs, or organizations your audience belongs to. Consider the socioeconomic status of audience members.
- Remember that your audience will be made up of diverse individuals.

---

to adapt your message to them. Knowing the educational background of your audience can also help you make decisions about your choice of vocabulary, your language style, and your use of examples and illustrations.

Psychological Audience Analysis

A **psychological audience analysis** explores an audience's attitudes toward a topic, purpose, and speaker, while probing the underlying beliefs and values that might affect these attitudes.

> An **attitude** reflects likes or dislikes.
> A **belief** is what you hold to be true or false. You may be able to address an underlying belief when trying to change an attitude or reinforce one.
> A **value** is an enduring concept of good and bad, right and wrong. More deeply ingrained than either attitudes or beliefs, values are also more resistant to change.

Analyze Attitudes toward Your Topic

Knowing how members of an audience feel about your topic lets you adjust your message accordingly. Try to categorize your audience and their attitudes according to the following three dimensions.

Interested-Uninterested With an interested audience, your task is simply to hold and amplify interest throughout the speech. If your audience is uninterested, you need to find ways to "hook" the members. Tell listeners why your message relates to their lives. Visual aids may also help you to gain and maintain the attention of apathetic listeners.

Favorable-Unfavorable Even if your general purpose is just to inform, it is useful to know whether your audience is predisposed to respond positively or negatively toward you or your message. Some audiences may be neither; instead, they may be neutral, apathetic, or simply uninformed about your topic. If they are already favorable, use their interest to move them closer to your speaking goal. If not, be realistic. Acknowledge their opposing point of view and consider refuting any misperceptions they have.

Captive-Voluntary A captive audience has externally imposed reasons for being there (such as a requirement to attend class). Your goal with a captive audience is to make your speech just as interesting and effective as one designed for a voluntary audience. You still have an obligation to address your listeners' needs and interests and to keep them engaged in what you have to say. If your audience is attending voluntarily, anticipate why they are coming and speak about the issues they want you to address.

Analyze Attitudes toward You, the Speaker

Your **credibility**—the degree to which you are perceived as trustworthy, knowledgeable, and dynamic—is one of the main factors that will shape your audience's attitude toward you. An audience's positive attitude toward you as a speaker can overcome negative or apathetic attitudes they may have toward your topic or purpose.

If you establish your credibility before you begin, your listeners will be more likely to believe what you say and to think that you are knowledgeable, interesting, and dynamic. If you have had personal experience with your topic, be sure to let the audience know. You will gain credibility instantly. If your analysis reveals that your audience does not recognize you as an authority on your subject, you will need to build your credibility into the speech.

Situational Audience Analysis

Situational audience analysis includes a consideration of the time and place of your speech, the size of your audience, and the speaking occasion. Table 6.1 summarizes situational audience analysis.

Analyze Your Audience After You Speak

After you have given your speech, evaluate your audience's positive or negative response to your message. Use your evaluation to help you prepare your next speech.

Nonverbal Responses

The most obvious nonverbal response is applause. Is the audience simply clapping politely, or is the applause robust and enthusiastic, indicating pleasure and acceptance? Responsive facial expressions, smiles, and nods are signs that the speech was well received. Remember, however, that listeners from different cultures respond to speeches with different behavior and levels of enthusiasm.[2]

Verbal Responses

If you have the chance, try to ask audience members how they responded to the speech in general, as well as to points you are particularly interested in. Their specific comments can indicate where you succeeded and where you need improvement.

TABLE 6.1 Analyzing the Situation

Factor	Importance
Time	
• What time of day will you speak? • At what point in the program will you speak? • For how long are you scheduled to talk?	• Listeners may be tired in the afternoon or after listening to several other speakers. • Be sure to end your talk right on time or a little early.
Location	
• Can you visit before you speak? • How will audience seating be arranged? • How close will you be to the audience? • Will you be on a stage or raised platform? • Will you speak from a lectern? • Do you need to use a microphone? • Will you have the appropriate equipment and lighting for your visual aids?	• Visit, if possible. Determine what you can and cannot change about the location. • Adapt your speech and visual aids to factors you cannot change. • Rehearse appropriate movements and gestures for the conditions. • Arrive early to practice with microphones and equipment.
Size of Audience	
• How many people are expected to attend?	• Larger audiences tend to expect a more formal style. • You can take questions during your talk from a group of ten or fewer.
Occasion	
• What is the occasion that brings the audience together?	• Knowing the occasion can help you predict audience demographics and state of mind.

Survey Responses

You can use the same survey techniques discussed earlier. Develop survey questions that will help you determine the general reactions to you and your speech, as well as specific responses to your ideas and supporting materials.

Behavioral Responses

Your listeners' actions are the best indicators of your speaking success. If you suggested that your listeners do something, did they ultimately behave as you intended?

STUDY GUIDE

MEET YOUR OBJECTIVES

1. **Describe informal and formal methods of gathering information about your audience.**
   Gather information through informally observing listeners and questioning people who know them. Use open-ended and close-ended questions to formally survey listeners.

2. **Explain how to analyze and use information to adapt to your audience.**
   Look for similarities and differences among listeners and common ground between you and the audience. Use information to ethically adapt your topic, content, and delivery to help the audience understand and to achieve your goal.

3. **List important demographic characteristics of audience members.**
   Adapt your speech to your listeners' ages, genders, sexual orientations, cultures and ethnicities, group memberships, and socioeconomic status.

4. **Discuss audience attitudes that can affect your speech.**
   Learn whether listeners attend your speech voluntarily or as a captive audience. Know their level of interest and support of your topic or position. You must also consider their opinions about your credibility.

5. **Analyze key aspects of the speaking situation.**
   Ethically adapt your speech depending on the time and location for it, the size of the audience, and the occasion.

Continued

6. **Identify methods of assessing audience reactions after your speech.**
Use nonverbal, verbal, survey, and behavioral responses to assess your effectiveness.

THINK ABOUT THESE QUESTIONS

1. **Self Assessment** After your next speech, describe the extent to which you accomplished your speaking goal, based on assessment techniques described on pages 54–56.

2. **Ethics Assessment** Tynisha wants to convince her audience to ban alcohol in all city parks. Her survey results suggest that 85 percent of her audience want to continue the current policy of permitting alcohol in city parks. Should she change her purpose to fit the existing attitudes of her audience? Why or why not?

3. **Critical Assessment** Dr. Ruiz thought the audience for her speech on birth control would be women of childbearing age. After writing her speech, however, she found out that all the women to whom she would be speaking were at least 20 years older than she expected. What changes, if any, should she make?

Adapting to Your Audience as You Speak

7

OBJECTIVES

1. Explain how to read nonverbal cues to understand listeners' reactions to your speech.
2. Describe several adaptations you can make to respond to listeners' nonverbal cues.
3. List several ways you can customize your message to your audience.
4. Discuss strategies for adapting to diverse groups of listeners.

Read Nonverbal Cues

Audience analysis and adaptation do not end when you have crafted your speech. They continue as you deliver your speech. Once you begin speaking, you must rely on nonverbal cues from the audience to judge how people are responding to the message. Learn to be aware of the often unspoken clues that your audience is either hanging on your every word or is bored.

Eye Contact

For most North American audiences, the best way to determine whether your listeners are maintaining interest in your speech is to note the amount of eye contact they have with you. The more contact they have, the more likely it is that they are listening to your message. If you find them looking down at the program (or, worse yet, closing their eyes), you can reasonably guess that they have lost interest. Realize, however, that audience members from different cultures respond to speeches in different ways.[1] For example, some Eastern European listeners may not maintain eye contact with you; they may look down at the floor when listening.

Facial Expression

Members of an attentive audience not only make direct eye contact but also have attentive facial expressions. Listeners from some cultures are more expressive than those of others. Japanese audience members, for example, are likely to show little expression. In any culture, however, beware of entirely frozen, unresponsive faces. Such audience members may be trying to look like they are interested while they are actually in a stupor of daydreaming. They also often have a slightly tilted head; a faint, frozen smile; and a hand holding up the chin.

Movement

An attentive audience doesn't move much. Squirming, feet shuffling, and general body movement often indicate that members of the audience have lost interest in your message.

Nonverbal Responsiveness

Frequent applause and nods of agreement with your message are indicators of interest and support. An interested audience also responds when encouraged or invited to do so by the speaker. If you ask for a show of hands and audience members sheepishly look at one another and eventually raise a finger or two, you can reasonably infer lack of interest and enthusiasm.

Verbal Responsiveness

Audience members may shout out a response or more quietly express agreement or disagreement to people seated next to them. A sensitive public speaker constantly listens for verbal reinforcement or disagreement.

Respond to Nonverbal Cues

After learning to "read" your listeners, you can use a repertoire of behaviors to help you connect with them.

HOW TO

Adapt Your Speech While You Are Speaking

- Watch the audience and notice listeners' non-verbal cues.
- If listeners seem interested, supportive, and attentive, continue speaking as you have planned, based on your prespeech analysis.
- If the audience is not interested and responsive, or is disagreeing with you, try one of the ideas listed in this chapter.
- If the audience's responses do not change, try another adaptation.
- If all else fails, you may need to abandon a formal speaker–listener relationship with your audience and open up your topic for discussion.
- Continue to listen and monitor so that you may learn more about the audience.

If your audience seems inattentive or bored:

> Tell a story.
> Use an example to which the audience can relate, or use a personal example.
> Remind your listeners why your message should be of interest to them.
> Eliminate some abstract facts and statistics.
> Use appropriate humor. Use audience demographics and the situation to help you decide what is appropriate.
> Make direct references to the audience.
> Invite the audience to participate by asking questions or asking for an example.
> Ask for a direct response, such as a show of hands, to see whether your listeners agree or disagree with you.
> Speed up the pace of your delivery, or pause for dramatic effect.

If your audience seems confused or doesn't seem to understand your point:

> Be more redundant. Repeat key points.
> Phrase your information in another way, or think of an example you can use to illustrate your point.
> Use a visual aid, such as a chalkboard or flipchart, to clarify your point.
> If you have been speaking rapidly, slow your speaking rate.
> Ask for feedback from an audience member to help you discover what is unclear.
> Ask someone in the audience to summarize the key points you are making.

If your audience seems to be disagreeing with your message:

> Provide additional data and evidence to support your point.
> Remind your listeners of your credibility, credentials, or background.
> Rely less on stories and more on facts to present your case. Write facts and data on a chalkboard, overhead transparency, or flipchart if one is handy.
> If you don't have the answers and data you need, tell listeners you will provide more information by mail, telephone, or email (and make sure you get back in touch with them).

Customize Your Message to Your Audience

Audiences prefer messages that are adapted just to them. What are some ways to communicate to your listeners that your message is designed specifically for them? Here are a few suggestions.

> Appropriately use audience members' names to relate information to specific people. Before you speak, ask those people for permission to use their names in your talk.

> Refer to the town, city, or community where you are speaking.
> Refer to a significant event that happened on the date of your speech. An Internet search for "this day in history" should reveal a number of interesting events. Link the event to the topic and audience. For example, "Today is the anniversary of one of the great battles of the Civil War. Today, I want to tell you about another battle in our country. The outcome will change all of our lives."
> Refer to a recent or local news event. Visit the Web site or local news source of an institution or group to whom you are speaking for stories that you can connect to the central idea of your talk.
> Refer to a group or organization. If you're speaking to an audience of service, religious, political, or work group members, make specific positive, but honest, references to that group.
> Find ways to apply facts, statistics, and examples to the people in your audience. For example, "Forty percent of women listening to me now are likely to experience gender discrimination. That means of the 20 women in this audience, 8 of you are likely to be discriminated against."

Adapt to Diverse Listeners

Audience diversity involves more factors than just ethnic and cultural differences. *Diversity* simply means differences. Audiences are diverse.

Because of your efforts to gather information about your audience, you should know something about the people who will likely be present for your talk. Based on your information, you may want to identify a **target audience,** a specific segment of your audience that you most want to address or influence.

Although you should avoid making generalizations based on cultural background, knowing that many people accept their culture's view on the following variables may help you adapt your message, supporting materials, and delivery.[2] You can use the suggested strategies to help you adapt to your diverse listeners. Be sure to assess your own cultural background and expectations, too. Avoid developing a message that would be effective with only people like you.

> **Individualistic or collectivistic**—Listeners from individualistic cultures focus more on the achievement of a single person. Emphasize how your information can help them as individuals. Collectivistic cultures tend to emphasize the accomplishments of a group or team. Point out the benefits of your information to their community.

> **High or low context**—High-context listeners pay closer attention to a variety of nonverbal cues than low-context ones, who will focus mainly on your words.

> **High or low need for certainty**—People with low tolerance for uncertainty need your speech to be clearly organized and may prefer a linear, step-by-step structure.

> **High or low power**—People from high-power cultures are attuned to status and power differences and prefer clearly defined roles and chains of command. They will not enjoy a consensus-seeking discussion, and they prefer that you clearly establish your credibility.

> **Long-term or short-term time orientation**—Listeners with a short-term orientation consider time an important resource. Show the immediate impact of any ideas you propose. In contrast, appeal to persistence and benefits to future generations for listeners who are concerned with the long term.

QUICK CHECK

Adapt to a Culturally Diverse Audience

- Tailor your speech primarily to your target audience.
- Avoid generalizations; assess a variety of cultural variables.
- Use a variety of strategies.
- Identify listeners' common values and assumptions.
- Use stories and examples that span cultures.
- Use visual aids with universal appeal.

STUDY GUIDE

MEET YOUR OBJECTIVES

1. **Explain how to read nonverbal cues to understand listeners' reactions to your speech.**
   While speaking, pay attention to your listeners' eye contact with you, their facial expressions and amount of movement, and their verbal and nonverbal responses to you.

2. **Describe several adaptations you can make to respond to listeners' nonverbal cues.**
   When you receive clues that listeners are bored, don't understand, or disagree with you, change what you are doing. You can try many strategies to communicate more effectively.

3. **List several ways you can customize your message to your audience.**
   Adapt to your specific audience by using audience members' names or mentioning the group they belong to; relating your speech to the location where you are speaking or to a historical or recent event; and relating statistics to your specific audience.

4. **Discuss strategies for adapting to diverse groups of listeners.**
   Adapt your speech to your listeners' cultural orientations toward individualism or collectivism, time, power, need for certainty, and attention to context. Consider directing your message toward a target audience.

Continued

THINK ABOUT THESE QUESTIONS

1. **Self Assessment** Consider a recent speech you gave. How did you adapt it to your specific audience? How could you have better customized the speech?
2. **Ethics Assessment** How can you ethically address the interests of all audience members if you direct your message toward a target audience?
3. **Critical Assessment** In the middle of a presentation, Brandon notices a few of the audience members losing eye contact with him, shifting in their seats, and glancing at their phones. What is happening, and what should Brandon do?

8

Developing Your Speech

OBJECTIVES

1. Select and narrow a topic for a speech.
2. Write an audience-centered specific-purpose statement for a speech.
3. State a central idea for a speech.
4. Apply three ways of generating main ideas from a central idea.

Select Your Topic

Your first task is to choose a topic for your speech. You will then need to narrow this topic to fit your time limits. But how do you go about choosing an appropriate, interesting topic?

Consider the Audience

As you search for potential speech topics, keep in mind each audience's interests and expectations. Your topic should be relevant to the *interests* and *expectations* of your listeners, and it should take into account the *knowledge* listeners already have about the subject.

Choose topics that are important—topics that matter to your listeners, as well as to yourself. Table 8.1 offers examples of topics appropriate for the interests, expectations, knowledge, and concerns of given audiences.

Consider Yourself

The best public-speaking topics are those that reflect your personal experience or that especially interest you. You can select a topic with which you are already familiar or one about which you would like to learn.

TABLE 8.1 Sample Audience-Centered Topics

Audience	Topic
Retirees	Preserving Social Security benefits
Civic organizations	The Special Olympics
Church members	Starting a community food bank
First graders	What to do in case of a fire at home
Teachers	Building children's self-esteem
College fraternities	Campus service opportunities

Your interest will motivate both your research and your eventual delivery of the speech.

Consider the Occasion

To be successful, a topic must be appropriate to the occasion. For example, you may not want to give a bawdy, humorous after-dinner speech at the birthday party of a dignified elder, or criticize an organization while speaking at the opening of its new headquarters.

Use Strategies

Contemplating your audience, yourself, and your occasion does not automatically yield a good topic. The following strategies can also help.

Brainstorm   Follow the guidelines in the How To box to use the time-tested technique of *brainstorming* to generate ideas for speech topics.[1]

Listen and Read   Very often, something you see, hear, or read triggers an idea for a speech. A current news story or social trend or issue you see on TV, read in your favorite news source, or receive via social media may suggest a topic. You can also consider randomly browsing the categories of a Web directory such as the Yahoo! directory (dir.yahoo.com) until you see a topic that piques your interest. Visit this chapter of MySearchLab (**www.mysearchlab.com**) for tools to help you select a topic. Chances are that a topic covered in

HOW TO

Brainstorm Speech Topics

- Write down the first topic that comes to mind. Do not allow yourself to evaluate it. Just write it down in a word or a phrase.
- Now jot down a second idea—again, anything that comes to mind.
- One topic may remind you of another possibility. Write it down. "Piggybacking" of ideas is okay.
- Continue without restraint. At this stage, anything goes.
- Make as long a list as you can think up in the time you have.
- Later, evaluate the list to choose a viable topic.

one medium has been covered in another as well, allowing extended research on the topic.

Just as you jotted down possible topics generated by brainstorming sessions, remember to write down topic ideas you get from media, class lectures, or informal conversations.

Don't Procrastinate!   For most brief speeches (under 10 minutes), you should allow at least one week from topic selection to speech delivery. A week gives you enough time to develop and research your speech. The whole process will be far easier than if you delay work until the night before you are supposed to deliver your speech.

QUICK CHECK

Selecting a Topic

- Is the topic relevant and important to your audience?
- How much does your audience know about the topic?
- Is the topic appropriate to the occasion?
- Is the topic of interest and importance to you?

Narrow the Topic

Now that you have a topic, you need to narrow it so that it fits within the time limits of your speech. Write your general topic—perhaps it is *Music*—at the top of a list. Add entries to the list, making each one more specific than the previous entry. Under "Music," for example, you might write, "Folk music," then "Irish folk music," and so on. Eventually, you will have a topic specific enough for the length of your speech. Be careful not to narrow your topic so much that you cannot find enough information for even a 3-minute talk. If you do, just go back a step to a broader topic.

Determine Your General Purpose

The **general purpose** of virtually any speech is either to inform, to persuade, or to entertain.

> Informative speakers give listeners information. They define, describe, or explain a thing, person, place, concept, process, or function to increase the knowledge of their listeners.
> Persuasive speakers try to get you to believe or do something. They may offer information, but they use the information to try to change or reinforce an audience's beliefs or to urge some sort of action.
> Entertaining speakers aim to get listeners to relax, smile, perhaps laugh, and generally enjoy themselves.

Determine Your Specific Purpose

Now that you have a topic and you know generally whether your speech should inform, persuade, or entertain, it is time for you to decide on its **specific purpose**. Unlike the general purpose, the specific purpose of your speech must be decided on by you alone, because it depends directly on the topic you choose.

Identify a Behavioral Objective

To arrive at a specific purpose for your speech, you must think in precise terms about what you want your audience to be able to do at the end of your speech. This kind of goal or purpose is called a **behavioral objective** because you specify the behavior you seek from the audience.

Formulate the Specific Purpose

Specific-purpose statements begin with the same nine words: "At the end of my speech, the audience will. . . ." The next word should be a verb that names an observable, measurable action that the audience should be able to do by the end of the speech.

Use verbs such as *list*, *explain*, *describe*, or *write*. Do not use words such as *know*, *understand*, or *believe*. You can discover what your listeners know, understand, or believe only by having them show you by performing some measurable activity.

Clarify the Specific Purpose

After you write your specific-purpose statement, make sure it follows these guidelines:

> Your specific purpose is important and reflects the interests, expectations, and knowledge level of your audience.
> Your specific-purpose statement expresses only one single idea. The purpose, "At the end of my speech, the audience will write a simple computer program and play the latest videogame," has more than one idea. If you try to achieve more than one specific purpose, you will have trouble covering all your ideas, and your speech may seem unfocused.
> Your specific-purpose statement does not say what you, the *speaker*, will do. It says what your *audience* will do.

Use the Specific Purpose

Everything you do while preparing and delivering the speech should contribute to your specific purpose. The specific purpose can help you assess the information you are gathering for your speech. For example, you may find that an interesting statistic, although related to your topic, does not help you achieve your specific purpose. In that case, you can substitute material that directly advances your purpose.

Develop Your Central Idea

The **central idea** is a one-sentence summary of your speech. The central idea (sometimes called the *thesis statement*), like the purpose statement, restates the speech topic. But whereas a purpose statement focuses on audience behavior, the central idea focuses on the content of the speech.

> The central idea should be a complete declarative sentence—not a phrase (such as *toxic waste dumping*) or clause (such as *stop dumping toxic waste*), and not a question ("Why is toxic waste a problem?").

> The central idea should use direct, specific language. An example of a good central idea is, "Toxic waste dumping is a major environmental problem in the United States today." Avoid qualifiers such as *in my opinion*. Avoid a central idea that is too vague, such as "Toxic waste is a reason to worry."

> The central idea should be a single idea. More than one central idea, like more than one idea in a purpose statement, will make your speech hard to understand.

> The central idea should reflect consideration of the audience. You considered your audience when selecting and narrowing your topic and when composing your purpose statement. In the same way, you should consider your audience's needs, interests, expectations, and knowledge when stating your central idea. If you do not consider your listeners, you run the risk of losing their attention before you even begin developing the speech.

Generate and Preview Your Main Ideas

Write the central idea at the top of a clean sheet of paper. Then ask these three questions:

1. Does the central idea have *logical divisions*? (These may be indicated by such phrases as "three types" or "four means.")
2. Can you think of several *reasons* why the central idea is true?
3. Can you support your central idea with a series of *steps* or a chronological progression?

You should be able to answer yes to one or more of these questions. These are your **main ideas**. Main ideas might, for example, be three *types* of birds of prey, four *reasons* the local park needs new lighting, or four *steps* in writing your own wedding vows.

Consult your specific-purpose statement as you generate your main ideas. If these main ideas do not help you achieve your purpose, you need to rethink your speech. You may change either your purpose or your main ideas. Whichever you do, be sure to synchronize these two elements. Remember, it is much easier to make changes at this point than after you have done your research and produced a detailed outline.

Once you have generated your main ideas, you can add a preview of those main ideas to your central idea (or thesis statement) to produce a **blueprint** for your speech. An example of a blueprint is, "Toxic waste dumping is a major environmental problem in the United States today. It endangers animals and poisons the water that humans drink." Preview the ideas in the same order you plan to discuss them in the speech.

STUDY GUIDE

MEET YOUR OBJECTIVES

1. **Select and narrow a topic for a speech.**
   Brainstorm, read, and listen to find topic ideas. Effective speech topics are appropriate for your audience, yourself, and your occasion.

2. **Write an audience-centered specific-purpose statement for a speech.**
   A specific-purpose statement begins, "At the end of my speech, the audience will . . ." and describes a single measurable action the audience should take. It should guide you during all speech preparation activities.

3. **State a central idea for a speech.**
   A central idea summarizes the topic of your speech with direct, specific language in a complete declarative sentence.

4. **Apply three ways of generating main ideas from a central idea.**
   Divide your central idea into main ideas by asking yourself if the central idea has logical divisions, if there are several reasons the central idea is true, and if the central idea can be supported with a series of steps.

THINK ABOUT THESE QUESTIONS

1. **Self Assessment** Turn back to Table 8.1 on page 67. For each of the audiences listed in the left-hand column, generate at least one additional audience-centered topic.

2. **Ethics Assessment** You overhear another student describing her paper about abolishing the death penalty and the book she used to research it. Would it be ethical to "borrow" her topic and consult the book she mentioned to prepare a speech for your public-speaking class?

Continued

3. **Critical Assessment** Use information from this chapter to critique and rewrite, if needed, the following specific-purpose statements. After you have made necessary corrections, pick one statement and use it to practice generating a central idea and main points.

   (1) At the end of my speech, the audience will know more about the Mexican Free-Tailed Bat.

   (2) I will explain some differences in nonverbal communication between Asian and Western cultures.

   (3) At the end of my speech, the audience will be able to list some reasons for xeriscaping one's yard.

   (4) At the end of my speech, the audience will be able to prepare a realistic monthly budget.

   (5) The advantages and disadvantages of living in a college dormitory.

9 Gathering Supporting Material

OBJECTIVES

1. Describe how personal knowledge and experience can serve as a source of supporting material for a speech.
2. Locate and evaluate Internet resources for a speech.
3. Explain how to use online databases to find supporting material for a speech.
4. Describe traditional library holdings that can provide supporting material for a speech.
5. Summarize how to conduct an effective interview.
6. Explain five strategies for a methodical research process.

Creating a successful speech requires knowledge of both the sources and the types of supporting material that speechmakers typically use.

Personal Knowledge and Experience

You might give a speech about a skill or hobby in which you are an expert. Or you might talk on a subject with which you have had some personal experience. In these cases, you may be able to provide some effective supporting materials from your own knowledge and experience. As an audience-centered speaker, you should realize that personal knowledge often has the additional advantage of heightening your credibility in the minds of your listeners.

The Internet

When facing a research task, most people turn first to the Internet. Knowing how to locate and evaluate various types of Internet resources can help make your search for supporting material more productive.

Locating Internet Resources

You have undoubtedly used Google to access material on the Web. If you feel overwhelmed by the number of sites a Google search can yield, a more specialized **vertical search engine** can help you narrow your search. For example, Google Scholar indexes academic sources, and Indeed indexes job Web sites.

Another strategy that can help you narrow your search is called a **Boolean search.** With a Boolean search, you can enclose phrases in quotation marks or parentheses so that the results include only those sites on which all words of the phrase appear in that order, rather than sites that contain the words at random. You can also insert "AND" or "+" between words and phrases to indicate that you wish to see only results that contain both phrases.

Similarly, Boolean searches let you exclude certain words and phrases from your search. And you can restrict the dates of your hits so that you see only documents posted within a specified time frame. These relatively simple strategies can help you to narrow a list of hits from, in some cases, millions of sites to a more workable number.

Exploring Internet Resources

As you go to the Web sites you have located, you will find a wide variety—from sites that try to sell you something, to the official sites of government agencies and news organizations. One clue to the type of site you have found is the **domain,** indicated by the last three letters of the site's URL (for example, *.com* or *.org*).

The following are common categories of Web sites.[1]

> **Commercial.** The purpose of this type of Web site is to sell products or services. The domain is often *.com*. News and entertainment sites also often have *.com* domains.

> **Country codes.** Web sites from countries other than the United States include a country code. For example, Great Britain is *.uk* and Canada is *.ca*.
> **Educational.** This type of site provides information about an educational entity. The domain is usually *.edu*.
> **Government.** The purpose of this type of Web site is to provide information produced by government agencies, offices, and departments. The domain is usually *.gov*.
> **Military.** Information about or from the military is usually indicated by Internet addresses that end in *.mil*.
> **Organizational.** The purpose of this type of Web site is to advocate a group's point of view. The domain is usually *.org*.

Evaluating Internet Resources

No search strategy can ensure the quality of the sites you discover. As you begin to explore sites, you need to evaluate them according to a consistent standard. The following six criteria can serve as such a standard.[2]

Accountability   Find out what individual or organization is responsible for the Web site.

> The individual or organization responsible for the site may be clear from the title of the site and/or its URL.
> See whether the site is signed.
> Follow links or search the author's name to determine the author's expertise and authority.
> If the site is unsigned, search for a sponsoring organization. Follow links, search the organization's name, or consider the domain to determine reputability.
> If you cannot identify or verify the author or sponsor of a Web site, be extremely wary of the site.

Accuracy   It may be difficult to determine whether the information a site contains is accurate unless you are an expert in the area the site addresses. These steps can help.

> Consider whether the author or sponsor is a credible authority. If so, the information is more likely to be accurate.
> Assess the care with which the site has been written. A site should be relatively free of writing errors.
> Conduct additional research into the information on the site. You may be able to verify or refute the information by consulting another resource.

Objectivity   Objectivity is related to accountability. Once you know who is accountable for a site, consider the interests, philosophical or political biases, and sources of financial support of that individual or organization. The more objective the author, the more credible the facts and information presented. Consider, too, any advertisements on the site that might influence its content.

Often, the first hit from your Web search is *Wikipedia*. Wikipedia can be useful for general and very current information, or as a source of other resources. Keep in mind, however, that anyone, regardless of expertise or level of objectivity, can add to or change the content of any entry. For this reason, many instructors consider Wikipedia an inappropriate source of information for student speeches.

Timeliness   Look for evidence that the site was posted recently or has been kept current. At the bottom of many sites, you will find a statement specifying when the site was posted and when it was last updated. When you are concerned with factual data, the more recent, the better.

Usability   The site should load fairly quickly. The layout and design of the site should facilitate its use. Also consider whether there is a fee to gain access to any of the information on the site.

QUICK CHECK

Evaluate Internet Resources

- I know who is accountable for the Web site.
- I can verify the accuracy of the information.
- The site is objective.
- The site is current.
- The site is easy to use and provides links to other sites.
- The site is culturally diverse and free of bias.

Diversity   An inclusive Web site will be free of material that communicates bias against any gender, ethnicity, race, culture, or sexual orientation; and against people with disabilities.[3]

Online Databases

Online databases provide access to bibliographic information, abstracts, and full texts for a variety of resources. Like Web sites, online databases are reached via a networked computer. Unlike Web sites, however, most databases are restricted to the patrons of libraries that subscribe to them. Your library may subscribe to several or all of the following popular full-text, searchable databases:

> **ABI/Inform Global.** This resource offers many full-text articles in business and trade publications from 1971 to the present.
> **Academic Search Complete.** This popular database offers many full-text articles from 1865 to the present, covering a wide variety of subjects.
> **JSTOR.** This is a multisubject, full-text database of journal articles from the first volume to the present.
> **LexisNexis Academic.** Focusing on business and law, this database provides many full-text articles from newspapers, magazines, journals, newsletters, and wire services. Dates of coverage vary.

> **Newspaper Source.** This database offers many full-text articles from more than 40 U.S. and international newspapers; more than 330 full-text television and radio news transcripts from CBS News, CNN, CNN International, FOX News, NPR, and others; and selected full-text articles from more than 330 regional (U.S.) newspapers.

Traditional Library Holdings

Despite the rapid development of Internet and database resources, the more traditional holdings of libraries, both paper and electronic, remain rich sources of supporting material.

The key to finding library materials is the *card catalog*. You can access the computerized card catalog of most libraries from your own computer before you ever enter the library. The catalog will supply each book's *call number*, which you will need in order to find the book. Once you have the call number, you are ready to venture into the library to obtain the item you want. It is a good idea to become familiar with your library's layout before you have to do research under the pressure of a deadline.

> **Books** Libraries' collections of books are called the **stacks.** The stacks are organized by call numbers. Many libraries offer a location guide or map to guide you to the floor or section of the stacks that houses the books with the call numbers in which you are interested.

  Do not wait until the last minute to conduct library research for your speech. Increasing numbers of libraries are beginning to house some of their stacks off-site. You may have to fill out a request form and allow some wait time before a book becomes available to you.

> **Reference resources** Many encyclopedias, dictionaries, directories, atlases, almanacs, yearbooks, books of quotations, and biographical dictionaries are now

available online. But if you are not able to find a specific reference resource online, you may be able to locate a print version in the reference section of your library. Reference librarians are often able to suggest print or electronic resources that you might otherwise overlook. Try to visit the library during hours when a librarian is available to help you.

Interviews

Consider interviewing a person who might know the answers to some of the important questions raised by your speech topic. Before you decide on an interview, be sure that your questions cannot be answered by doing online or library research. If you decide that only an interview can give you the material you need, you should prepare for it in advance.

Preparing for the Interview

Determine Your Purpose Specifically, what do you need to find out? Do you need hard facts that you cannot obtain from other sources? Do you need the interviewee's expert testimony on your subject? Or do you need an explanation of some of the information you have found in online or print sources?

Arrange a Meeting Once you have a specific purpose for the interview, decide whom you need to speak with, and arrange a meeting. Telephone or email the person in advance, explain briefly who you are and why you are calling, and ask for an appointment. Most people are flattered to have their authority and knowledge recognized and willingly grant interviews if their schedules permit.

Using your electronic device to record audio or video of the interview can free you from having to take copious notes and make it easy to refer to the interviewee's exact words. If you are considering recording the interview, ask for the interviewee's okay during this initial contact. If the person does not grant permission, be prepared to gather your information without electronic assistance.

Plan Your Questions   Before your interview, find out as much as you can about both your subject and the person you are interviewing. Prepare questions that take full advantage of the interviewee's specific knowledge of your subject. You can do this only if *you* already know a good deal about your subject.

Combine closed-ended and open-ended questions. Open-ended questions often follow closed-ended questions: When the person you are interviewing answers a closed-ended question with a simple "yes" or "no," you may wish to follow up by asking "Why?"

Conduct the Interview

Follow the suggestions in the How To box to conduct effective interviews.

Conduct an Effective Interview

- **Dress appropriately.** Conservative, business-like clothes show that you are serious about the interview and that you respect the norms of your interviewee's world.
- **Bring note-taking supplies.** Even if you plan to record the interview, you may want to turn off the recording at some point during the interview or your device may malfunction, so you'll need an alternative.
- **Arrive a few minutes ahead of schedule.** Be prepared, however, to wait patiently, if necessary.
- **Remind the interviewee of your purpose.** Restate why you chose that person to interview. If you admire the interviewee's work, feel free to tell him or her.
- **Prepare your equipment.** If you have decided to use a recorder, set up your device as needed. You may keep it out of sight once the interviewee has seen it, but never try to hide a recorder at the outset—such a ploy

is unethical. If you are going to take written notes, get your supplies ready.

- **Follow your plan.** Use the questions you have prepared as a guide. Listen carefully to the person's answers, and ask for clarification of any ideas you don't understand.

- **Be ready to adjust the plan.** Listen closely to the person's words and their intended meaning. If the interviewee mentions something you did not think of, don't be afraid to pursue the point.

- **End the interview on time.** Thank your interviewee for his or her contribution, and leave.

Follow Up the Interview

As soon as possible after the interview, read through your notes carefully and revise any portions that may be illegible or unclear. If you recorded the interview, save and label the file with the date and the interviewee's name.

Research Strategies

Well-organized research strategies can make your efforts easier and more efficient. You need to develop a preliminary bibliography, locate resources, evaluate the usefulness of resources, take notes, and identify possible presentation aids.

Develop a Preliminary Bibliography

Creating a **preliminary bibliography** or list of promising resources should be your first goal. You will probably discover more resources than you actually look at or refer to in your speech; at this stage, the bibliography simply serves as a menu of possibilities. How many resources should you list in a preliminary bibliography for, say, a 10-minute speech? A reasonable number might be 10 or 12 that look promising. If you have many more than that, you may feel overwhelmed. If you have fewer, you may have too little information.

You will need to develop a system for keeping track of your resources. You can bookmark Web sites; print out or save screenshots of a record from online catalogs or articles from databases. You may also be able to email files containing articles to yourself or store them via an online service such as Dropbox.

Locate Resources

You should have no trouble obtaining the actual texts of resources from the Web and online databases. For all the other items in your preliminary bibliography, you will need to locate the resources yourself. Refer back to the discussion earlier in this chapter on traditional library holdings.

Evaluate the Usefulness of Resources

It makes sense to gauge the potential usefulness of your resources before you begin to read more closely and take notes. The instructions in the How To box can help you.

HOW TO

Evaluate Source Material

Before you read in depth and take notes from your resources, take a little time to figure out which ones are likely to be of most use for your speech.

- Glance over the tables of contents of books.
- Flip quickly through books or scroll Web sites or database articles to note any charts, graphs, or other visual materials that could be used as visual aids.
- Skim a key chapter or two of books. Skim Web sites and articles as well.

To choose the most useful materials, think critically about these questions:

- Is the resource likely to help you achieve your specific purpose?
- How effective is the information likely to be with your audience?

Take Notes

Once you have located, previewed, and ranked your resources, you are ready to begin more careful reading and note-taking.

> Beginning with the resources that you think have the greatest potential, record any examples, statistics, opinions, or other supporting material that might be useful to your speech. Depending on the resources, you can photocopy them, cut and paste them or save them into a computer file, and/or print them out.

> If you copy a phrase, sentence, or paragraph verbatim from a source, be sure to put quotation marks around it. You may need to know later whether it is a direct quote or a paraphrase. (This information will be obvious, of course, on printouts or photocopies.)

> Record the source of the supporting material. In Chapter 4, we discuss the ethical importance of crediting all sources of ideas and information. If you consistently keep track of your sources as you take notes, you will avoid the possibility of committing unintentional plagiarism.

> If you need to compile a formal bibliography, or list of sources, to submit to an instructor, use the type of formatting specified by your instructor. You can find detailed instructions for the most common methods of formatting bibliographic citations at the Purdue Online Writing Lab (OWL): http://owl.english.purdue.edu.

Identify Possible Presentation Aids

In addition to discovering verbal supporting material in your sources, you may also find charts, graphs, photographs, and other potentially valuable visual material.

Even if you are not certain that you will use presentation aids in your speech, it can't hurt to save, photocopy, and/or print out any good possibilities. Then, when the time comes to consider if and where presentation aids might enhance your speech, you will have some at hand.

Be sure to record the sources of visual materials just as you did for your written materials, so that you can find them again without frustration if you need them.

QUICK CHECK

Research Strategies
- Develop a preliminary bibliography.
- Locate sources.
- Consider the potential usefulness of sources.
- Take notes.
- Identify possible presentation aids.

STUDY GUIDE

MEET YOUR OBJECTIVES

1. **Describe how personal knowledge and experience can be a source of supporting material for a speech.**
   Personal experiences and knowledge can provide some of your source material and can raise your credibility with the audience.

2. **Locate and evaluate Internet resources for a speech.**
   Vertical search engines and Boolean searches can narrow results of an Internet search. Use the domain to help you evaluate the accountability, accuracy, objectivity, timeliness, usability, and diversity of Internet materials.

3. **Explain how to use online databases to find supporting material for a speech.**
   Online databases offer abstracts and full-text of articles, news, and more. They are typically available through libraries that subscribe to them.

4. **Describe traditional library holdings that can provide supporting material for a speech.**
   Books, stored in the library's stacks, and references, stored in the reference room, can provide information unavailable online. Be sure to allow plenty of time for library research.

Continued

5. **Summarize how to conduct an effective interview.**
Prepare carefully for an interview by researching and creating a list of questions. Treat interviewees' time with respect, and listen carefully to their responses to questions in order to follow up with clarification questions.

6. **Explain five strategies for a methodical research process.**
To conduct an efficient search, you need to develop a preliminary bibliography, locate resources, evaluate the usefulness of resources, take notes, and identify possible presentation aids.

THINK ABOUT THESE QUESTIONS

1. **Self Assessment** Explain how you might use each of the five key sources of supporting material to help you develop an informative speech on how to choose a new computer.

2. **Ethics Assessment** Electronic and print indexes and databases sometimes include abstracts of books and articles rather than full texts. If you have read only the abstract of a source, is it ethical to include that source in your preliminary bibliography?

3. **Critical Assessment** You neglected to record complete bibliographic information for one of your best information sources, a journal article you found on a database. You discover your omission as you are reviewing your outline just before you deliver your speech, and now you have no way to look up the information. How can you solve your problem in an ethical way? What are some ways you could have avoided this problem?

10 Supporting Your Speech

OBJECTIVES

1. Explain the importance and best practices for using illustrations in a speech.
2. Differentiate how descriptions and explanations are used in speeches.
3. Summarize how to give definitions in a speech.
4. Describe how to use analogies in a speech.
5. Recap effective ways to present statistics in a speech.
6. Describe the value of using opinions in a speech.
7. Select the best supporting material for a speech.

Once you have gathered a variety of appropriate supporting material, you will need to decide how to use your information to best advantage in your speech. Be sure to use oral or written citations as described in Chapter 4 and at MySearchLab (**www.mysearchlab.com**) to properly acknowledge sources of supporting material.

Use Illustrations

Everybody likes to hear a story. An **illustration**—a story or anecdote that provides an example of an idea, issue, or problem you are discussing—almost always ensures audience interest.

> **Brief illustrations** are often no longer than a sentence or two. A series of brief illustrations can sometimes have more impact than either a single brief illustration or a more detailed, extended illustration. In addition, although an audience could dismiss a single illustration as an exception, two or more strongly suggest a trend or norm.

> **Extended illustrations** are longer and more detailed than brief illustrations; they resemble a story. They are vividly descriptive, and they have a plot—which includes an opening, complications, a climax, and a resolution. Longer stories take more time, but they can be very dramatic and emotionally compelling. Extended illustrations can work well as speech introductions.

> **Hypothetical illustrations** may be either brief or extended. They describe situations or events that have not actually occurred but that *might* happen. Remember from Chapter 4 that ethical speakers introduce hypothetical illustrations with a phrase such as, "Imagine that . . ."

To use illustrations effectively, be certain that your stories are directly relevant to the idea or point they are supposed to support. They should be typical of a situation or represent a trend. The best illustrations are personal ones that your listeners can imagine experiencing themselves. Include enough details to make the story vivid and specific to listeners.

Use Descriptions and Explanations

A **description** tells you what something is like. Descriptions provide the details that allow audience members to develop mental pictures of what speakers are talking about. Good descriptions are vivid, accurate, and specific; they make people, places, and events come alive for the audience.

An **explanation** is a statement that makes clear how something is done or why it exists in its present form or existed in its past form. Speakers who discuss or demonstrate processes of any kind rely at least in part on explanations of *how* those processes work. Explaining *why* involves giving causes or reasons for a policy, principle, or event. Explaining why some condition or event exists provides an analysis that often leads to better solutions.

HOW TO

Use Descriptions and Explanations

- Avoid overuse. Alternate descriptions and explanations with other types of support.
- Keep them brief. Supply only the necessary details.
- Be specific. Use vivid, concrete words that appeal to the senses.

Provide Definitions

Definitions have two uses in speeches. First, a speaker should be sure to define any and all specialized, technical, or little-known terms in his or her speech. Such definitions are usually achieved by *classification*, the kind of definition you would find in a dictionary. Second, a speaker may define a term by showing how it works or how it is applied in a specific instance—what is known as an *operational definition*. For example, a speaker may define a disease such as rickets by explaining the effects on people who develop it, rather than using a dictionary definition.

HOW TO

Use Definitions Effectively

- Use a definition only when needed.
- Make definitions immediately and easily understandable to your audience.
- Be certain that your definition and your use of a term are consistent throughout a speech.

Use Analogies

An **analogy** is a comparison. Like a definition, an analogy increases understanding; unlike a definition, it deals with relationships and comparisons—between the new and the old, the unknown and the known, or any other pair of ideas or things. Analogies can help your listeners understand unfamiliar ideas, things, and situations by showing how these are similar to something they already know.

Literal Analogies

A **literal analogy** is a comparison between two similar things. But because it is creative, it is inherently interesting and should help grab an audience's attention. One speaker compared crustaceans, such as shrimp, to insects, noting that both are in the same group of animals.[1] Literal analogies can help listeners from a different culture understand terms they may not be familiar with. To help the audience understand, make sure the two things you compare in a literal analogy are very similar.

Figurative Analogies

If you describe the relationships among a group of coworkers as a seething snake pit, filled with hissing gossip and sharp-fanged attacks, you are using a **figurative analogy**. A figurative analogy relies on imaginative insights, rather than on facts or statistics, so it is not considered hard evidence. Be sure that the essential similarity between the two objects in a figurative analogy is readily apparent. For example, the main similarity between the snake pit and the work group is the strife between those in the same group. If the comparison is unclear, your audience can end up wondering what in the world you are talking about.

Use Statistics as Support

Just as three or four brief examples may be more effective than just one, a *statistic* that represents hundreds or thousands of individuals may be more persuasive still. Statistics can help a speaker express the magnitude or seriousness of a situation. Or statistics can express the relationship of a part to the whole.

Use Reliable Sources

Statistics can be exploited to support almost any conclusion desired. As an ethical speaker, your goal is to cite *reputable*, *authoritative*, and *unbiased* sources.

> Reputable sources are those known to have expertise in research or the subject of the statistics.
> The most authoritative source is the **primary source**—the original collector and interpreter of the data. Go to the primary source as often as possible. Do not assume that a secondhand account, or **secondary source**, has reported the statistic accurately and fairly.
> Unbiased sources have no special interest in their statistics supporting any particular viewpoint. Government statistics and those from independent sources are generally considered unbiased.

As you evaluate your sources, try to find out how the statistics were gathered. For example, if a statistic relies on a sample, how was the sample taken? Sample sizes and survey methods do vary widely, but most legitimate polls involve samples of 500 to 2,000 people, selected at random from a larger population.

Interpret Statistics Accurately

People are often swayed by statistics that sound good but have, in fact, been wrongly calculated or misinterpreted. Both as a user of statistics in your own speeches and as a consumer of statistics in articles, books, and speeches, be constantly alert to what the statistics actually mean.

Make Your Statistics Understandable and Memorable

You can make your statistics easier to understand and more memorable in several ways.

> Dramatize statistics with your choice of viewpoint. Does a genetic condition protect 10 percent of people from high blood pressure or, more dramatically, make it easier for 90 percent to develop high blood pressure?[2]
> Compact statistics or express them in limits that are more meaningful or more easily understandable to your audience. For example, you might express the amount of the national debt as the number of dollars per American adult.[3]

> Explode statistics. Exploded statistics are created by adding or multiplying related numbers—for example, cost per unit times number of units. Because it is larger, the exploded statistic seems more significant than the original figures from which it was derived.
> Compare statistics. Comparing your statistic with another heightens its impact.
> Round off numbers, but do so without distorting or falsifying the statistic.
> Use visual aids to present your statistics. Displaying numbers in a table or graph in front of your listeners enables them to more easily grasp the statistics.

QUICK CHECK

Select Effective Statistics

- Are the data from primary sources?
- Are the sources reputable, unbiased, and authoritative?
- Did you interpret the statistics accurately?
- Are the statistics easy to understand?
- Are they memorable?
- Can you convert the statistics into visual aids?

Use Opinions

Expert testimony, the testimony of a recognized authority, can add a great deal of weight to your arguments. You may quote experts directly or paraphrase their words, as long as you are careful not to alter the intent of their remarks.

Like illustrations, **lay testimony,** the opinions of non-experts, can stir an audience's emotions. And, although neither as authoritative nor as unbiased as expert testimony, lay testimony is often more memorable.

To make a point memorable, include a **literary quotation** in your speech. You can easily access quotation dictionaries on the Web and in the reference sections of most libraries. Brief, pointed quotations usually have greater audience impact than longer ones.

Here are a few suggestions for using opinions effectively in your speeches.

> Be certain that any authority you cite is unbiased and an expert on the subject you are discussing.
> Cite your source properly, and be sure to quote accurately.
> Use opinions that are representative of prevailing opinion.
> Limit quotations to one or two per speech.

Select the Best Supporting Material

You should consider accountability, accuracy, objectivity, recency, usability, and diversity in evaluating any supporting material you hope to use. How do you decide what to use and what to eliminate?

> **Magnitude.** Bigger is better. The larger the numbers, the more convincing your statistics will be. The more experts who support your point of view, the more your expert testimony will command your audience's attention.
> **Proximity.** The best supporting material is whatever is the most relevant to your listeners, or "closest to home."
> **Concreteness.** If you need to discuss principles and theories, explain them with concrete examples and specific statistics.
> **Variety.** A mix of illustrations, opinions, definitions, and statistics is much more interesting and convincing than the exclusive use of any one type of supporting material.
> **Humor.** Unless the topic is very serious or somber, audiences usually appreciate a touch of humor in an example or opinion.
> **Suitability.** Your final decision about whether to use a certain piece of supporting material will depend on its suitability to you, your speech, the occasion, and your audience.

STUDY GUIDE

MEET YOUR OBJECTIVES

1. **Explain the importance and best practices for using illustrations in a speech.**
   Illustrations catch listeners' interest. Brief, extended, and hypothetical illustrations can also help your audience understand your message.

2. **Differentiate how descriptions and explanations are used in speeches.**
   Use vivid descriptions to help listeners visualize people, places, things, or events. Use specific, concrete explanations to show *how* something works or the reasons *why* something occurs or exists.

3. **Summarize how to give definitions in a speech.**
   Use easily understandable dictionary and operational definitions to help audiences understand unfamiliar terms.

4. **Describe how to use analogies in a speech.**
   Use literal analogies to compare two similar things and imaginative figurative analogies to help listeners understand things that share fewer similar characteristics.

5. **Recap effective ways to present statistics in a speech.**
   Use statistics from reliable sources, interpret them accurately, and make them understandable to listeners by dramatizing, compacting, exploding, comparing, or showing visuals of them.

6. **Describe the value of using opinions in a speech.**
   Expert and lay testimony and literary quotations can help you use the opinions of others to support your own message.

7. **Select the best supporting material for a speech.**
   The best supporting materials are those with the most magnitude, proximity to the audience, concreteness, variety, and suitability to the audience. Some humor is usually welcome.

Continued

THINK ABOUT THESE QUESTIONS

1. **Self Assessment** Describe how you can use each of the six types of supporting material described in this chapter in your next speech.
2. **Ethics Assessment** Before adding to your speech an illustration that shares personal information about a friend, should you ask permission from your friend?
3. **Critical Assessment** Tony found just the statistics he needs on the Internet. What information does he need in order to evaluate the statistics?

11

Organizing Your Speech

OBJECTIVES

1. List and describe five patterns for organizing the main ideas of a speech.
2. Explain how to integrate supporting material into a speech.
3. Use verbal and nonverbal signposts to organize a speech for the ears of others.

You must organize your ideas in logical patterns to ensure that your audience can follow, understand, and remember what you say.

Organize Your Main Ideas

In Chapter 8, you learned how to generate a preliminary plan for your speech by determining whether your central idea had logical divisions, could be supported by several reasons, or could be explained by identifying specific steps.

Now you are ready to decide which of your main ideas to discuss first, which one second, and so on. Five organizational patterns are most common:

> topical
> chronological
> spatial
> cause and effect
> problem–solution

Organize Ideas Topically

If your central idea has natural divisions, you can often organize your speech topically. Speeches on such diverse

97

topics as factors to consider when selecting a mountain bike, types of infertility treatments, and the various classes of ham-radio licenses all could reflect **topical organization.**

Natural divisions are often basically equal in importance. It may not matter which point you discuss first, second, or third. You can simply arrange your main points as a matter of personal preference.

At other times, you may wish to emphasize one point more than the others. You can use one of the following guidelines.

> **Recency** According to the principle of **recency,** audiences tend to remember best what they hear last, so when you organize by recency, you order your points from least to most important.
> **Primacy** To use the principle of **primacy,** put your most important or convincing idea first. Organize your main points according to primacy if your topic is controversial and you know or suspect your audience will be skeptical or hostile to your ideas.
> **Complexity** If your main points range from simple to complicated, it makes sense to arrange them in order of **complexity,** progressing from the simple to the most complex.

Order Ideas Chronologically

When your central idea can be supported by a series of steps, chronological organization often makes sense. **Chronological organization** is organization by time or sequence; your steps are ordered according to when each occurred or should occur. A speech on the history of the modern Olympic games might be organized chronologically.

You can choose to organize your main points either from earliest to most recent (forward in time) or from recent events back into history (backward in time). The progression you choose depends on your personal preference and on whether you want to use the principles of primacy or recency to emphasize the beginning or the end of the sequence. However, how-to explanations are usually arranged forward in time, as a sequence or series of steps to follow from beginning to end.

Arrange Ideas Spatially

A speaker who relies on **spatial organization** arranges ideas according to their physical locations or directions. A speech about the Lewis and Clark expedition might be arranged spatially to describe the team's various camp sites. It does not usually matter whether the speaker chooses to progress up or down, east or west, forward or back, as long as ideas are developed in a logical order.

Organize Ideas to Show Cause and Effect

A speech organized to show **cause and effect** might first identify a situation and then discuss the effects that result from it (cause→effect). For example, a speaker might describe a recent drought and then discuss its effects.

A speech could also present a situation and then seek its causes (effect→cause). Such a speaker might describe the recent drought and then talk about factors that created it.

According to the recency principle, the cause–effect pattern emphasizes the effects; the effect–cause pattern emphasizes the causes.

Organize Ideas by Problem and Solution

If you want to emphasize how best to *solve* a problem, you will probably use a **problem–solution pattern** of organization. Like causes and effects, problems and solutions can be discussed in either order:

> If listeners are already fairly aware of a problem but uncertain how to solve it, you will probably discuss the problem first and then the solution(s).
> If your audience knows about an action or program that has been implemented but does not know the reasons for its implementation, you might select a solution–problem pattern of organization.

Combine Multiple Patterns

You can combine several of these patterns. For example, you may use an overall cause–effect pattern, discussing a drought and then its effects. However, you may order your points about the effects topically—talking first about effects on crops, then on animals, and then on people—or spatially, talking about effects in different geographical areas. Visit this chapter of MySearchLab (**www.mysearchlab.com**) to practice determining the organizational patterns of speeches.

Acknowledge Cultural Differences in Organization

Although the five patterns just discussed are typical of the way speakers in the United States are expected to organize and process information, they are not necessarily typical of all cultures.[1] In fact, each culture teaches its members patterns of thought and organization that are considered appropriate for various occasions and audiences.

On the whole, U.S. speakers tend to be more linear and direct than speakers from other cultures. Semitic speakers support their main points by pursuing tangents that might seem "off topic" to many U.S. speakers. Speakers in some Asian cultures might never overtly state their main ideas. They would expect the audience to determine the main ideas by analyzing the themes and messages of stories the speaker shared. Speakers from Romance and Russian cultures may tend to begin with a basic principle and then move to facts and illustrations that they only gradually connect to a main point.

Of course, these are very broad generalizations. But as an audience member, recognizing the existence of cultural differences when you are listening to a speech can help you appreciate and understand the organizational pattern of a speaker from a culture other than your own.

Organize Your Supporting Material

Suppose you have decided what supporting material to use and have identified the ideas in your speech that require support. Now you realize that in support of your second main idea you have an illustration, two statistics, and an opinion. In what order should you present these items?

You can sometimes use the five standard organizational patterns to arrange your supporting material, as well as your main ideas and subpoints. Illustrations, for instance, may be organized chronologically, as one speaker did when discussing technology:

> . . . miracle has followed upon miracle—from a television in every home in the 1950s, to the launching of the first communications satellite in the 1960s, to the introduction of cable TV in the 1970s, the rise of personal computers in the 1980s, the Internet in the 1990s, and social media in the 2000s.[2]

At other times, however, none of the five patterns may seem suited to the supporting materials you have. In those instances, you may need to turn to an organizational strategy more specifically adapted to your supporting materials. These strategies include (1) primacy or recency, (2) specificity, (3) complexity, and (4) "soft" to "hard" evidence.

Primacy or Recency

As we've discussed, the principles of primacy and recency can help you determine whether to put a main idea at the beginning or the end of your speech. You can use these principles to order your supporting material, too.

Suppose that you have several statistics to support a main point. All are relevant and significant, but one is especially gripping. You might opt to arrange the statistics in your speech according to recency, saving the most dramatic one for last.

Specificity

Sometimes your supporting material will range from very specific examples to more general overviews of a situation. You may either offer your specific information first and end with your general statement or make the general statement first and support it with specific evidence.

Complexity

You've seen that moving from the simple to the complex is one way you can organize your main ideas. The same method of organization may also be applied to supporting material. In many situations, it makes sense to start with the simplest ideas, which are easy to understand, and work up to more complex ones. For example, you might give a definition of an unfamiliar term before presenting a graph of statistics related to that term.

Soft to Hard Evidence

Supporting material can also be arranged from "soft" to "hard."

> **Soft evidence** rests on opinion or inference. Hypothetical illustrations, descriptions, explanations, definitions, analogies, and opinions are usually considered soft.
> **Hard evidence** includes factual examples and statistics.

To organize supporting materials in this order, you might tell a brief story about your own experience trying to use less water during a drought and then present expert opinions about the best ways to use less water, followed by statistics about which methods actually do use the least water. Soft to hard organization of supporting material relies chiefly on the principle of recency—that the last statement is remembered best. In this example, your listeners would be likely to remember the most effective ways they can save water.

QUICK CHECK

Organizing Your Supporting Material

- Primacy: most important material first
- Recency: most important material last
- Specificity: from specific information to general overview or from general overview to specific information
- Complexity: from simple to more complex material
- Soft to hard evidence: from opinion or hypothetical illustration to fact or statistic

Organizing Your Presentation for the Ears of Others: Signposting

You have a logically ordered, fairly complete plan for your speech. But if you delivered the speech at this point, your audience might become frustrated or confused as they tried to figure out your organizational plan. So your next task is to develop **signposts**—organizational cues for your audience's ears. Signposts include previews, transitions, and summaries.

One significant difference between writing and public speaking is that public speaking is more repetitive. Audience-centered speakers need to remember that listeners, unlike readers, cannot go back to review a missed point. Using previews, summaries, and transitions not only helps your audience follow the organization of your speech but also builds repetition of key points into your speech, so that audience members are less likely to miss them.

Previews

As its name indicates, a **preview** is a statement of what is to come. Previews help to ensure that audience members will first anticipate and later remember the important points of a speech. Two types of previews are usually used in speeches: *initial previews* and *internal previews*.

Initial Previews An initial preview is a statement of what the main ideas of the speech will be. As discussed in Chapter 8, it is usually presented in conjunction with the central idea at or near the end of the introduction, as a *blueprint* for the speech. For example, your blueprint might be, "The recent drought is the cause of severe problems for all living things in our area. It has produced ill effects on crops, on animals, and on people."

Internal Previews In addition to using previews near the beginning of their speeches, speakers also use them at various points throughout. These internal previews introduce and outline ideas that will be developed as the speech progresses.

Sometimes speakers phrase internal previews in the form of questions they plan to answer. The question in this example provides an internal preview.

> . . . the question remains, what can we do, as potential travelers and potential victims, to protect ourselves?[3]

Just as anticipating an idea helps audience members remember it, so mentally answering a question helps them plant the answer firmly in their minds.

Transitions

A **transition** is a verbal or nonverbal signal that a speaker has finished discussing one idea and is moving to another.

Verbal Transitions Speakers can use a variety of different verbal transitions, including (1) repeating a key word; (2) using well-known transitional phrases; and (3) enumerating, or numbering, points.

A speaker can sometimes make a verbal transition simply by repeating a key word from an earlier statement or by using a synonym or a pronoun that refers to an earlier key word or idea. This type of transition is often used to make one sentence flow smoothly into the next. (The previous sentence itself is an example: "This type of transition" refers to the sentence that precedes it.)

Well-known transitional words or phrases, such as the following, show relationships between ideas.

> *In addition to* transitions, previews and summaries are *also* considered to be signposts.
> *Not only* does plastic packaging use up our scarce resources, but it contaminates them *as well*.
> *In other words*, as women's roles have changed, they have *also* contributed to this effect.
> *In summary*, Fanny Brice is probably the best remembered star of Ziegfeld's Follies.

> *Therefore*, I recommend that you sign the grievance petition.

Simple enumeration (*first, second, third*) can also point up relationships between ideas and provide transitions.

HOW TO

Transition to Your Conclusion

One type of transitional signpost that can occasionally backfire and do more harm than good is one that signals the end of a speech. The words *finally* and *in conclusion* give the audience implicit permission to stop listening, and they often do. If the speech has been too long or has otherwise not gone well, the audience may even audibly express relief.

Better strategies for moving into your conclusion include the following:

* Repeat a key word or phrase.
* Use a synonym or pronoun that refers to a previous idea.
* Offer a final summary.
* Refer back to the introduction of your speech.

Nonverbal Transitions You can use several types of nonverbal transitions, either alone or in combination with verbal transitions. A change in facial expression, a pause, an altered vocal pitch or speaking rate, and a movement all may indicate a transition.

For example, a speaker talking about the value of cardiopulmonary resuscitation began his speech with a powerful anecdote about a man suffering a heart attack at a party. No one knew how to help, and the man died. The speaker then looked up from his notes and paused, while maintaining eye contact with his audience. His next words were, "The real tragedy of Bill Jorgen's death was that it should not have happened." His pause, as well as the words that followed, indicated a transition into the body of the speech.

Like this speaker, most good speakers use a combination of verbal and nonverbal transitions to move from one point to another through their speeches. You can learn more about nonverbal communication in Chapter 17.

Summaries

Like a preview, a **summary,** or recap of what has been said, provides your listeners with additional exposure to your ideas and can help ensure that they will grasp and remember your message. Most speakers use two types of summaries: *the final summary* and *the internal summary.*

Final Summary A final summary restates the main ideas of a speech and gives an audience their *last* exposure to those ideas. It occurs just before the end of a speech, often doing double duty as a transition between the body and the conclusion. Your final summary should leave listeners in no doubt as to the important points of your speech.

Internal Summary Internal summaries, as their name suggests, occur within and throughout a speech. An internal summary restates ideas that you have developed before that point. You can use an internal summary after discussing two or three points, to keep those points fresh in the minds of the audience as the speech progresses.

Speakers often combine an internal summary and internal preview to create a transition. For example, you might say, "Now that I've detailed the devastating crop losses caused by the drought and the large losses in animal populations, I want to tell you what the drought has done to us humans."

Supplement Signposts with Presentation Aids

One way in which you can increase the likelihood of your listeners' attending to your signposting is to prepare and use presentation aids to supplement your signposts.

QUICK CHECK

Types of Signposts

Initial previews
Internal previews
Verbal transitions
Nonverbal transitions
Final summaries
Internal summaries

For example, you could display a PowerPoint slide showing a bulleted or numbered outline of your main ideas as you preview them in your introduction and summarize them in your conclusion. Some speakers like to use one slide for each main point, and display them to emphasize transitions between points.

Visual support for your signposts is especially helpful for your audience if your speech is long or its organization is complex.

STUDY GUIDE

MEET YOUR OBJECTIVES

1. **List and describe five patterns for organizing the main ideas of a speech.**

   For North American audiences, the five most common patterns of organization include topical, chronological, spatial, cause and effect, and problem–solution. These patterns are sometimes combined. Other organizational patterns may be favored in different cultures.

2. **Explain how to integrate supporting material into a speech.**

   You can organize the supporting material for each main idea according to one of the five common patterns: primacy, recency, specificity, complexity, or soft-to-hard evidence.

Continued

3. **Use verbal and nonverbal signposts to organize a speech for the ears of others.**

   Signposts include verbal and nonverbal transitions, previews, and summaries. They are used to help you communicate your organization to your audience. Reinforce signposts visually with presentation aids.

THINK ABOUT THESE QUESTIONS

1. **Self Assessment** Take notes while listening to either a live or recorded speech. Try to determine the speaker's organizational strategy, the reasons for it, and its effectiveness. Note whether the speaker used signposts to help you follow the organization.

2. **Ethics Assessment** Is there an ethical distinction between primacy and recency? If a speaker has a statistic that offers overwhelming evidence of the severity of a given problem, for example, is it ethical for the speaker to save that statistic for last? Should the speaker reveal immediately to the audience how severe the problem really is?

3. **Critical Assessment** Which organizational pattern is most appropriate for the main points suggested in the following central ideas?

   - There are at least three distinct theories about what happened to the dinosaurs.
   - The new university multipurpose sports center will be divided into several zones to serve students' activity needs.

12 Developing an Introduction

OBJECTIVES

1. Explain the functions of a speech introduction.
2. List and discuss methods for introducing a speech.

Purposes of Introductions

Many speakers think that drafting an introduction is the first task in preparing a speech, but it is actually more often the last. A key purpose of your introduction is to provide an overview of your message. How can you do that until you know what the message is going to be? Nonetheless, the introduction is too important to the overall success of your speech to be left to chance or last-minute preparation.

The introduction provides your audience with important first impressions of you and your speech, and its main job is to convince your audience to listen to you. Specifically, a good introduction must perform five important functions:

1. Get the audience's attention.
2. Introduce the subject.
3. Give the audience a reason to listen.
4. Establish your credibility.
5. Preview your main ideas.

Get the Audience's Attention

A key purpose of the introduction is to gain favorable attention for your speech. Because listeners form their first impressions of a speech quickly, the introduction must capture their attention and cast the speech in a favorable light or the rest of the speech may be wasted on them.

We emphasize *favorable* attention for a good reason. It is possible to gain an audience's attention with words or presentation aids that alienate them or disgust them so that they become irritated instead of interested in what you have to say.

Be creative in your speech introductions. But also use common sense in deciding how best to gain the favorable attention of your listeners. Alienating them is even worse than boring them.

Introduce the Subject

The most obvious purpose of an introduction is to introduce the subject of a speech. Within a few seconds after you begin your speech, the audience should have a pretty good idea of what you are going to talk about.

The best way to ensure that your introduction does indeed introduce the subject of your speech is to include a statement of your central idea in the introduction.

Give the Audience a Reason to Listen

After you have captured the attention of your audience and introduced the topic, you have to give the audience some reason to want to listen to the rest of your speech. An unmotivated listener quickly tunes out.

You can help establish listening motivation by showing the members of your audience how the topic affects them. One criterion for determining the effectiveness of your supporting material is *proximity*, the degree to which the information affects your listeners directly. Just as proximity is important to supporting materials, it is also important to speech introductions. "This concerns me" is a powerful reason to listen.

It does not matter so much *how* or *when* you demonstrate proximity. But it is essential that you do at some point establish that your topic is of vital personal concern to your listeners.

HOW TO

Establish Credibility during Your Introduction

1. **Prepare well.** Thorough research and good organization help give the audience confidence that you know what you are talking about.
2. **Appear confident.** Speaking fluently while maintaining eye contact does much to convey a sense of confidence. If you seem to have confidence in yourself, your audience will have confidence in you.
3. **Tell the audience of your personal experience with your topic.** Instead of considering you boastful, most audience members will listen to you with respect.

Establish Your Credibility

Credibility is a speaker's believability. A credible speaker is one whom listeners judge to be a believable authority and a competent speaker. A credible speaker is also someone listeners believe they can trust. If you can establish your credibility early in a speech, it will help motivate your audience to listen.

Preview Your Main Ideas

A final purpose of the introduction is to preview the main ideas of your speech. An initial preview statement

QUICK CHECK

Purposes of Introductions

Purpose	Method
Get the audience's attention.	Avoid alienating, disgusting, or irritating listeners.
Introduce the subject.	Present your central idea to your audience.
Give the audience a reason to listen	Tell your listeners how the topic directly affects them.
Establish your credibility.	Prepare, look confident, and offer your credentials.
Preview your main ideas.	Tell your audience what you are going to tell them.

usually comes near the end of the introduction, included in or immediately following a statement of the central idea. The preview statement allows your listeners to anticipate the main ideas of your speech, which in turn helps ensure that they will remember those ideas after the speech.

As we discussed in Chapter 11, an initial preview is a signpost. Just as signs posted along a highway tell you what is coming up, a signpost in your speech tells the listeners what to expect by enumerating the ideas or points that you plan to present. Identifying your main ideas helps organize the message and enhances listeners' learning.

Effective Introductions

There are several effective methods for developing speech introductions. Not every method is appropriate for every speech, but chances are that you can discover among these alternatives at least one type of introduction to fit the topic and purpose of your speech, whatever they might be. View effective introductions at MySearchLab (**www.mysearchlab.com**).

Use Illustrations or Anecdotes

An illustration or **anecdote** can provide the basis for an effective speech introduction. In fact, if you have an especially compelling illustration that you had planned to use in the body of the speech, you might do well to use it in your introduction instead. A relevant and interesting anecdote will introduce your subject and almost invariably gain an audience's attention. And a personal illustration can help establish your credibility.

Provide Startling Facts or Statistics

A second method of introducing a speech is to use a startling fact or statistic. Startling an audience with the extent of a situation or problem invariably catches their attention and motivates them to listen further, as well as helping them remember afterward what you had to say.

Use Quotations

Using an appropriate quotation to introduce a speech is a common practice. Quotations are easy to find on the Internet, and often, in the past, a writer or speaker has expressed an opinion on your topic that is more authoritative, comprehensive, or memorable than what you can say. However, quotes should be used only if they are extremely interesting, compelling, or very much to the point. Using a quotation to open every speech can become a lazy habit.

Use Humor

Humor, handled well, can be a wonderful way to get an audience's attention. It can help relax your audience and win their goodwill for the rest of the speech.

If your audience is linguistically diverse or composed primarily of listeners whose first language is not English, you may want to choose an introduction strategy other than humor. Much humor is created by verbal plays on words and may not translate well with people who do not speak the same language.

Certain subjects are also inappropriate for humor. It would hardly be appropriate to open a speech on world hunger, Sudden Infant Death Syndrome, or rape, for example, with a funny story. Used with discretion, however, humor can provide a lively, interesting, and appropriate introduction for many speeches.

Ask Questions

Questions are commonly combined with another method of introduction. Either by themselves or in tandem with another method of introduction, questions can provide effective openings for speeches. For example, you may ask, "Do you know how many of today's college graduates hold over $100,00 in student debt?" and then present a startling statistic that answers your question.

When using a question to open a speech, you will generally use a **rhetorical question**, the kind to which you don't expect an answer. Pause briefly after you deliver a rhetorical question, in order to "hook" the attention of listeners as they try to answer your question in their minds. Opening questions prompt the audience's participation in a mental dialogue with you that can enhance their attention throughout your speech.

Refer to Historical Events

Perhaps you could begin a speech by drawing a relationship between an historic event that happened on this day and your speech objective. An Internet search for "this date in history" will reveal many possible events. Be sure the historical reference you choose is clearly linked to the purpose of your speech.

Refer to Recent Events

If your topic is timely, a reference to a recent event can be a good way to open your speech. An opening taken from a recent news story can take the form of an illustration, a startling statistic, or even a quotation. Referring to a recent event increases your credibility by showing that you are knowledgeable about current affairs.

"Recent" does not necessarily mean a story that broke just last week or even last month. An event that occurred within the past year or so can be considered recent. Even a particularly significant event that is slightly older can qualify.

Use Personal References

A reference to yourself can take several forms. You might reveal your reason for interest in the topic. You might express appreciation at having been asked to speak. Or you might share a personal experience. Whatever form of personal reference you use, the purpose is to establish a bond between you and your audience.

Refer to the Occasion

References to the occasion are often made at weddings, birthday parties, dedication ceremonies, and other such events. It is customary to make a personal reference as well, placing oneself in the occasion. For example, you might open a wedding toast by saying how happy you are to witness the marriage of your friends. Referring to the occasion can also be combined with other methods of introduction, such as an illustration or a rhetorical question.

Refer to Preceding Speeches

If your speech is one of several being presented on the same occasion, you will usually not know until shortly before your own speech what other speakers will say. Few experiences will make your stomach sink faster than hearing a speaker just ahead of you speak on your topic. Worse still, that speaker may even use some of the same supporting materials you had planned to use. When this situation occurs, it may be wise to refer to a preceding speech. If the other speaker has spoken on a topic closely related to your own, you can draw an analogy. In a sense, your introduction becomes a transition from that earlier speech to yours.

QUICK CHECK

Effective Introduction Techniques

- Use an illustration or anecdote.
- Present startling facts or statistics.
- Use an appropriate quotation.
- Use humor.
- Begin with a rhetorical question.
- Refer to historical events or recent events.
- Use personal references.
- Refer to the occasion or to preceding speeches.

◯ STUDY GUIDE

MEET YOUR OBJECTIVES

1. **Explain the functions of a speech introduction.**
   A good introduction gets the audience's attention, gives the audience a reason to listen, introduces your subject, establishes your credibility, and previews your main ideas.

2. **List and discuss methods for introducing a speech.**
   Effective introduction methods include illustrations, startling facts or statistics, quotations, humor, questions, references to historical events, references to recent events, personal references, references to the occasion, or references to preceding speeches, used alone or in combination.

THINK ABOUT THESE QUESTIONS

1. **Self Assessment** How could you motivate your classroom audience to listen to you on each of these topics: cholesterol, Elvis Presley, the history of greeting cards, ozone depletion, distracted driving?

2. **Ethics Assessment** Mardi tells her public-speaking classmate Shanna about an illustration she thinks will make an effective introduction. Shanna thinks it would make a great introduction for her own speech, which is on a different topic. Shanna learns that she is scheduled to speak before Mardi. She badly wants to use the illustration that Mardi discovered. Can she ethically do so?

3. **Critical Assessment** Nikai is planning an informational speech in which he will demonstrate Native American musical instruments. What is a good way for Nikai to introduce his speech?

Developing a Conclusion

13

1. Explain the functions of a speech conclusion.
2. List and discuss methods for concluding a speech.

Purposes of Conclusions

Just as most fireworks displays end with a grand finale, your speech should end, not necessarily with fireworks, but with a conclusion worthy of your well-crafted message. Long after you finish speaking, your audience is likely to remember the effect, if not the content, of your closing remarks. An effective conclusion will serve two purposes: It will summarize the speech, and it will provide closure.

Summarize the Speech

The end of your speech is your last chance to impress the central idea on your audience, and it provides you the opportunity to do it in such a way that they cannot help but remember. The conclusion is also your last chance to repeat your main ideas for the audience.

Reemphasize the Central Idea in a Memorable Way   Many of the most memorable quotations from famous speakers were the conclusions of their speeches. For example, close to 250 years later, we remember Patrick Henry's famous closing line, "Give me liberty or give me death!"[1] With practice, most people can prepare similarly effective conclusions. Begin by using the ideas in Chapter 15 for using language to make your statements more memorable. You could also use a final illustration, quotation, or personal reference to make your closing memorable.

Restate the Main Ideas   Most speakers summarize their main ideas in the first part of the conclusion or as part of the transition between the body of the speech and its conclusion.

Provide Closure

Probably the most obvious purpose of a conclusion is to provide **closure**—to let the audience know that the speech has ended. Use the verbal and nonverbal signals, such as those described in the How To box, to let your audience know you are closing your speech.

HOW TO

Signal the End of Your Speech

Verbal Signals
- Use such transition words and phrases as *finally, for my last point, in conclusion*, and so on.
- Avoid giving listeners permission to "tune out" too soon.
- Follow transition quickly with the final statement of the speech.

Nonverbal Signals
- Pause between the body of your speech and its conclusion.
- Slow your speaking rate.
- Move out from behind the podium to make a final impassioned plea.
- Use a falling vocal inflection for your final statement.

Motivate the Audience to Respond   At the beginning of your speech, your goal was to motivate your audience to listen to you. At the end, you want to motivate listeners to respond to your message. If your speech is informative, you may want the audience to think about the topic or to research it further. If your speech is persuasive, you may want your audience to take some sort of appropriate action—write a letter, buy a product, make a telephone call, or get involved in a cause. In fact, an *action* step is essential to the persuasive organizational strategy called the *motivated sequence*, discussed in Chapter 24. If audience members feel that they are or could be personally involved or affected, they are more likely to respond to your message.

QUICK CHECK

Purposes of Conclusions

Summarize the Speech
- Make your central idea memorable.
- Restate your main ideas.

Provide Closure
- Use verbal and nonverbal signals.
- Motive listeners to respond.

Effective Conclusions

Effective conclusions may employ illustrations, quotations, personal references, or any of the other methods used for introductions. In addition, there are at least two other distinct ways of concluding a speech: with a reference to the introduction and with an inspirational appeal or challenge. Visit MySearchLab (**www.mysearchlab.com**) to analyze speeches with effective conclusions.

Refer to the Introduction

The following are excellent ways to provide closure in the conclusion:

> Finish a story from your introduction.
> Answer your opening rhetorical question.
> Remind the audience of the startling fact or statistic you presented in the introduction.

Alluding to the introduction in your conclusion will also make your speech memorable and motivate the audience to respond.

Issue an Inspirational Appeal or Challenge

Another way to end your speech is to issue an inspirational appeal or challenge to your listeners, rousing
them to a high emotional pitch. An inspiring conclusion
should reemphasize your central ideas in a memorable
way, motivate your audience to respond, and provide
closure to your speech.

Dr. Martin Luther King Jr. stirred his audience
with the famous inspirational closing to his "I Have a
Dream" speech, which you can view at MySearchLab
(**www.mysearchlab.com**). When you use this method,
the conclusion becomes the climax toward which your
entire speech builds.

STUDY GUIDE

MEET YOUR OBJECTIVES

1. **Explain the functions of a speech conclusion.**
   The two main purposes of the conclusion are to summarize your speech in a memorable way and to provide closure.
2. **List and discuss methods for concluding a speech.**
   Conclusions may take any one of the forms used for introductions. In addition, you can refer to the introduction or make inspirational appeals or challenges.

THINK ABOUT THESE QUESTIONS

1. **Self Assessment** Knowing that you have recently visited the Vietnam Veterans Memorial in Washington, D.C., your American history professor asks you to make a brief presentation to the class about the Wall: its history; its symbolic meaning; and its impact on the families, comrades, and friends of those memorialized there. Write both an introduction and a conclusion for this speech.
2. **Ethics Assessment** You believe the closing words used by a famous speaker would provide the most effective conclusion for your own speech. How could you ethically use the famous speaker's inspirational words?
3. **Critical Assessment** Many public-speaking instructors advise against saying, "in conclusion."[2] Why should you avoid this transitional phrase?

Outlining and Revising Your Speech

OBJECTIVES

1. Develop a preparation outline for a speech.
2. Prepare speaking notes for a speech.

Develop a Preparation Outline

Although few speeches are written in paragraph form, most speakers develop a detailed **preparation outline** that includes the following:

> central idea
> main ideas
> supporting material
> the speech's specific purpose
> introduction
> conclusion
> signposts
> references (optional)

To begin your outlining task, you might try a technique known as **mapping** or clustering. Write on a sheet of paper all the main ideas, subpoints, and supporting material for the speech. Then use geometric shapes and arrows to indicate the logical relationships among them.

Whatever technique you choose to begin your outline, your ultimate goal is to produce a plan that lets you judge the unity and coherence of your speech, see how well the parts fit together, and see how smoothly the speech flows. The following suggestions will help you complete your preparation outline. However, keep in mind that different instructors may have different expectations for both outline content and outline format. Be sure to understand and follow your own instructor's guidelines.

Write Your Preparation Outline in Complete Sentences

Unless you write your preparation outline in complete sentences, you will have trouble judging the coherence of the speech. Moreover, complete sentences will help during your early rehearsals. If you write cryptic phrases, you may not remember what they mean.

Use Standard Outline Form

Although you did not have to use standard outline form when you began to outline your ideas, you need to do so now. **Standard outline form** lets you see at a glance the exact relationships among the various main ideas and supporting material in your speech. It is an important tool for evaluating your speech. To produce a correct outline, follow the instructions in the How To box and the model in Figure 14.1. To see models of outlines and use a handy outlining tool, visit this chapter of MySearchLab (**www.mysearchlab.com**).

Write and Label Your Specific Purpose at the Top of Your Outline

Do not work the specific purpose into the outline itself. Instead, label it and place it at the top of the outline. Your specific purpose can serve as a yardstick by which

```
 I. First main idea
     A. First subpoint of I
     B. Second subpoint of I
         1. First subpoint of B
         2. Second subpoint of B
             a. First subpoint of 2
             b. Second subpoint of 2
II. Second main idea
```

FIGURE 14.1 Standard Outline Form. It is unlikely that you will subdivide beyond the level of lowercase letters (a, b, c) in most speech outlines, but next would come numbers in parentheses and then lowercase letters in parentheses.

> **HOW TO**
>
> ### Use Standard Outline Form
>
> - Properly indent main ideas, subpoints, and supporting material, as shown in Figure 14.1.
> - Use at least two subpoints, if any, for each main idea. Logic dictates that you cannot divide anything into one part.
>   - If you have only one piece of supporting material, incorporate it into the subpoint or main idea that it supports.
>   - If you have only one subpoint, incorporate it into the main idea above it.
> - If you have more than five subpoints, you may want to place some of them under another point. An audience will remember your ideas more easily if they are divided into blocks of no more than five.

to measure the relevance of each main idea and piece of supporting material. Everything in the speech should contribute to your specific purpose.

Add the Blueprint, Key Signposts, Introduction, and Conclusion to Your Outline

Place the introduction after the statement of your specific purpose, the blueprint immediately following the introduction, the conclusion after the outline of the body of the speech, and other signposts within the outline.

Analyze Your Preparation Outline

Once you have completed your preparation outline, you can use it to help you analyze and possibly revise the speech. The following questions can help you in this critical thinking task.

> **Does the speech as outlined fulfill the purpose you have specified?** If not, revise the specific purpose or change the direction and content of the speech itself. If you need to reduce the length of your speech, consider narrowing your specific purpose. If, for

example, your purpose is to have your audience be able to list and describe five advantages of organic foods, you may have to be less ambitious and describe only three—pick your best three.

> **Are the main ideas logical extensions (natural divisions, reasons, or steps) of the central idea?** If not, revise either the central idea or the main ideas. Like the first question, this one relates to the unity of the speech and is critical to making certain the speech "fits together" as a whole.

> **Will the signposts help listeners understand the flow of each idea into the next?** If not, change or add previews, summaries, or transitions. If signposts are not adequate, the speech will lack coherence.

> **Does each subpoint provide support for the point under which it falls?** If not, then either move or delete the subpoint.

> **Have you chosen the best supporting material?** Make sure all material relates clearly to the point it is intended to support. If you need to reduce the length of your speech, scan your preparation outline for supporting material that can be cut.

> **Is your outline form correct?**

Having considered these questions, you are ready to rehearse your speech, using the preparation outline as your first set of notes.

Prepare Speaking Notes

As you rehearse your speech, you will find that you need your preparation outline less and less. Both the structure and the content of your speech will become set in your mind. At this point, you are ready to prepare a shorter outline to serve as your **speaking notes**.

This outline should provide enough clearly formatted detail to ensure that you can make your presentation as you have planned in your preparation outline. However, your speaking notes should not be so detailed that you will be tempted to read rather than speak to your audience. Use the following suggestions for developing speaking notes.

Choose Your Technology

You may decide to display your outline on a laptop or electronic tablet—perhaps utilizing one of several apps available for speaking notes—or you may opt to use old-fashioned note cards. Regardless of which technology you select, make sure your letters and words are large enough to be read easily.

Even if you plan to use an electronic option, you may want to have a backup outline on note cards in case of technical difficulty. Note cards don't rustle as paper does, and they are small enough to hold in one hand. Write on one side only, and number your note cards in case they get out of order just before or during your speech.

Use Standard Outline Form

Make your introduction, each main idea, and your conclusion distinct. Standard outline form will help you find your exact place when you glance down at your speaking notes. You will know, for example, that your second main idea is indicated by "II."

Include Shortened Versions of Your Introduction and Conclusion

Even if your instructor does not require you to include your introduction and conclusion on your preparation outline, include abbreviated versions of them in your speaking notes. You might feel more comfortable delivering the presentation if you have your first and last sentences written out in front of you.

Include Your Central Idea, Not Your Purpose Statement

Be sure to include your central idea. Do not put your specific-purpose statement in your speaking notes because you will not actually say it during your presentation.

Include Supporting Material and Signposts

Write out in full any statistics and direct quotations and their sources. Write your key signposts—your initial preview, for example—to ensure that you will not have to grope awkwardly as you move from one idea to another.

Include Delivery Cues

Write in your speaking notes such cues as "Louder," "Pause," or "Walk two steps left." However, be sure to write delivery cues in a different color or font so that you don't confuse them with your verbal content.

QUICK CHECK

Preparation Outline and Speaking Notes

Preparation	Delivery
Use complete sentences.	Use single words and phrases.
Write out full introduction and conclusion.	Write first and last sentences only.
Add blueprint, all signposts.	Keep only statistics, direct quotations, and key signposts.
Place specific-purpose statement at the top.	Omit specific-purpose statement.

◉ STUDY GUIDE

MEET YOUR OBJECTIVES

1. **Develop a preparation outline for a speech.**
   A preparation outline includes your carefully organized main ideas, subpoints, and supporting material; it may also include your specific purpose, introduction, blueprint, internal previews and summaries, transitions, and conclusion. Write each of these elements in complete sentences and standard outline form. Use the preparation outline to begin rehearsing your speech and to help you revise it, if necessary.

2. **Prepare speaking notes for a speech.**
   Speaking notes are less detailed than a preparation outline and usually include supporting material, signposts, and delivery cues.

THINK ABOUT THESE QUESTIONS

1. **Self Assessment** Different instructors have different expectations for outline content and format. Obtain your own instructor's guidelines and compare them to the advice in this chapter.

2. **Ethics Assessment** Can a speaker legitimately claim that a speech is extemporaneous if he or she has constructed a detailed preparation outline?

3. **Critical Assessment** Myorka thinks it is silly to worry about using correct outline form for either her preparation outline or her speaking notes. Do you agree with her? Why or why not?

15 Using Words Well

OBJECTIVES

1. Describe three differences between oral and written language styles.
2. List and explain three ways to use words effectively.
3. Discuss how to adapt your language style to diverse listeners.
4. List and explain three types of memorable word structures.

Oral versus Written Language Style

Your instructor has probably told you not to write your speech out word for word. Instructors say this because there are at least three major differences between oral and written language styles.

> **Oral style is more personal.** When speaking, you can look your listeners in the eye, talk to them directly, and interact. If you see that they don't like or don't understand what you are saying, you can adjust your statements and explanations to gain greater acceptance. As a speaker, you are likely to use more pronouns (*I, you*) than you would in writing.
> **Oral style is less formal.** Memorized speeches usually sound as if they were written because, in much writing, words and phrases are longer, more complex, and more formal than those used by most speakers. Oral style, on the other hand, is characterized by "looser construction, repetition, rephrasing, and comment clauses ('you know'). . . ."[1]
> **Oral style is more repetitious.** When you're listening to a speech, you don't have opportunities to

stop and reread, look up unfamiliar words, or ask for help if you don't understand. For this reason, an oral style is and should be more repetitious. Speakers build in repetition in previews, transitions, and summaries to make sure that listeners will grasp their messages.

Use Words Effectively

Your challenge as a speaker is to use words well so that you can communicate your intended message. Ideally, language should be specific and concrete, simple, correct, and concise.

Use Specific, Concrete Words

Specific words are often concrete words, which appeal to one of our five senses, whereas general words are often abstract words, which refer to ideas or qualities. A linguistic theory known as *general semantics* holds that the more concrete your words, the clearer your communication.

Specific, concrete nouns create memorable images; likewise, specific, concrete verbs can be especially effective. It is more memorable, for example, to say, "The leaves of plants in the fields are shredded to tatters," than to say, "The hailstorm severely damaged crops."

Use Simple Words

When searching for a specific, concrete word, you may want to consult a thesaurus, but do not feel that you have to choose an obscure or unusual term. Your words should be immediately understandable to your listeners. Don't try to impress them with jargon and pompous language. The best language is often the simplest. Used wisely, simple words communicate with great power and precision.

Use Words Correctly

Your effectiveness with your audience depends in part on your ability to use the English language correctly.

If you are unsure of a grammatical rule, seek assistance from a good English usage handbook. If you are unsure of a word's pronunciation, you can hear recordings of correct pronunciations at major online dictionaries. Consult dictionaries to confirm word meanings, too, but remember that language operates on two levels.

1. The **denotation** of a word is its literal meaning, the definition you find in a dictionary. For example, the denotation of the word *notorious* is "famous."
2. The **connotation** of a word is the meaning we associate with the word, based on our past experiences. *Notorious* connotes fame resulting from some dire deed. *Notorious* and *famous* are not really interchangeable. It is just as important to consider the connotations of the words you use as it is to consider the denotations. When considering connotations, remember these two points:
   - Audience members may have their own private connotations for words, based on their own experiences. Private meanings are difficult to predict, but as a public speaker, you should be aware of the possibility of triggering your audience members' private connotations, especially when you are discussing highly emotional or controversial topics.
   - If your audience includes people whose first language is not English, to whom the nuances of connotation may not be readily apparent, explain your intentions in more detail, rather than relying on word associations.

Use Words Concisely

Your goal should be to use only as many words as are necessary to convey your message. The How To box offers suggestions for using language concisely.

HOW TO

- Eliminate phrases that add no meaning to your message, such as "In my opinion" (just state the opinion) or "Before I begin, I'd like to say" (you've already begun—just say it).
- Avoid narrating your speaking technique. There is no need to say, "Here's an interesting story that I think you will like." Just tell the story.
- Avoid using a long phrase when a short one will do. Here are some examples:

Instead of saying	Say
So, for that reason	So
Due to the fact	Because
But at the same time	But
In the final analysis	Finally

Adapt Your Language Style to Diverse Listeners

To communicate successfully with the diverse group of listeners who comprise your audience, make sure your language is understandable, appropriate, and unbiased.

Use Understandable Language

Even if you and all your public-speaking classmates speak English, you probably speak many varieties of the language, including the following.

> **Ethnic vernacular,** such as "Spanglish," African American Vernacular English (AAVE), or Cajun
> **Regionalisms,** words or phrases specific to one part of the country but rarely used in quite the same way in other places
> **Jargon,** the specialized language of a particular profession or hobby

If you give a speech to others who share your ethnic, regional, or professional background, you can communicate successfully with them using these specialized varieties of English. However, if you give a speech to an audience as diverse as the members of your public-speaking class, use **standard U.S. English.** Standard U.S. English is the language taught by schools and used in the media, business, and the government in the United States. "Standard" does not imply that standard U.S. English is inherently right and all other forms are wrong, but only that it conforms to a standard that most speakers of U.S. English will readily understand.

Use Appropriate Language

A speaker whose language defames any subgroup—people of particular ethnic, racial, and religious backgrounds, genders, sexual orientations, or ability statuses—or whose language might be otherwise considered offensive or risqué runs a great risk of antagonizing audience members.

Use Unbiased Language

Even speakers who would never dream of using overtly offensive language may find it difficult to avoid language that stereotypes or discriminates more subtly. Sexist language falls largely into this second category.

For example, not many years ago, a sentence such as, "Everyone should bring his book to class tomorrow" was considered appropriate to refer to people of all genders. Now we use both pronouns ("Everyone should bring his or her book to class tomorrow") or reword the sentence so that it is plural and thus gender neutral ("All students should bring their books to class tomorrow").

Now also considered sexist is the use of the masculine noun *man* to refer to all people. Instead of such masculine nouns as *waiter*, *chairman*, *fireman*, and *congressman*, choose such gender-neutral alternatives as *server*, *chair*, *firefighter*, and *member of Congress*.

In addition, you should avoid sexist language that patronizes or stereotypes people. It is not always easy to avoid biased language. For example, suppose that Dr. Pierce is a young, African American, female M.D. If you don't mention her age, race, and gender, you may reinforce your listeners' stereotypical image of a physician as middle-aged, white, and male. But if you *do* mention these factors, you may be suspected of implying that Dr. Pierce's achievement is unusual. There is no easy answer to this dilemma or others like it. You will have to consider your audience, your purpose, and the occasion when deciding how best to identify Dr. Pierce.

QUICK CHECK

Use Words Well

- Are your words specific and concrete?
- Do you use the English language correctly?
- Are your words concise?
- Is your language immediately understandable to your listeners?
- Is your language appropriate for your audience?
- Is your language unbiased?

Craft Memorable Word Structures

Memorable speeches are stylistically distinctive. They create arresting images. And they have what a marketing-communication specialist has termed "ear appeal."[2] Visit MySearchLab (www.mysearchlab.com) to hear speakers deliver memorable word structures. Learn in Chapter 25 about creating humor with words.

Create Figurative Images

A **figure of speech** deviates from the ordinary, expected meanings of words to make a description or comparison unique, vivid, and memorable. Common figures of speech include metaphors, similes, and personification.

Use Metaphors and Similes   A **metaphor** is an implied comparison. For example, "He is a snake." A **simile** is a less direct comparison that includes the word *like* or *as*. For example, "His lies make him as slippery as a snake."

Speakers often turn to metaphors and similes in times that are especially momentous or overwhelming—times when literal language seems insufficient. In the hours and days after the September 11, 2001, terrorist attacks on the United States, various speakers used metaphorical phrases, including "one more circle of Dante's hell," "nuclear winter," and "the crater of a volcano" to describe the site of the destroyed World Trade Center in New York City.[3]

Use Personification Personification is the attribution of human qualities to inanimate things or ideas. If, for example, you say that the sun smiles upon your city, you are personifying the sun.

Create Drama

Another way you can make phrases and sentences memorable is to use them to create drama in your speech—to keep the audience in suspense or to catch them slightly off guard by phrasing something in a way that differs from the way they expect you to say it.

Sentence Length Use a short sentence to express a vitally important thought. Short, simple sentences can have much the same power as short, simple words.

Omission Use **omission**. Leave out a word or phrase that the audience expects to hear. For example, a speaker might omit the words *mountain climbers* to add drama, saying, "Only 5 of the 16 who set out to scale the peak would ever return." When you use omission, be sure listeners will understand the words you leave out.

Inversion Use **inversion**. Reverse the normal word order of a phrase or sentence. John F. Kennedy used inversion by changing the usual subject-verb-object sentence pattern to object-subject-verb in this brief declaration from his inaugural speech: "This much we pledge."[4]

Suspension   When you read a mystery novel, you are held in suspense until you reach the end and learn "who did it." The stylistic technique of verbal suspension does something similar, using a key word or phrase at the end of a sentence, rather than at the beginning.

Some years ago, the Coca-Cola Company used **suspension** as the cornerstone of its worldwide advertising campaign by making *Coke* the last word in the slogan, "Things go better with Coke," rather than the expected order, "Coke goes better with everything."

Create Cadence

Rhythms are memorable. Take advantage of language rhythms, not by speaking in singsong patterns, but by using such stylistic devices as repetition, parallelism, antithesis, and alliteration.

Repetition   Using a key word or phrase more than once gives rhythm and power to your message and makes it memorable. Perhaps the best-known modern example of **repetition** in a speech is the declaration that became the title of Martin Luther King Jr.'s most famous civil rights speech.

Parallelism   Parallelism occurs when two or more clauses or sentences have the same grammatical pattern. In a 2013 speech to Israeli students in Jerusalem, Barack Obama used parallelism by starting sentences with the words *we are*:

> We are enriched by faith. We are governed not simply by men and women, but by laws. We are fueled by entrepreneurship and innovation. And we are defined by a democratic discourse. . . .[5]

Antithesis   The word *antithesis* means "opposition." In language style, a sentence that uses **antithesis** has two parts with parallel structures but contrasting meanings. Speakers have long realized the dramatic potential of antithesis. In Franklin D. Roosevelt's first inaugural address, he declared,

Our true destiny is not to be ministered unto but to minister to ourselves and to our fellow men.[6]

An antithetical statement is a good way to end a speech. The cadence will make the statement memorable.

Alliteration Alliteration is the repetition of a consonant sound (usually an initial consonant) several times in a phrase, clause, or sentence (for example, *discipline and direction*; *confidence and courage*).

STUDY GUIDE

MEET YOUR OBJECTIVES

1. **Describe three differences between oral and written language styles.**
   Oral language is more personal and less formal than written language. Speakers must also provide their audiences with more repetition than writers need to use.

2. **List and explain three ways to use words effectively.**
   Effective speakers use specific, concrete words to evoke clear mental images in their listeners. They also choose simple, respectful, unbiased words. As a speaker, be sure to use words correctly and to keep in mind the connotations of words, as well as their dictionary definitions. And, finally, eliminate unnecessary words and phrases.

3. **Discuss how to adapt your language style to diverse listeners.**
   Use language your listeners can understand. Use appropriate language to avoid offending your audience. Use unbiased language to communicate in a sensitive way.

Continued

4. **List and explain three types of memorable word structures.**

Create arresting images through such figures of speech as metaphors, similes, and personification. Create drama by using short sentences for important ideas, strategically omitting words, and structuring sentences with key words at the end to create suspense. Use repetition, alliteration, parallelism, and antithesis to create memorable rhythm or cadence.

THINK ABOUT THESE QUESTIONS

1. **Self Assessment** A friend asks for advice on making the word choices in her speech as effective as possible. Offer her at least three suggestions, based on this chapter, for using words effectively.
2. **Ethics Assessment** Is it ethical to change your variety of English in order to adapt to your listeners' expectations? Why or why not?
3. **Critical Assessment** How would a 750-word paper and a 3- to 5-minute speech that both have the same topic, central idea, main idea, and supporting material differ?

16 Methods of Delivery

OBJECTIVES

1. Explain how to effectively deliver a manuscript speech.
2. Summarize the advantages and disadvantages of memorizing a speech.
3. Describe how to deliver an effective impromptu speech.
4. Explain the benefits of delivering a speech extemporaneously.

There are four basic methods of delivery from which a speaker can choose: manuscript speaking, memorized speaking, impromptu speaking, and extemporaneous speaking. Table 16.1 found at the end of this chapter on page 143 offers an overview of the advantages and disadvantages of each method.

Manuscript Speaking

Reading from a manuscript is usually a poor way to deliver a speech. Although it may provide some insurance against forgetting the speech, **manuscript speaking** is rarely done well enough to be interesting.

However, some speeches should be read. For example, during times of crisis, statements to the press by government or business leaders should be crafted precisely, rather than tossed off casually. One advantage of reading from a manuscript is that you can choose words very carefully when dealing with a sensitive and critical issue.

The key to giving an effective manuscript speech is to sound as though you are not giving a manuscript speech. Use the tips in the How To box to help you.[1]

HOW TO

Deliver a Manuscript Speech

- Make as much eye contact with the audience as possible; look directly at them, not over their heads.
- Type your speech in short, easy-to-scan phrases and make eye contact at the ends of sentences.
- Use your index finger to keep your place in the manuscript when you look up.
- Do not read your speech too quickly; use the same pace you normally speak.
- Vary the rhythm and inflection of your voice to sound natural.
- Mark your manuscript to remind you to pause or to emphasize certain words.
- Use appropriate and natural gestures and movement.

Memorized Speaking

Memorized speaking sounds stiff, stilted, and over-rehearsed. You also run the risk of forgetting parts of your speech and awkwardly searching for words in front of your audience. And you won't be able to make on-the-spot adaptations to your listeners if your speech is memorized. Memorized speaking does, however, have the advantage of allowing you to have maximum eye contact with the audience.

If you are accepting an award, introducing a speaker, making announcements, or delivering other brief remarks, a memorized delivery style is sometimes acceptable. But, as with manuscript speaking, you must take care to make your presentation sound lively and interesting.

Impromptu Speaking

You have undoubtedly already delivered many impromptu presentations. Your response to a question posed by a teacher in class and your unrehearsed rebuttal to a comment made by a colleague during a meeting are examples of impromptu presentations. The impromptu method is often described as "thinking on your feet" or "speaking off the cuff." The advantage of **impromptu speaking** is that you can speak informally and maintain direct eye contact with the audience. But unless you are extremely talented or have learned and practiced the techniques of impromptu speaking, an impromptu speech usually lacks logical organization and thorough research. When you are called on to deliver an improvised or impromptu speech, the guidelines in the How To box can help ease you through it.

Because there is no opportunity to conduct any kind of research before delivering an impromptu speech, you will have to speak from your own experience and knowledge. Remember, audiences almost always respond favorably to personal illustrations, so use any appropriate and relevant ones that come to mind. Of course, the more knowledge you have about the subject to be discussed, the easier it will be to speak about it off the cuff. But do not make up information or provide facts or figures you're not certain about.

HOW TO

Make an Impromptu Speech

- **Consider your audience.** What are listeners' common characteristics and interests? What do they know about your topic? What do they expect you to say? What is the occasion of your speech?
- **Be brief.** One to three minutes is a realistic time frame for most impromptu situations. Some spur-of-the-moment remarks, such as press statements, may be even shorter.
- **Organize!** Effective impromptu speakers organize their ideas into an introduction, body, and conclusion. Consider using a simple topical organization or chronological order. A variation on the chronological pattern is the past, present, future model; you discuss (1) what happened in the past, (2) what is happening now, and (3) what may happen in the future.

An honest "I don't know" or a very brief statement is more appropriate. No matter how much knowledge you have, be cautious about the information you share, especially if your subject is sensitive or your information is classified. If asked about a controversial topic, give an honest but noncommittal answer. You can always elaborate later, but you can never take back something rash you have already said. It is better to be careful than sorry!

Extemporaneous Speaking

In **extemporaneous speaking,** you speak from a written or memorized general outline, but you do not have the exact wording in front of you or in memory. You have rehearsed the speech so that you know key ideas and their organization, but not to the degree that the speech sounds memorized.

The extemporaneous method reflects the advantages of a well-organized speech delivered in an interesting and vivid manner. An extemporaneous style is conversational; it gives your audience the impression that the speech is being created as they listen to it, because to some extent it is. Audiences prefer to hear something live rather than something prepared yesterday or weeks ago. Seeing something happening *now* provides added interest and excitement.

You develop an extemporaneous style by first rehearsing your speech, using many notes or perhaps looking at your preparation outline. After going over your speech a few times, you will find that you have internalized the overall structure of the speech, although the exact way you express your ideas may vary. You will rely less on your notes and focus more on adapting your message to your listeners. The final draft of your speaking notes may be an abbreviated outline or a few key words and essential facts or statistics that you want to remember. Visit this chapter of MySearchLab (**www.mysearchlab.com**) for more tips on effective extemporaneous speaking.

TABLE 16.1 Advantages and Disadvantages of Methods of Delivery

	Advantages	Disadvantages
Manuscript: reading a speech from a prepared text	You can choose words carefully when dealing with sensitive or critical issues; you can be precise.	Rarely done well enough to maintain audience interest.
Memorized: giving a speech from memory without using notes	This method enables you to have maximum eye contact with the audience.	May sound stiff, stilted, and overrehearsed; you may forget parts of your speech; you cannot make on-the-spot adaptations.
Impromptu: delivering a speech without preparing in advance	You can speak informally and maintain direct eye contact with the audience.	May lack logical organization and thorough research; may be unimpressive.
Extemporaneous: speaking from a written or memorized general outline, knowing the major ideas but not the exact wording	Style is conversational; speech sounds live rather than rehearsed, is well organized, and is delivered in an interesting and vivid manner.	Could become repetitive; you may forget certain points; new thoughts may increase the length.

STUDY GUIDE

MEET YOUR OBJECTIVES

1. **Explain how to effectively deliver a manuscript speech.**
When precision wording is important, you may need to read a speech from a prepared text. Make your voice and gestures as natural as possible, and make eye contact at the ends of sentences.

2. **Summarize the advantages and disadvantages of memorizing a speech.**
Giving a speech from memory allows maximum eye contact with the audience, but you risk sounding stiff, forgetting part of the speech, and being unable to adapt the speech to the audience.

Continued

3. **Describe how to deliver an effective impromptu speech.**
   An unrehearsed speech allows informality and eye contact. Consider the audience, and organize your remarks accordingly. Keep your talk brief, use your own knowledge, and share information cautiously.
4. **Explain the benefits of delivering a speech extemporaneously.**
   Because it seems spontaneous and is customized to the audience, the extemporaneous method is the most desirable in most situations. Speak from an outline without memorizing the exact words.

THINK ABOUT THESE QUESTIONS

1. **Self Assessment** Imagine you are an executive for a corporation. What business situations would call for you to deliver each of the four types of speeches described in this chapter?
2. **Ethics Assessment** Is it ethical to present a manuscript or memorized speech when you have been asked to present an extemporaneous speech?
3. **Critical Assessment** Roger was so nervous about his first speech that he practiced it until he could have given it in his sleep. He had some great examples, and his instructor had praised his outline. But as he gave his speech, he saw his classmates tuning out. What might he have done wrong, and how could he have rescued his speech?

17 Nonverbal Communication

OBJECTIVES

1. Make effective eye contact during a speech.
2. Use gestures effectively while speaking.
3. Move purposefully in ways that enhance your message while speaking.
4. Display an appropriate posture while delivering a speech.
5. Use facial expressions to enhance verbal messages.
6. Choose appropriate attire for making a speech.

Eye Contact

Of all the aspects of delivery discussed in this chapter, the most important one in a public-speaking situation for North Americans is eye contact.[1] Eye contact with your audience lets your audience know you are interested in them and want to talk to them. It keeps your audience interested, helps them remember your message, and enhances your credibility. Eye contact also provides you with feedback about how your speech is coming across, so you can adapt it if needed. Each of these functions contributes to the success of your delivery. The How To box offers advice for effective eye contact.

Gestures

Important points are emphasized with gestures. You can gesture to indicate places, to enumerate items, and to describe objects.

Make Eye Contact with Your Audience

- When it's your time to speak, walk to the lectern or to the front of the audience, pause briefly, and look at your audience before you say anything.
- Have your opening sentence well enough in mind that you can deliver it without looking at your notes or away from your listeners.
- Establish eye contact with the entire audience, not just with those in the front row or only one or two people.
- Look to the back as well as the front and from one side of your audience to the other, but avoid following a predictable pattern.
- Look at individuals, establishing person-to-person contact with them—not so long that it will make a listener feel uncomfortable, but long enough to establish the feeling that you are talking directly to that individual.
- Don't look over your listeners' heads; establish eye-to-eye contact.
- When delivering your speech via video, such as in a videoconference, look at the camera to give the impression of eye contact with viewers.

Problem Gestures

Many people who gesture easily and appropriately in the course of everyday conversations aren't sure what to do with their hands when they find themselves in front of an audience. Following are some common problem poses and gestures. It can be natural to adopt these stances momentarily, but holding them for long periods during a speech looks awkward and unnatural, and may keep you from using other, more appropriate gestures.

> **Parade rest.** Keeping your hands behind your back can make you look like a soldier standing at "parade rest."

> **Broken wing.** Another common position is standing with one hand on the hip in a "broken wing" pose. Worse than the "broken wing" is both hands resting on the hips in a "double broken wing."

> **Arm clutch.** Few poses are more awkward looking than when a speaker clutches one arm, as if grazed by a bullet. The audience half expects the speaker to call out reassuringly, "Don't worry, Ma; it's only a flesh wound."
> **Hands in pockets.** Keeping your hands in your pockets can make you look as if you were afraid to let go of your change or your keys.
> **Fig leaf clutch.** Some students clasp their hands and let them drop in front of them in a distracting "fig leaf clutch."

Gestures can distract your audience in various other ways as well. Grasping the lectern until your knuckles turn white or just letting your hands flop around without purpose or control does little to help you communicate your message. Sometimes, it may be better to use no gestures—to just put your hands comfortably at your side—than to use awkward, distracting gestures.

Functions of Gestures

If you don't know what to do with your hands, think about the message you want to communicate. Your gestures can lend strength to or detract from what you have to say by repeating, contradicting, substituting, complementing, emphasizing, or regulating your verbal message.

> **Repeating.** You can say "I have three major points to talk about today" while holding up three fingers. Or you can describe an object as 12 inches long while holding your hands about a foot apart.
> **Contradicting.** Because your audience will believe what you communicate nonverbally sooner than what you communicate verbally, monitor your gestures to make sure that you are not contradicting what you say.
> **Substituting.** Without uttering a word, you can hold up the palm of your hand to calm a noisy crowd. Flashing two fingers to form a V for "victory" and raising a clenched fist are other common

examples of gestures that can substitute for a verbal message.

> **Complementing.** A politician who declines to comment on a reporter's question while holding up her hands to augment her verbal refusal is relying on the gesture to complement or provide further meaning to her verbal message.

> **Emphasizing.** A shaking fist or a slicing gesture with one or both hands helps emphasize a message. So does pounding your fist into the palm of your hand. Other gestures can be less dramatic but still lend emphasis to what you say. Try to allow your gestures to arise from the content of your speech and your emotions.

> **Regulating.** Gestures can also regulate the exchange between you and your audience. If you want the audience to respond to a question, you can extend both palms to invite a response. During a question-and-answer session, your gestures can signal when you want to talk and when you want to invite others to do so.

Using Gestures Effectively

Here are some guidelines to consider when working on your delivery.

> **Relax.** Gestures should be *relaxed,* not tense or rigid. Although you should monitor your gestures, avoid appearing stiff and self-conscious as you do so.

> **Stay natural.** Your gestures should flow from your message. Avoid sawing or slashing through the air with your hands unless you are trying to emphasize a particularly dramatic point.

> **Be definite.** Gestures should appear *definite* rather than as accidental brief jerks of your hands or arms. If you want to gesture, go ahead and gesture. Avoid minor hand movements that will be masked by the lectern.

> **Use gestures that are consistent with your message.** If you are excited, for example, gesture more vigorously.
> **Match gestures to your speaking situation.** When delivering a speech via video, such as in a videoconference, you may need to use smaller gestures that viewers can see on-screen.
> **Vary your gestures.** Try not to use just one hand or one all-purpose gesture; try to use gestures for a variety of purposes.
> **Don't overdo it.** Your purpose is to communicate a message to your audience, not to perform for your listeners to the extent that your gestures receive more attention than your message.
> **Coordinate the timing of gestures with your message.** For example, when you announce that you have three major points, hold up your three fingers at the same moment you say the word *three*.
> **Use gestures that work best for you.** Your gestures should fit your personality.

Keep one important principle in mind: Your nonverbal delivery should flow from your message. Make your gestures appropriate to your audience and situation. In more formal speaking situations, particularly when speaking to a large audience, bolder, more sweeping, and more dramatic gestures are appropriate. A small

---

QUICK CHECK

Gestures

The most effective gestures are
- natural and relaxed
- definite and varied
- consistent with your message
- unobtrusive
- coordinated with what you say
- appropriate to your audience and situation

audience in a less formal setting calls for less formal gestures. Cultural expectations can help you make decisions about your approach to using gestures. Many Asian listeners may prefer a quieter, less flamboyant use of gestures. Many European listeners are accustomed to speakers who are less animated in their use of gestures, movement, and facial expressions than is typical for Americans.

Movement

Should you walk around during your speech, or should you stay in one place? If there is a lectern, should you stand behind it, or would it be acceptable to stand in front or to the side of it? Is it all right to sit down while you speak? Can you move among the audience? The following discussion may help you answer these questions.

Move Purposefully

Your movement should be consistent with the verbal content of your message. It should make sense rather than appear as aimless wandering. Your movement should not detract from your message. If the audience focuses on your movement rather than on what you are saying, it is better to stand still.

Reduce Physical Barriers

If barriers such as a lectern, rows of chairs, a chalkboard, an overhead projector, or other audiovisual aids act as obstacles between you and your audience, you may want to rearrange or remove them, or move closer to the audience.

Establish Immediacy

Movements such as standing or moving closer to listeners or coming out from behind a lectern can help to create a perception of closeness or **immediacy** between you and your audience, which may enhance your credibility and help you effectively communicate your message.[2] Pay close attention to your listeners to determine the appropriate amount of immediacy so that you do not violate cultural expectations or make listeners uncomfortable.

Signal Transitions

As you begin a new idea or major point, make a transitional statement, or change from a serious subject to a more humorous one, movement can be a good way to signal that your approach to the speaking situation is changing.

As a general principle, your use of movement during your speech should make sense to your listeners.

Posture

Although there have been few formal studies of posture in relation to public speaking, there is evidence that the way you carry your body communicates significant information.[3] Your face and voice show your audience *which* emotion you are feeling; your posture communicates the *intensity* of that emotion.

In general, avoid slouched shoulders, shifting from foot to foot, or drooping your head. Your posture should not call attention to itself. Instead, it should come about naturally, as a result of what you have to say and your interest in the speaking event, as well as the speaking occasion and environment. For example, during a very informal presentation, it may be perfectly appropriate as well as comfortable and natural to sit on the edge of a desk.

Facial Expression

Your audience sees your face before they hear what you are going to say. Thus, you have an opportunity to set the emotional tone for your message before you start speaking. Try for a pleasant facial expression that helps establish a positive emotional climate, but do not adopt a phony smile that looks insincere and plastered on your face.

Your face plays a key role in expressing your thoughts, especially your emotions and attitudes.[4] Although humans are technically capable of producing thousands of different facial expressions, we most often express only six primary emotions: happiness, anger, surprise, sadness, disgust, and fear. According to cross-cultural studies by social psychologist Paul Ekman, the facial expressions of these emotions are virtually universal, so even a culturally diverse audience usually will be able to read your emotional expressions clearly.

Your facial expressions should naturally vary to be consistent with your message. Present somber news with a serious expression. To communicate interest in your listeners, keep your expression alert and friendly.

Personal Appearance

There is considerable evidence that your personal appearance affects how your audience will respond to you and your message, particularly during the opening moments of your presentation. Appropriate wardrobe varies depending on climate, custom, culture, and audience expectations. Most people have certain expectations about the way a speaker should look. Use your audience analysis to identify and avoid violating your audience's expectations.

STUDY GUIDE

MEET YOUR OBJECTIVES

1. **Make effective eye contact during a speech.**
   To communicate effectively with North American audiences, make eye contact with the entire audience before and during your speech.

2. **Use gestures effectively while speaking.**
   Use natural, definite, and varied gestures that fit your personality and help you communicate your message to your particular audience.

Continued

3. **Move purposefully in ways that enhance your message while speaking.**
Use movement to emphasize your verbal messages, to make your audience feel closer to you, and to help listeners understand the transitions and organization of your speech.

4. **Display an appropriate posture while delivering a speech.**
Posture communicates the intensity of your emotions and your interest in your audience and speech. Avoid slouching and drooping.

5. **Use facial expressions to enhance verbal messages.**
Rehearse using universally recognized facial expressions that match the emotions of your verbal messages.

6. **Choose appropriate attire for making a speech.**
Analyze your audience and speaking situation to determine what to wear when you deliver your speech.

THINK ABOUT THESE QUESTIONS

1. **Self Assessment** Record and analyze a video of yourself rehearsing your next speech. Did you follow the advice given in this chapter? How can you improve your eye contact, gestures, posture, and use of movement and facial expressions?

2. **Ethics Assessment** Many politicians hire image consultants to coach them in nonverbal skills. Is it ethical for a speaker to use such consultants to attempt to gain more credibility with voters?

3. **Critical Assessment** Monique is self-conscious about her hand gestures, and she often just puts her hands behind her back. What advice would you give Monique to help her use gestures more effectively?

18 Verbal Communication

OBJECTIVES

1. Use effective vocal delivery when giving a speech.
2. Explain how to use a microphone when speaking in public.
3. Describe the steps to follow when rehearsing your speech.

Vocal Delivery

Your credibility as a speaker and your ability to communicate your ideas clearly to your listeners will in large part depend on your vocal delivery. It is primarily through the quality of our voices, as well as our facial expressions, that we communicate whether we are happy, sad, bored, or excited. If your vocal clues suggest that you are bored with your topic, your audience will probably be bored also.

Vocal delivery includes pitch, speaking rate, volume, pronunciation, articulation, pauses, and general variation of the voice. A speaker has at least two key vocal obligations to an audience: Speak to be understood, and speak with vocal variety to maintain interest.

Speak to Be Understood

To be understood, you need to consider four aspects of vocal delivery: volume, articulation, dialect, and pronunciation.

Volume The fundamental goal in your vocal delivery is to speak loudly enough so that your audience can hear you. The **volume** of your speech is determined by the amount of air you project through your larynx, or voice box. More air equals more volume of sound.

Your diaphragm, a muscle in your upper abdomen, helps control sound volume by increasing airflow from your lungs through your voice box. Breathing from your diaphragm—that is, consciously expanding and contracting your abdomen as you breathe in and out—can increase the volume of sound, as well as enhance the quality of your voice.

Articulation The process of producing speech sounds clearly and distinctly is **articulation**. If you do not clearly articulate the sounds that make up words, your listeners may not understand you or may fault you for simply not knowing how to speak clearly and fluently. Here are some commonly misarticulated words:[1]

dint	instead of	*didn't*
lemme	instead of	*let me*
mornin	instead of	*morning*
seeya	instead of	*see you*
soun	instead of	*sound*
wanna	instead of	*want to*
whadayado	instead of	*what do you do*

Such speech flaws may not keep your audience from understanding you, but poor enunciation does reduce your credibility as a speaker. Many errors in articulation result from simple laziness. Often, we get into bad habits of mumbling, slurring, and abbreviating.

The best way to improve your articulation of sounds is first to identify words or phrases that you have a tendency to slur or chop. Once you have identified them, practice saying the words correctly. Consult an online dictionary to make sure you can hear the difference between the improper and proper pronunciations. A speech teacher can help you check your articulation.

Dialect A **dialect** is a consistent style of pronouncing words that is common to an ethnic group or a geographic region. In the southern part of the United States, people prolong some vowel sounds when they speak. And in the northern Midwest, the word *about* sometimes sounds a bit like "aboat." Research suggests that listeners tend to prefer a dialect similar to their own.[2]

Although a speaker's dialect may pigeonhole that person as being from a certain part of the country, it won't necessarily affect the audience's comprehension of the information unless the dialect is so pronounced

---

HOW TO

Modify a Dialect

You can adapt your dialect by changing your intonation pattern, vowel production, consonant production, or speaking rate.

- **Use proper intonation.** A typical North American intonation pattern is predominantly a rising and falling pattern. The pattern looks something like this:

  "Good ᵐᵒʳⁿning.   How ᵃʳᵉ you?"

  For North American audiences, speakers of other languages may want to modify intonation patterns that listeners would find distracting.
- **Pronounce vowels clearly.** Clipping or shortening vowel sounds can make comprehension challenging. If you need to stretch or elongate your vowels, consider recording your speech and then comparing it with standard American pronunciations.
- **Pronounce consonants appropriately.** Consonant production varies, depending on which language you are speaking. Although it is sometimes difficult to produce clear consonants that are not overdone, avoid consonants that are so soft as to be almost unheard. They can produce a blur of unintelligible sound rather than crisply articulated words.
- **Use an appropriate speaking rate.** A rate that is too fast can contribute to problems with clipped vowels, soft or absent consonants, and an intonation pattern that is on one pitch level rather than comfortably varied. Slowing your rate just a bit can enhance comprehension.

that the listeners can't understand the speaker's words. We don't recommend that you eliminate your own mild dialect, but if you get negative feedback or suspect that your word pronunciation is significantly distracting to your listeners, you might consider modifying it, using the suggestions in the How To box.

Pronunciation   Whereas articulation relates to the clarity of sounds, **pronunciation** concerns the degree to which the sounds conform to those assigned to words in standard English. Mispronouncing words can detract from a speaker's credibility. If you are uncertain about how to pronounce a word, look it up in an online dictionary. Most popular dictionaries provide recordings of the correct pronunciations of words. Often, however, we are not aware that we are not using standard pronunciation unless someone points it out.

Some speakers reverse speech sounds, saying "aks" instead of "ask," for example. Some allow an *r* sound to intrude into some words, saying "warsh" instead of "wash," or leave out sounds in the middle of a word, as in "ackchally" instead of "actually" or "Febuary" instead of "February." Some speakers also accent syllables in nonstandard ways; they say "po' lice" instead of "po lice'" or "um' brella" rather than "um brel'la."

If English is not your native language, you may have to spend extra time working on your pronunciation and articulation. Here are two useful tips to help you. First, make an effort to prolong your vowel sounds. Speeee-ak tooooo proooooolooooong eeeeeeach voooooowel soooooound yooooooooou maaaaaaaake. Second, to reduce choppy-sounding word pronunciation, blend the end of one word into the beginning of the next. Make your speech flow from one word to the next, instead of separating it into individual chunks of sound.[3]

Speak with Variety

Appropriate variation in vocal pitch and rate, as well as appropriate use of pauses, can add zest to your speech and help maintain audience attention.

Pitch Vocal **pitch** is how high or low your voice sounds. Everyone has a habitual pitch. This is the range of your voice during normal conversation. Some people have a habitually high pitch, whereas others have a low pitch.

Your voice has **inflection** when you raise or lower the pitch as you pronounce words or sounds. Your inflection helps determine the meaning of your utterances. A surprised "ah!" sounds different from a disappointed "ah" or inquisitive "ah?" Your vocal inflection is thus an important indicator of your emotions and gives clues as to how to interpret your speech.

In some cultures, vocal inflection plays a major role in helping people interpret the meaning of words. For example, Thai, Vietnamese, and Mandarin Chinese languages purposely use monotone and low, falling, high, and rising pitches.[4] If you are a native speaker of a language in which pitch influences meaning, be mindful that pitch does not have the same effect in many Western languages, although all languages rely on inflection to provide nuances of meaning.

The best public speakers vary their inflection considerably. Variation in your vocal inflection and overall pitch helps you communicate the subtlety of your ideas and keeps your listeners interested. Lack of variation in pitch has been consistently identified as one of the most distracting characteristics of ineffective speakers. An unvarying monotone is boring.

Record your speech as you rehearse, and evaluate your use of pitch and inflection critically. If you are not satisfied with your inflection, consider practicing your speech with exaggerated variations in vocal pitch. Although you would not deliver your speech this way, it might help you explore the expressive options available to you.

Rate How fast do you talk? Most speakers average between 120 and 180 words per minute. There is no one "best" speaking rate. The best rate depends on two factors: your speaking style and the content of your message.

One symptom of speech anxiety is the tendency to rush through a speech to get it over with. You can use feedback from others or record and listen critically to your message to help you assess whether you are speaking at the proper speed.

Fewer speakers have the problem of speaking too slowly, but a turtle-paced speech will almost certainly make it more difficult for your audience to maintain interest. Remember, your listeners can grasp information much faster than you can speak it.

Pauses An appropriate pause can often do more to accent your message than any other vocal characteristic. President Kennedy's famous line, "Ask not what your country can do for you; ask what you can do for your country," was effective not only because of its language, but also because it was delivered with a pause dividing the two thoughts. Try delivering that line without the pause; without it, that statement just doesn't have the same power.

Effective use of pauses, also known as *effective timing*, can greatly enhance the impact of your message. Whether you are trying to tell a joke, a serious tale, or a dramatic story, your use of a pause can determine the effectiveness of your anecdote. A well-timed pause, coupled with eye contact, can also powerfully accent a particular word or sentence. Silence is a way of saying to your audience, "Think about this for a moment."

QUICK CHECK

Good Vocal Delivery

- Use adequate volume.
- Articulate speech sounds clearly and distinctly.
- Pronounce words accurately.
- Vary your pitch.
- Vary your speaking rate.
- Pause to emphasize ideas.

Beware, however, of the vocalized pause. Many beginning public speakers are uncomfortable with silence, and so, rather than pausing where it seems natural and normal, they vocalize sounds such as "umm," "er," "you know," and "ah." However, such vocalized pauses will annoy your audience and detract from your credibility. You can download apps that help you count and eliminate vocalized pauses, or you can ask a listener to point them out to you as you rehearse.

Using a Microphone

No matter how polished your gestures or well intoned your vocal cues are, if you are inaudible or use a microphone awkwardly, your speech will not have the desired effect.

There are three kinds of microphones. The **lavaliere microphone** is the clip-on type often used by news people and interviewees. Worn on a collar or lapel, it requires no particular care other than not thumping it or accidentally knocking it off. The **boom microphone,** used by makers of movies, hangs over the heads of the speakers and is remote controlled.

The most common microphone is the **stationary microphone**. This is the type that is most often attached to a lectern, sitting on a desk, or standing on the floor. The microphones in most electronic devices used to deliver speeches via videoconferencing are also usually stationary. Generally, the stationary microphones used today are multidirectional. You do not have to remain frozen in front of a stationary microphone while delivering your speech. However, you do need to take some other precautions when using one.

> First, check to make sure that your microphone is indeed multidirectional and can pick up your voice even if you aren't speaking directly into it.
> Second, speak clearly and crisply. You may need to pronounce B, P, and S sounds with less intensity than usual.

> Third, if you must test a microphone, count or ask the audience whether they can hear you. Blowing on a microphone produces an irritating noise! Do not tap, pound, or shuffle anything near the microphone. If you are using note cards, quietly slide them aside as you progress through your speech.

> Finally, continue to speak at your normal volume. Some speakers lower their volume and become inaudible when they have a microphone in front of them.

If you have the chance to rehearse with the microphone you will use, figure out where to stand for the best sound quality and how sensitive the microphone is to extraneous noise. Practice will accustom you to any voice distortion or echo that might occur so that these sound qualities do not surprise you during your speech.

Rehearsing Your Speech: Some Final Tips

Rehearsal is the key to effective verbal and nonverbal delivery of your speech. The following suggestions can help you make the most of your rehearsal time.

> Finish drafting your speech outline at least two days before your speech performance.

> Before you prepare the speaking notes to use in front of your audience, rehearse your speech aloud to help determine where you will need notes to prompt yourself.

> Revise your speech as necessary to keep it within the time limits set by your instructor or whoever invited you to speak.

> Prepare your speaking notes. Use whatever system works best for you. Some speakers use pictorial symbols to remind themselves of a story or an idea. Others use complete sentences or just words or phrases in an outline pattern to prompt them. Many teachers advocate using note cards for speaking notes. Some speakers use an iPad or other electronic display. If you do use electronic notes, it is wise to have a hard-copy backup.

> Rehearse your speech standing up so that you can get a feel for your use of gestures as well as your vocal delivery. Do not try to memorize your speech or plan specific gestures. As you rehearse, you may want to modify your speaking notes to include reminders to gesture or pause at key points.

> If you can, present your speech to someone else so that you can practice establishing eye contact. Seek feedback from your captive audience about both your delivery and your speech content.

> If possible, record audio or video of your rehearsals. Most smartphones, computers, and computer tablet have a built-in camera and microphone. When listening to or viewing the recording, observe your vocal and physical mannerisms and make necessary changes. Many speakers still find it useful to practice before a mirror so that they can observe their body language—it's low-tech, but it still works.

> Rehearse using all your presentation aids. Don't wait until the last minute to plan, prepare, and rehearse with computer-generated slides or other aids that you will need to manipulate as you speak.

> Your final rehearsals should re-create, as much as possible, the speaking situation you will face. If you will be speaking in a large classroom, find a large classroom in which to rehearse your speech. If your audience will be seated informally in a semicircle, then this should be the context in which you rehearse your speech. The more realistic the rehearsal, the more confidence you will gain.

> Practice good delivery skills while rehearsing. Remember this maxim: Practice *makes* perfect if practice *is* perfect.

STUDY GUIDE

MEET YOUR OBJECTIVES

1. **Use techniques of effective vocal delivery when giving a speech.**
   To be effective, speak to be understood, with enough volume, clear articulation, and correct pronunciation, modifying your dialect only if necessary. Maintain your listeners' interest by speaking with vocal variety, including proper pitch and inflection, an appropriate rate, and effective use of pauses.

2. **Explain how to use a microphone when speaking in public.**
   Try to rehearse with your microphone before your speech to determine how much you can move. Avoid making annoying sounds, but use your normal speaking volume.

3. **Describe the steps to follow when rehearsing your speech.**
   Allow at least two days after finishing your speech outline to practice your speech delivery and develop your speaking notes. As much as possible, re-create the speech environment when you rehearse. Record your rehearsal or recruit a listener to provide feedback on your performance.

THINK ABOUT THESE QUESTIONS

1. **Self Assessment** Review the tips for rehearsing your speech presented on pages 161 to 162. Rate yourself on a scale of 1 to 5 (1 = poor; 5 = excellent) on each of the suggestions. Use your self-ratings to develop a plan to improve your rehearsals.

2. **Ethics Assessment** Is it ethical to cultivate a highly emotional vocal delivery style to use when attempting to persuade listeners?

3. **Critical Assessment** Professor Murray speaks slowly and in a monotone; consequently, many of her students do not enjoy her music history lectures. What can she do to give her voice some variety?

19

Adapting and Delivering Your Speech

OBJECTIVES

1. Describe how to adapt a speech for listeners whose cultures are different from yours.
2. Take steps to prepare for a successful speech delivery.
3. Prepare to answer questions after delivering a speech.

Adapt Your Delivery to a Diverse Audience

You need to adapt your presentation to the expectations of your listeners, especially those whose cultural backgrounds differ from yours. Consider the following suggestions to help you develop strategies for adapting both your verbal and your nonverbal messages.

Avoid an Ethnocentric Mind-Set

Ethnocentrism is the assumption that your own cultural approaches are superior to those of other cultures. When considering how to adapt your delivery style to your audience, try to view different approaches and preferences not as right or wrong but merely as different from your own.

Use a Less Dramatic Style for High-Context Listeners

Because a high-context culture places considerable emphasis on unspoken messages, you need not be overly expressive for audiences from such a culture. For example, to many Japanese people, a delivery style that includes exuberant gestures, overly dramatic facial expressions, and frequent movements might seem overdone. A more subtle, less demonstrative approach would create less "noise" and be more effective.

Monitor Your Level of Immediacy with Your Audience

Speaker **immediacy** depends on how close you are to your listeners, the amount of eye contact you display, and whether you speak from behind or in front of a lectern. According to the immediacy principle, we move closer to things we like, and we move away from things we don't like.[1]

Some cultures expect less immediacy; the key is not to violate what listeners expect.[2] For example, Japanese audiences don't expect speakers to move from behind a lectern and stand very close to listeners.

Monitor Your Expression of Emotion

Not all cultures interpret and express emotions the same way. People from the Middle East and the Mediterranean are typically more expressive and animated in their conversation than are Europeans.[3] People from a high-context culture place greater emphasis on delivery of a message than do people from a low-context culture (such as North Americans), and high-context audiences rely heavily on your unspoken message to help them interpret what you are saying.[4] Remember, however, that even low-context listeners attend to your nonverbal clues.

Use Gestures with Care

Even subtle nonverbal messages communicate feelings, attitudes, and cues about the nature of the relationship between you and your audience, so it is important to

---

QUICK CHECK

Adapt Your Delivery to a Diverse Audience

Consult people who know the culture and refrain from ethnocentrism as you adapt:

- nonverbal delivery
- immediacy behaviors
- emotional expressiveness
- gestures and verbal expressions

avoid gestures or expressions that would offend your listeners. There is no universal dictionary of nonverbal meaning, so spend some time asking people who are from the same culture as your prospective audience about what gestures and expressions your audience will appreciate.

Our general advice is to become sensitive and responsive to cultural differences and to keep cultural expectations in mind when you rehearse and deliver a speech. The How To box gives suggestions for getting the information you need.

Successfully Deliver Your Speech

When you are ready to deliver your speech, your task is to calmly and confidently communicate with your audience. Consider the following suggestions to help you prepare for a successful performance.

> **Get plenty of rest before your speech.** Last-minute, late-night final preparations can take the edge off your performance.
> **Watch what you eat.** A heavy meal or too much caffeine before you speak can have a negative effect on your performance.
> **Acknowledge normal prespeech jitters.** Remember that most speakers are nervous. But if you have developed a well-organized, audience-centered message

---

HOW TO

Gather Cultural Advice

Talk with people you know who are familiar with the cultural expectations of the audience you will address. Ask specific questions:

- Do listeners like direct eye contact?
- Where does the audience expect me to stand while speaking?
- When will the audience expect me to start and end my talk?
- Will listeners find particular gestures offensive?

on a topic of genuine interest to you, you're doing all the right things to make your speech a success.

> **Review the suggestions in Chapter 2 for becoming a confident speaker.** Re-create the speech environment when you rehearse. Use deep-breathing techniques to help you relax. Make sure you are especially familiar with your introduction and conclusion. Act calm so that you will feel calm. Visit MySearchLab (**www.mysearchlab.com**) for more tips on overcoming anxiety.

> **Arrive early for your speaking engagement.** If the room is in an unfamiliar location, give yourself plenty of time to find it. You may also want to rearrange the furniture or make other changes in the speaking environment.

> **Check your equipment.** After checking your equipment, set up your presentation aids carefully.

> **Relax before you deliver your message.** Budget your time so that you do not spend the moments before you speak frantically trying to attend to last-minute details.

> **Visualize success.** Picture yourself delivering your speech in an effective way. Also, remind yourself of the effort you have spent preparing for your speech. A final mental rehearsal can boost your confidence and help ensure success.

Keep in mind that speech delivery is an art rather than a science. Adapt these tips and your delivery to reflect your personality and individual style.

Responding to Questions

A question-and-answer session may be scheduled after your speech. During this Q&A period, your delivery method changes from extemporaneous to impromptu speaking. Here are some tips to make the question-and-answer period less challenging. Chapter 26 offers additional suggestions for answering questions after group presentations.

> **Prepare.** Analyze your audience. Think of possible questions those particular listeners might ask you, and then rehearse your answers.

> **Repeat or rephrase the questions.** Repeating a question ensures that everyone can hear the question. It also ensures that you understand the question. It lets you succinctly summarize a rambling question. And repeating the question gives you just a bit of time to think about your answer.

> **Stay on message.** Keep bringing the audience back to your central idea. If a listener asks a question unrelated to your talk, guide your questioner back to the message you have prepared.

> **Give a "double-barreled" talk.** Some seasoned speakers suggest that you save a bit of your speech to deliver during the Q&A session.[5] You present your speech, and then when an appropriate question is asked, you give your second, much briefer speech as your answer.

> **Ask the first question yourself.** As you transition between the end of your speech and the Q&A, prime the audience by asking and answering an initial challenging question.

> **Listen nonjudgmentally.** Give your full attention to the questioner. Listen politely and respond courteously.

> **Neutralize hostile questions.** Restate the question and acknowledge the questioner's emotions. Focus your answer on the heart of the questioner's issue or problem.

> **When you don't know the answer, admit it.** You can promise to find out more information and then get back to the person later. When you make a promise, follow through on it.

> **Be brief.** Even if you've planned a "double-barreled" talk, make your answers short and to the point.

> **Use organized signposts.** Use verbal signposts to help listeners understand your answer. For example, you can say, "I have two answers to that question. First, ..." Then, when you get to your second point, say, "My second point is . . . ."

> Indicate when the Q&A period is ending. For example, warn your audience, "I only have time for two more questions."

STUDY GUIDE

MEET YOUR OBJECTIVES

1. **Describe how to adapt a speech for listeners whose cultures are different from yours.**
   Get advice from people who are familiar with your audience, and avoid ethnocentrism. Adapt verbal and nonverbal delivery.

2. **Take steps to prepare for a successful speech delivery.**
   Rest and eat well before a speech. Take steps to boost your confidence. Arrive early, and visualize your successful speech.

3. **Prepare to answer questions after delivering a speech.**
   Consider your audience and plan for questions they might ask. Listen politely to questions and repeat or rephrase them, especially hostile questions. Keep answers brief, organized, and to the point.

THINK ABOUT THESE QUESTIONS

1. **Self Assessment** Review the tips on pages 166 to 167 for getting ready to deliver your speech. Rank the suggestions in order of how much they can help you before your next speech.

2. **Ethics Assessment** How can you ethically adapt to an audience of listeners from many different cultures?

3. **Critical Assessment** Muriel, who has been a church organist for 35 years, is planning on speaking to her music club about her experiences playing the pipe organ. How would you advise Muriel to prepare for questions after her speech?

20 Selecting Presentation Aids

OBJECTIVES

1. Discuss four ways in which presentation aids help communicate ideas to an audience.
2. Describe the types of presentation aids and how to use them effectively.
3. Use criteria to choose presentation aids to include in a speech.

The Value of Presentation Aids

A presentation aid is any object that reinforces your point visually so that your audience can better understand it. Presentation aids can help your listeners do all of the following:[1]

> **Focus**—Presentation aids grab the attention of your listeners and keep their interest when words alone might not.

> **Understand**—Of your five senses, you learn more from sight than from all the others combined.[2] Demonstrating or showing procedures or events step-by-step is an especially effective way to help listeners understand them.[3]

> **Remember**—It is well known that you remember most what you understand best. In addition, receivers better retain material they get via both audio and video "channels" of communication.[4]

> **Organize**—Listing your major ideas on a computer-generated slide, chart, or poster can help your audience grasp your main ideas and follow your transitions.

Types of Presentation Aids

You can choose from a huge variety of presentation aids. We group them into four categories for discussion: three-dimensional aids, two-dimensional aids, computer-generated aids, and audiovisual aids.

Three-Dimensional Presentation Aids

Three-dimensional aids include actual objects, models, and people.

Objects Objects add interest because they are tangible. They can be touched, smelled, heard, and even tasted, as well as seen. Objects are real, and audiences like the real thing.

If you use an object to illustrate an idea, make sure that you can handle the object with ease. If an object is too large, it can be unwieldy and difficult to show to your audience. Tiny objects can be seen only close up. Avoid objects that are dangerous to handle.

Models If it is not possible to bring the object you would like to show your audience, consider showing them a **model**. Make sure, however, that any model you use is large enough to be seen by all members of your audience.

People Using people to illustrate your message can be tricky. Before your presentation, choose someone you trust so that you can fully inform him or her about what needs to be done. Rehearse your speech using your live presentation aid.

If you don't need the person to demonstrate something during your opening remarks, wait and introduce the person to your audience when needed. Remember, your presentation aids are always subordinate to your speech. You must remain in control.

Two-Dimensional Presentation Aids

Two-dimensional presentation aids—including drawings, photos, maps, graphs, charts, flipcharts, and chalkboards and whiteboards—are used very commonly by speakers.

Drawings Drawings are easy and inexpensive to make, and they can be tailored to your specific needs. As a rule, large and simple line drawings are more effective for stage presentations than are detailed images. One way to view drawings at large sizes is to incorporate them into computer-generated presentation aids.

Photographs Photographs can show objects or places that cannot be illustrated with drawings or that an audience cannot view directly. Photos can easily be incorporated into computer-generated slides. If you must use a printed photograph, enlarge it or scan and project it.

Maps Most maps are designed to be read from a distance of no more than two feet. To make a map large enough for your audience to see, you can enlarge it using a color copier, draw a simplified large-scale version, or embed it in a computer-generated slide.

Graphs A **graph** is a pictorial representation of statistical data in an easy-to-understand format. Most listeners find that graphs help make data more concrete. Graphs are particularly effective in showing overall trends and relationships among data. The four most common types of graphs are bar graphs, pie graphs, line graphs, and picture graphs.

> A **bar graph** consists of flat areas—bars—whose various lengths represent information.
> A **pie graph** shows the individual shares of a whole. Pie graphs are especially useful in helping your listeners to see quickly how data are distributed in a given category or area.
> **Line graphs** show relationships between two or more variables. Like bar graphs, line graphs organize statistical data to show overall trends. A line graph can cover a greater span of time or numbers

than a bar graph without looking cluttered or confusing. A simple line graph communicates better than a cluttered one.

> **Picture graphs** look somewhat less formal and less intimidating than other kinds of graphs. One of the advantages of picture graphs is that they need few words or labels, which makes them easier for your audience to read.

Charts Charts, or tables, summarize and present a great deal of information in a small amount of space. They are easy to use, reuse, and enlarge. They can also be displayed in a variety of ways. You can use a flip-chart, a poster, or a computer-generated slide, which can project a giant image of your chart on a screen. Charts must be simple and easy to read. Do not try to put too much information on one chart.

Flipcharts A flipchart consists of a large pad of paper resting on an easel. You can either prepare your visual aids on the paper before your speech or draw on the paper while speaking. Flipcharts are easy to use; during your presentation, you need only flip the page to reveal your next visual. Flipcharts are best used when you have brief information to display or when you want to summarize comments from audience members during a presentation.

Chalkboards and Whiteboards Most public-speaking teachers discourage overuse of chalkboards and white-boards, because you must turn your back to the audience to write. If you use the board, use it only for brief phrases or very simple diagrams that can be drawn in just a few seconds.

Computer-Generated Presentation Aids

Most audiences, especially those in the corporate world, expect a speaker to use computer-generated presentation aids. The most popular presentation software programs include the widely known PowerPoint; Prezi™, which stores files in the Internet "cloud" and allows users to zoom in and out of slides; and Keynote, popular with many users of Apple devices for its sleek, contemporary appearance.

Although computer-generated graphics can be overused and, like any presentation aid, can distract from your message if used improperly, they nonetheless open up professional-looking possibilities for illustrating your speech. **Clip art** consists of images that are either in printed form or stored as electronic images in a computer file. Copyright-free clip art and photos are available at no cost from many Internet sources. Presentation software allows you to easily incorporate these images into your visual aids.

Be sure to consider your audience when you use computer-generated presentation aids.[5] As with any presentation aid, the images or clips that you choose to display must help develop your central idea; otherwise, they will distract your audience from it. The following tips can help.[6]

Keep Sights and Sounds Simple Many users attempt to shovel too much information into their slides and overwhelm listeners. Keep in mind that presentation aids *support* your message; they are not your message.

> Limit the number of words on each slide.
> Use slides to present images rather than merely repeat your words.
> Resist the urge to add sound effects. *You* should be the sound track, not your computer.

Repeat Elements to Unify Your Presentation Use a common visual element, such as a bullet or visual symbol, at the beginning of each word or phrase in a list. Use common color schemes and spacing to give your visuals coherence. Use fonts consistently, rather than mix them. Use a similar visual style for each of your images to achieve a professional, polished look. Use repetition of key words (such as *use* at the beginning of each sentence in this paragraph).

Choose a Font with Care   Several types of **fonts** are shown in Figure 20.1. Use **sans serif fonts** for titles. **Serif fonts** are easier to read for longer passages. Although interesting and dramatic, **script fonts** should be used sparingly because they are hard to read. Use **decorative fonts** only when you want to communicate a certain special tone or mood. Regardless of which font style you use, don't use more than one or two on a single visual.

Font Types

Serif
Poster
Bodoni
Garamond
Americana

Sans Serif
Abadi
Herald
Denmark
Garrison Sans

Script
Quill
Kauflinn
Mariah
Kunstler Script

Decorative
Pablo
Curlz
PAPER CLIP
Stars and Stripes

FIGURE 20.1 | Typefaces grouped by font type.

Make Informed Decisions about Using Color   Color communicates. Choose colors that will support and reinforce the topic and purpose of your speech. To unify your presentation, use the same background color on all visuals and no more than two colors for words. Using a dark background with lighter-colored words can have a pleasing effect and make the words easy to see.

Allow Plenty of Time to Prepare Your Presentation Aids   Prepare your presentation aids well in advance of your speaking date so that you can make them as attractive and polished looking as possible. A sloppy,

---

QUICK CHECK

Design Effective PowerPoint Aids

- Use clip art to give your visuals a professional touch.
- Keep sights and sounds simple.
- Repeat elements to unify your presentation.
- Choose a typeface with care.
- Avoid mixing many different fonts.
- Make informed decisions about using color.
- Finish preparing your presentation aids early.

---

amateurish presentation aid will convey the impression that you are not a credible speaker, even if you have spent many hours preparing the verbal part of your speech.

Audiovisual Presentation Aids

Audiovisual aids combine sound and images to communicate ideas. We also discuss audio aids in this category.

Video Aids   It's now easy to record video images and audio clips to support speech ideas; digital video cameras are inexpensive, widely available, and a standard feature of smartphones. If you are using video from movies or TV to support your talk, you'll likely get the images from YouTube or other Internet sources, or from commercially prerecorded digital video disks (DVDs).

Before you decide to use a video image, think about whether or not it will really enhance your speech. Short, well-selected clips are most likely to be effective.

You can use a variety of technologies to store your videos and play them back during your speech:

> **DVD player.** Simply play back part of a prerecorded movie or TV show.
> **Computers and devices.** You can store and play video clips on your computer, smartphone, computer tablet, such as an iPad, or your iPod or other MP3

player. Embedding the video in computer-generated presentation aids can give you more control over precisely what clip you are showing, as well as the visual context and timing when you play it. Unless the audience is very small, all of these options require you to hook your device to a monitor or a projection system. Make sure monitors are available and compatible with your device, or bring your own.

› **The Internet.** If the room in which you are delivering your speech has Internet access, you can skip storing your video, and instead, play the video directly from YouTube or another Internet source. You can also retrieve your video or audio material from the "cloud," computer storage that is in a remote location. Playing video directly from the Internet or from cloud storage does, however, carry the risk of losing an Internet connection prior to or during your speech.

When using any of these technologies, you'll want to practice using your video and make sure all of the equipment you need is available. We also recommend that, before you give your speech, you do a technical run-through, ensuring that your video image will be ready when you want it to be.

Audio As with video, you can either create your own audio content or use a variety of prerecorded sources. You also have a number of options for storage and playback. As with video, be sure to rehearse with and master any technology involved with audio aids, and don't let your sound track overwhelm or distract from your own speech.

Select the Right Presentation Aids

Because there are so many choices, you may wonder, "How do I decide which presentation aid to use?" Use the suggestions in the How To box to help you. Get more advice about choosing and using presentation aids at MySearchLab (**www.mysearchlab.com**).

> ### Choose Presentation Aids
>
> - **Consider your audience.** The age, interests, and attitudes of your audience should affect your selection of audiovisual support.
> - **Estimate the size of the audience.** Choose presentation aids that everyone will be able to see clearly.
> - **Think of your speech objective.** Don't select a presentation aid until you have decided on the purpose of your speech.
> - **Evaluate your own skill and experience.** Use only equipment with which you are comfortable or have had practical experience.
> - **Know the room in which you will speak.** If the room has large windows with no shades and no other way to dim the light, do not consider using visuals that require a darkened room.

STUDY GUIDE

MEET YOUR OBJECTIVES

1. **Discuss four ways in which presentation aids help communicate ideas to an audience.**
   Presentation aids help you gain and maintain the audience's attention and communicate the organization of your ideas. They can improve listeners' understanding and recollection of those ideas.

2. **Describe the types of presentation aids and how to use them effectively.**
   Three-dimensional presentation aids include objects, models, and people. Two-dimensional presentation aids include drawings, photographs, slides, maps, graphs, charts, flipcharts, and chalkboards. Software

Continued

presentation packages can be used to produce many presentation aids inexpensively and efficiently. Audiovisual aids include video clips and audio clips or performances that help communicate ideas to your listeners.

3. **Use criteria to choose presentation aids to include in a speech.**
   Consider the audience, your topic and purpose, your own skills, and the location of your speech when choosing presentation aids.

THINK ABOUT THESE QUESTIONS

1. **Self Assessment** Identify several public-speaking situations that would lend themselves well to using presentation aids. What are some situations in which using presentation aids would *not* be beneficial?

2. **Ethics Assessment** Tom is preparing a speech on driver safety. He plans to begin his speech with a series of graphic pictures showing traffic accident victims. Is it ethical to show graphic images that arouse audience fears?

3. **Critical Assessment** Professor Chou uses only the chalkboard to illustrate her anthropology lectures and then only occasionally writes a word or two. What other types of visual or auditory aids could Professor Chou use in teaching?

21 Preparing and Using Presentation Aids

OBJECTIVES

1. Follow three guidelines for developing effective presentation aids.
2. Identify guidelines for effectively using presentation aids.

Guidelines for Preparing Presentation Aids

A speech should be more than just what a speaker says, with a few PowerPoint slides or other visual aids added as an afterthought. Spend time carefully developing your **visual rhetoric** as well as your words. Three guiding principles for effective presentations are to keep them easy to see, keep them simple, and keep them safe.

Keep Them Easy to See

To communicate your ideas clearly, everyone in the audience must be able see your presentation aids clearly. Our most important advice is this: *Write big!*

Keep Them Simple

Your presentation aid should convey to your audience information that you think is important, but your speech should provide the majority of your message.

Simple, well-designed, and well-planned drawings and pictures can be valuable additions to your presentation. Choose images carefully to ensure that the image you display complements the mental image created by your spoken words.

Computer-generated graphics should be simple and uncluttered. Limit text to key words or phrases. If you have a great deal of information, use two or three simple charts or slides rather than putting all your words on one visual. Slides loaded with fancy fonts, clip art, and outlandish colors can quickly become distracting and hard to read. Instead of supporting your presentation, they will actually confuse your audience and detract from your message.

Each element in your visual aid should serve a clear and specific purpose that is appropriate to your audience, topic, and setting.

Keep Them Safe!

While demonstrating how to string a bow during a speech on archery, one student accidentally launched the bow over the heads of his startled audience. Not only did he lose credibility because he was not able to string the bow successfully, but he also endangered his audience.

We cannot emphasize this point enough: Do not use dangerous or illegal presentation aids! They are never worth the risk of a ruined speech or an injured audience member. Substitute a picture, chart, or other representational device.

Using Presentation Aids

Here are some tips to help you use presentation aids for maximum audience impact.

Rehearse with Your Presentation Aids

Your appearance before your audience should not be the first time you deliver your speech while holding up an object, using a flipchart, or showing your Power-Points. Practice with your presentation aids until you feel at ease with them.

Make Eye Contact with Your Audience, Not with Your Presentation Aids

Of course, you will need to glance at your visual aid to make sure that it isn't upside down or that it is the proper one. But do not face the image or object while giving your talk. Keep looking your audience in the eye.

Explain Your Presentation Aids

Always set your visuals in a verbal context. Don't just unceremoniously announce, "Here are the recent statistics on birth rates in the United States," and hold up your visual without further explanation. Tell the audience how to interpret the data.

Do Not Pass Objects among Members of Your Audience

What can you do if your object is too small to be seen without passing it around? If no other speaker follows your speech, you can invite audience members to come up and see your object when your speech is over. If your audience is only two or three rows deep, you can even hold up the object and move in close to the audience to show it while you maintain control.

Use Animals with Caution

Most actors are unwilling to work with animals—and for good reason. At best, they may steal the show. And most often, they are unpredictable. You may think you have the smartest, best-trained dog in the world, but you really do not know how your dog will react to a strange environment and an unfamiliar audience. The risk of having an animal detract from your speech may be too great to make planning a speech around one worthwhile.

Use Handouts Effectively

Many speech instructors believe that you should not distribute handouts during a speech—handing out papers during your presentation will only distract your audience. However, many audiences in business and other types of organizations expect a summary of your key ideas in written form. If you do find it necessary to use written material to reinforce your presentation, consider using the suggestions in the How To box.

Use Handouts

HOW TO

- **Make sure handouts are really necessary.** Do not distribute handouts that have only a marginal relevance to your verbal message. They will defeat your purpose.
- **If your listeners do not need the information during your presentation, save handouts for the end.** Don't distribute your handout during the presentation unless your listeners must refer to the material while you're talking about it.
- **After distributing your handouts, tell audience members to keep the material face down until you're ready to talk about the material.**
- **Control your listeners' attention.** Tell them where in the handout you want them to focus. For example, you could say, "I see that many of you are interested in the second and third pages of the report. I'll discuss those items in just a few moments. I'd like to talk about a few examples before we get to page 2."
- **Clearly number handout pages.** This will make it easy for you to direct audience members to specific pages.
- **Prepare images of each page of the handouts.** Show the image when you talk about the page, to make sure listeners know where to focus. Don't try to economize by *only* displaying material and not providing handouts, however. The print will undoubtedly be too small to be seen clearly.
- **Distribute a summary of the key ideas at the end of your talk.** Your summary handout might also refer to the specific action you want your audience to take.

Time the Use of Visuals to Control Your Audience's Attention

A skillful speaker knows when to show a supporting visual and when to put it away. For example, it's not wise to begin your speech with all your charts, graphs, and drawings in full view, unless you are going to refer to them in your opening remarks. Time the display of your visuals to coincide with your discussion of the information contained in them.

> **If possible, use a remote control device to advance computer-generated images.** Because you do not need to stay anchored near the computer to advance each slide, you can move around.

> **Show a blank slide to return the audience's focus to you.** You could also turn off the projection altogether. Just don't allow an image or bulleted list of words unrelated to your message to compete with you for your listeners' attention when you are making a point or telling a story.

> **Consider arranging for someone to help you.** The person can be a presentation aid, hold other aids, turn the pages of your flipchart, or change the slides on the projector. Make sure you rehearse with your assistant so that all goes smoothly during your presentation.

Use Technology Effectively

Some novice speakers are tempted to overuse presentation aids simply because they can quickly produce eye-catching visuals. Resist this temptation.

Also consider that many classrooms and lecture rooms are not equipped with the necessary hardware. Don't assume that the hardware and software you need will be available in the room where you are speaking. Be sure to ask what kinds of technology exist.

Remember Murphy's Law

According to Murphy's Law, if something can go wrong, it will. When you use presentation aids, you increase the chances that problems or snags will develop when you present your speech. The chart may fall off the easel, you may not find the chalk, or the computer in the room may not be compatible with your software. Be prepared. Bring backup supplies and have an alternative plan in case your original plans go awry.

If something doesn't go as you planned, do your best to keep your speech on track. If the chart falls, pick it up and keep talking; don't offer lengthy apologies. If

22 Informative Speaking

OBJECTIVES

1. Describe three goals and five different types of informative speeches.
2. Effectively and appropriately use four strategies to enhance audience understanding.
3. Effectively and appropriately use three strategies to maintain audience interest.
4. Effectively and appropriately use four strategies to enhance audience recall of information presented in an informative speech.
5. Develop an audience-centered informative speech.

Goals and Types of Informative Speeches

When you inform someone, you assume the role of a teacher. A **speech to inform** shares information with others to enhance their knowledge or understanding of concepts and ideas. The skill of teaching and enhancing understanding is important to virtually any profession. When you speak to inform, you typically attempt to achieve three goals:

> *You speak to enhance understanding.* Understanding occurs when a listener accurately interprets the intended meaning of a message.
> *You speak to maintain interest.* If your listeners are bored and not focusing on your message, you won't achieve your informative-speaking goal.
> *You speak to be remembered.* The day after hearing a presentation, most listeners remember only about 50 percent of what they were told. By two days

later, they recall only about 25 percent. Your job as an informative speaker is to improve those statistics.

Informative speeches can be classified according to the subject areas they cover. As Table 22.1 shows, classifying your speech can help you decide how to organize the information you want to present. Good organization will help your audience process your message.

Strategies to Enhance Audience Understanding

At the heart of creating understanding in someone is the ability to describe both old and new ideas to the person.

Speak with Clarity

To speak with clarity is to express ideas so that the listener understands the intended message accurately. Speaking clearly is an obvious goal of an informative speaker. What is not so obvious is *how* to speak clearly. Whether it's how to drive a car or how to care for an aardvark, if you are already familiar with a topic, you're likely to think your task of communicating an idea to someone is easier than it is.

Give careful thought to how you will help listeners understand your message. Communication researcher Joseph Chesebro has summarized several research-based strategies you can use to enhance message clarity.[1]

> Preview your main ideas in your introduction.
> Tell your listeners how new information relates to a previous point.
> Frequently summarize key ideas.
> Provide a visual outline to help listeners follow your ideas.
> Provide a handout prior to your talk with the major points outlined; leave space so that listeners can jot down key ideas.
> Once you announce your topic and outline, stay on message.

TABLE 22.1 Types of Informative Speeches

	Description	Typical Organization Patterns	Sample Topics
A Speech about Objects	Presents information about tangible things	Topical Spatial Chronological	The Rosetta Stone Museums International Space Station Voting machines
A Speech about Procedures	Reviews how something works or describes a process	Chronological Topical Complexity	How to . . . Fix a carburetor Operate a nuclear power plant Buy a quality used car Trap lobsters
A Speech about People	Describes either famous people or personal acquaintances	Chronological Topical	Sojourner Truth Nelson Mandela Indira Gandhi Your granddad Your favorite teacher
A Speech about Ideas	Presents abstract information or discusses principles, concepts, theories, or issues	Topical Complexity Chronological	Communism Success Buddhism Reincarnation
A Speech about Events	Describes an event that either has happened or will happen	Topical Spatial	Assassination of Abraham Lincoln Inauguration Day Cinco de Mayo

Another important suggestion to enhance message clarity is *don't present too much information too quickly.* If you need to share highly detailed information, put that information in writing.

Use Principles and Techniques of Adult Learning

Andragogy is the art and science of teaching adults. The How To box summarizes some effective andragogical, or adult-learning, principles found by researchers and scholars.[2]

Clarify Complex Processes

Research suggests that you can demystify a complex process if you first provide a simple overview of the process with an analogy, a vivid description, or a word picture.[3]

Analogies *Analogies*, or comparisons, can help listeners understand unfamiliar ideas or processes by comparing them to something they already know. To comprehend the vastness of the Milky Way galaxy, for instance, you might point out that if the Milky Way

---

HOW TO

Use Adult-Learning Principles

- **Give adults information they can use right away.** Listeners are more likely to focus on and understand information they can apply immediately to their mental "in-basket" or to-do list.
- **Actively involve adult learners in the learning process.** Consider asking them questions to think about or, in some cases, to respond to on the spot.
- **Connect adult learners' life experiences with new information.** First, know the kinds of experiences that your listeners have had, and then refer to those experiences as you present your ideas.
- **Explain how new information is relevant to listeners' needs and their busy lives.**
- **Seek ways to relate the ideas you present to listeners' problems.**

were the size of North America, our entire solar system would fit inside a coffee cup.[4]

Vivid Descriptions You can also *describe* a complex process, providing more detail than when you just define something. Descriptions answer questions about the who, what, where, why, and when of the process. Who is involved? What is the process, idea, or event that you want to describe? Where and when does it take place? Why does it occur, or why is it important to the audience? (Not all of these questions apply to every description.)

Word Pictures You may want to clarify a process with a **word picture**. Word pictures are lively descriptions that help your listeners form a mental image by appealing to their senses of sight, taste, smell, sound, and touch. To create an effective word picture, begin by forming your own clear mental image of the person, place, object, or process before you try to describe it. See it with your "mind's eye."

> What would a listener see if he or she were looking at it?
> What would listeners hear?
> If they could touch the object or do the process, how would it feel to them?
> If your listeners could smell or taste it, what would that be like?

To describe these sensations, choose the most specific and vivid words possible. Onomatopoeic words—words that sound like the sounds they name—such as *buzz, snort, hum, crackle,* or *hiss,* are powerful. So are similes and other comparisons. "The rock was as rough as sandpaper" and "the pebble was as smooth as a baby's skin" appeal to both the visual and the tactile senses.

Be sure to describe the emotions that a listener might feel if he or she were to experience the situation you relate. If you experienced the situation, describe your own emotions. Use specific adjectives rather than general terms such as *happy* or *sad*.

One speaker, talking about her first speech assignment, described her reaction this way: "My heart stopped. Panic began to rise up inside. For the next week, I lived in dreaded anticipation of the event."[5] Note how effectively her choices of such words and phrases as "my heart stopped," "panic," and "dreaded anticipation" describe her terror at the prospect of making a speech—much more so than if she had said, "I was scared." The more vividly and accurately you can describe emotion, the more intimately involved in your description the audience will become.

Appeal to a Variety of Learning Styles

As you develop your speech and supporting materials, consider how you can appeal to the variety of **learning styles** among your listeners, including the following:

> **Auditory learners** learn best by *hearing* material.
> **Visual print learners** would much rather *read* material than listen to it presented orally.
> **Visual learners** depend on more than words alone to help them remember ideas and information. They learn best with words *and* images. Your presentation aids can assist both kinds of visual learners.
> **Kinesthetic learners** learn best by moving while learning. They would rather try something than hear it, watch it, or read about it. Ponder ways to allow listeners to move, such as asking for a show of hands.

QUICK CHECK

Strategies to Enhance Audience Understanding

- Speak with clarity.
- Use principles and techniques of adult learning.
- Clarify complex processes.
- Appeal to a variety of learning styles.

Strategies to Maintain Audience Interest

Before you can inform an audience, you must gain and maintain their interest. No matter how carefully crafted your definitions, skillfully delivered your description of a process, or visually reinforcing your presentation aid, if your listeners aren't paying attention, you won't achieve your goal. Strategies for gaining and holding interest are vital in achieving your speaking goal.

Establish a Motive for Your Audience to Listen to You

Most audiences probably will not be waiting breathlessly for you to talk to them. You will need to motivate them to listen to you. Unless you hold the power to reward or punish your listeners, you will need to find more creative ways to get your audience to listen to you. Pique their interest with a story. Tell them how the information you present will be of value to them. Use an unexpected twist or rhetorical question.

Tell a Story

Good stories with interesting characters and riveting plots have fascinated listeners for millennia; the words "Once upon a time" are usually a surefire attention getter. Stories are also a way of connecting your message to people from a variety of cultural backgrounds.

The characteristics of a well-told tale are simple yet powerful. A good story includes conflict, incorporates action, creates suspense, and may also include humor.

> **Conflict.** Stories that pit one side against another and describe opposing ideas and forces in government, religion, or personal relationships foster attention.
> **Action.** An audience is more likely to listen to an action-packed message than to one that listlessly lingers on an idea too long. The key to maintaining interest is a plot that moves along to hold attention. Good stories have a beginning that sets the stage, a heart that moves to a conclusion, and an ending that ties up all the loose ends.

> **Suspense.** Suspense is created when the characters in the story may do one of several things. Keeping people on the edge of their seats because they don't know what will happen next is an element in good storytelling.

> **Humor.** Using a bit of humor makes the point while holding the listener's attention. Not all stories have to be funny. Stories may be sad or dramatic without humor. But adding humor at appropriate times usually helps maintain interest and attention.

Present Information That Relates to Listeners

Being an audience-centered informative speaker means being aware of information that your audience can use. If, for example, you are going to teach your audience about recycling, be sure to talk about specific recycling efforts on your campus or in your community. Adapt your message to the people who will be in your audience.

Use the Unexpected

Advertisers know that listeners will focus on the unexpected. If you add a surprise twist to a quotation or story, audience members will increase their attention. You can also create a "mini-mystery" by asking a rhetorical question to get listeners to actively process your words.[6]

Strategies to Enhance Audience Recall

Some speakers are better than others at presenting information in a memorable way. Here are some strategies that will help your audiences remember you and your message.

Build In Redundancy

When you speak, repeat key points. Give a clear preview at the beginning of your talk as well as a summary statement in your conclusion. Include internal summaries—short summaries after key points during your speech—to help audiences remember key ideas. Use numeric signposts (numbering key ideas verbally by saying, "My first point is. . . . My second point is. . . ."\) to make sure your audience can identify and remember key points.

A reinforcing visual aid that displays your key ideas can also enhance recall. If you really want to ensure that listeners come away from your speech with essential information, consider preparing a handout or an outline of key ideas.

Make Your Key Ideas Short and Simple

Don't bombard listeners with lengthy lists. One classic research study concluded that people can hold only about seven pieces of information in their short-term memories.[7] Remember to crystallize the central idea of your speech into a one-sentence statement. Phrase your central-idea statement, as well as your main points, as simply as possible. Try to make them short enough to fit on a bumper sticker.

Pace Your Information Flow

Organize your speech so that you present an even flow of information, rather than bunching up a number of significant details around one point. If you present too much new information too quickly, you may overwhelm your audience.[8]

Make sure that your audience has time to process any new information. Use supporting materials both to help clarify new information and to slow down the pace of your presentation. Do not try to see how much detail and content you can cram into a speech.

Reinforce Key Ideas

Reinforcing key ideas is one of the most powerful techniques of all.

Reinforce Ideas Verbally You can reinforce an idea by using such phrases as "This is the most important point" or "Be sure to remember this next point." Suppose you have four suggestions for helping your listeners avoid serious sunburn, and your last suggestion is the most important. How can you make sure your audience knows that? Just tell them. "Of all the suggestions I've given you, this last tip is the most important one. The higher the SPF level on your sunscreen, the better." Be careful not to overuse this technique. If you claim that every other point is a key point, soon your audience will not believe you.

Reinforce Ideas Nonverbally You can also signal the importance of a point with nonverbal emphasis. Gestures serve the purpose of accenting or emphasizing key phrases, as italics do in written communication.

> A well-placed pause can provide emphasis and reinforcement to set off a point. Pause just before or just after making an important point to focus attention on it.
> Raising or lowering your voice can also reinforce a key idea.
> Movement can help emphasize major ideas. Moving from behind the lectern to tell a personal anecdote can signal that something special and more intimate is about to be said.
> Your movement and gestures should be meaningful and natural, rather than seemingly arbitrary or forced. Your need to emphasize that an idea can provide the motivation to make a meaningful movement.

Developing an Audience-Centered Informative Speech

Use the audience-centered speaking model, shown in Figure 3.1 on page 17, to guide you step-by-step through the process of preparing an informative speech. Visit MySearchLab (**www.mysearchlab.com**) to analyze these key elements in examples of informative speeches.

Consider Your Audience

As with any type of speech, you need to consider three general questions about audience analysis when preparing an informative talk:

> *To whom are you speaking?* Find out as much as you can about what they already know and their preferred learning styles.
> *What are their interests, attitudes, beliefs, and values?* Determining listeners' interests, attitudes, beliefs, and values can help you balance your use of strategies to enhance understanding and recall with your need for strategies to maintain interest.
> *What do they expect from you?* Careful consideration of the audience's expectations can help you maintain their interest, perhaps by surprising them with something they do not expect.

Select and Narrow Your Informational Topic

To choose what you will say about a topic, ask yourself, and answer, the question, "What do my listeners already know about my topic?" You also should consider the question, "How interested are they in my topic?" If your audience is both knowledgeable and interested in your topic, you can provide more details and build on the information they already have. If they are likely to be uninterested or uninformed, then you'll need to establish, early on in your message, a clear and engaging reason they should tune you in.

Determine Your Informative Purpose

You already know that your general purpose is to inform. You also need to develop a behavioral specific-purpose statement that says what you want your audience to *state*, *describe*, *identify*, *list*, or otherwise *do* to demonstrate what they learn from your speech. Although you may never actually ask it, it may help to think of your specific-purpose sentence as a test question that you're writing for your audience.

Develop Your Central Idea

With a clear and precise specific-purpose sentence, you'll be better prepared to identify your central idea— a one-sentence summary of your message. As we noted earlier in the chapter, you should state your central idea as simply as possible.

Generate Your Main Ideas

The type of informative talk you are planning will influence your central and main ideas. A speech about an object may lend itself to certain main ideas—such as history, features, and uses of the object—whereas a speech about a person might be more likely to have main ideas related to the person's accomplishments or relationship to you, the speaker.

Gather Your Supporting Materials

The type of informative speech you make will often give you ideas about supporting materials. Biographical details and stories will most likely support a speech about a person. Stories, examples, or statistics may help you teach your audience about an event or idea. Supporting visual aids often make "how-to" speeches about procedures effective. Speeches about objects also often benefit from visual aids, especially if the actual object is appropriate to show.

Organize Your Speech

As shown in Table 22.1 on page 189, different types of informative speeches lend themselves to different organizational patterns.

Rehearse Your Presentation

Rehearse your speech out loud while standing. Re-creating the experience of actually delivering your speech helps you not only polish your delivery, but also better manage any apprehension you may have.

For informative speeches, it is especially helpful to rehearse in front of people who are similar to your listeners. Seek their feedback about whether you are effectively teaching them about your topic. To determine whether your speech is meeting your learning objectives, you may even actually ask your sample audience the "test question" you developed as your specific-purpose statement.

Deliver Your Speech

Effective audience-centered speakers are continually looking for ways to adapt and modify their message as they speak. This is especially important in informative speaking. As you speak, watch your audience closely for puzzled facial expressions or other signs that may indicate they do not understand your informative message. Be alert, too, for any signs of wandering attention, such as fidgeting or lack of eye contact. Be prepared to adapt your message, using the strategies discussed earlier in this chapter for enhancing listeners' understanding and maintaining their attention.

STUDY GUIDE

MEET YOUR OBJECTIVES

1. **Describe three goals and five different types of informative speeches.**
   Informative speakers must enhance listeners' understanding, maintain their interest, and be remembered. They can make speeches about objects, procedures, people, events, and ideas.

2. **Effectively and appropriately use four strategies to enhance audience understanding.**
   To enhance your listeners' understanding, define ideas clearly, use adult-learning principles, clarify unfamiliar ideas or complex processes, use descriptions effectively, and address listeners' variety of learning styles.

3. **Effectively and appropriately use three strategies to maintain audience interest.**
   To gain and maintain listeners' interest, you must motivate your audience to listen to you. Tell a story, present information that relates to listeners, or use the unexpected.

Continued

4. **Effectively and appropriately use four strategies to enhance audience recall of information.**
   Help your listeners remember what you tell them by being redundant, keeping your ideas short and simple, pacing the flow of information, and reinforcing important points.
5. **Develop an audience-centered informative speech.**
   You can apply principles of informative speaking at every step of the the audience-centered method of speaking.

THINK ABOUT THESE QUESTIONS

1. **Self Assessment** What strategies do your instructors use in class to motivate students to listen, enhance listeners' understanding, and improve their recall?
2. **Ethics Assessment** In order to give your 5-minute speech about nuclear energy, you must greatly simplify a very complex process. How can you avoid misrepresenting your topic? Should you let your audience know how much you are simplifying the process?
3. **Critical Assessment** You have been asked to speak to a kindergarten class about your chosen profession. How can you make your message clear, interesting, and memorable to your audience?

23 Understanding Principles of Persuasive Speaking

OBJECTIVES

1. Describe the goals of persuasive messages.
2. Explain classic and contemporary theories of how persuasion occurs.
3. Describe four ways to motivate listeners to respond to a persuasive message.
4. Prepare and present an audience-centered persuasive speech.

The Goals of Persuasion

Persuasion is the process of changing or reinforcing attitudes, beliefs, values, or behaviors. In a persuasive speech, the speaker explicitly asks the audience to make a choice, rather than just informing them of the options. To advocate a particular view or action successfully, you must understand your listeners' positions before you speak.

Attitudes

Our attitudes represent our likes and dislikes. Stated more precisely, an **attitude** is a learned predisposition to respond favorably or unfavorably toward something. Attitudes (likes and dislikes) are easier to change than either beliefs or values.

Beliefs

A **belief** is what you understand to be true or false. If you believe in something, you are convinced that it exists or is true. Beliefs are typically based on past experiences or evidence, but some beliefs are based on faith—we haven't directly experienced something, but we believe anyway. A belief is more susceptible to change than a value is, but it is still difficult to alter. Beliefs are changed by evidence. Usually it takes a great deal of evidence to change a belief and alter the way your audience structures reality.

Values

A **value** is an enduring conception of right or wrong, good or bad. If you value something, you classify it as good or desirable, and you tend to think of its opposite or its lack as bad or wrong. If you do not value something, you are indifferent to it. Speeches that focus on changing or reinforcing audience values emphasize how and why something is better than something else. Values form the basis of our life goals and the motivating force behind our behavior, and listeners' values are difficult to change. Understanding what your listeners value can, however, help you adapt the content of your speech to their values.

Behavior

Persuasive messages often attempt to do more than change or reinforce attitudes, beliefs, or values—they attempt to change behavior. Several factors motivate us to respond to persuasive messages with a change in behavior: our actual and perceived needs, our tendency to avoid pain and seek pleasure, our emotional reactions, and our compulsion to seek psychological balance and order in our lives.

How Persuasion Works

There are many theories and considerable research on how persuasion works. We'll discuss two approaches here: (1) a classic approach identified by the ancient Greek rhetorician Aristotle; and (2) the elaboration likelihood model (ELM), a contemporary theory that builds on the classic approach. Both suggest that persuasion is a complex process, and that not all of us are persuaded in the same way. Aristotle's theory emphasizes what a *speaker* should do to influence an audience, however, while ELM theory describes how *listeners* process the messages they hear.

Aristotle's Traditional Approach: Using Ethos, Logos, and Pathos to Persuade

Aristotle, a Greek philosopher and rhetorician who lived and wrote in the fourth century BCE, defined *rhetoric* as the process of discovering, in any particular case, the available means of persuasion. He identified three general methods (or, using his language, "available means") of persuasion. They are ethos, logos, and pathos.

Ethos   To use **ethos** to persuade, an effective communicator must be credible. Not only must the information be credible, Aristotle believed the speaker also should be ethical, possess good character, have common sense, and be concerned for the well-being of the audience. The more credible and ethical a speaker is perceived to be, the greater the chances are that a listener will believe in, trust, and respond positively to the speaker's persuasive message.

Logos   The word **logos** literally means "the word." Aristotle used this term to refer to the rational, logical arguments that a speaker uses to persuade someone. A skilled persuader not only reaches a logical conclusion, but also supports the message with evidence and reasoning.

Pathos   Aristotle used the term **pathos** to refer to the use of appeals to emotion in persuasion. Emotion-arousing stories and examples, as well as pictures and music, all appeal to listeners' emotions.

ELM's Contemporary Approach: Using a Direct or Indirect Path to Persuade

The **elaboration likelihood model (ELM) of persuasion** has a long name but is actually a simple idea that explains how you are persuaded to do or think about something.[1]

To **elaborate** means that you *think* about the information, ideas, and issues related to the content of the message. When you elaborate on a message, you are critically evaluating what you hear by paying special attention to the arguments and evidence the speaker is using. The likelihood of whether you elaborate on a message or not (hence, the name *elaboration likelihood model*) varies from person to person and depends on the topic of the message. The theory suggests that there are two ways you can be persuaded:

1. A **direct persuasion route** that you follow when you elaborate on, or critically evaluate, a message.
2. An **indirect persuasion route**, in which you don't elaborate and are more influenced by the peripheral factors of the message and messenger. You might, for example, be persuaded by your emotional reaction to the speaker's examples or by your liking of the speaker.

ELM theory suggests that, as a speaker, you need not only to present well-reasoned arguments with credible evidence, but also to be attuned to indirect factors that can influence your listeners, such as your delivery, appearance, and your audience's general impression of how prepared you are.

QUICK CHECK

Theories of Persuasion

Aristotle	**ELM**
Focus is on speaker's actions:	Focus is on listeners' actions:
• Logos—logic, evidence	• Direct route—elaboration on logic, evidence
• Ethos—speaker credibility and ethics	• Indirect route—no elaboration, persuaded by factors such as credibility and emotion
• Pathos—emotion	

How to Motivate Listeners

Motivation is the underlying internal force that drives people to achieve their goals. Persuasion works because listeners are motivated to respond to a message. An audience is more likely to be persuaded if you help members solve their problems or otherwise meet their needs. They can also be motivated if you convince them that good things will happen to them if they follow your advice, or that bad things will occur if they don't.

Use Dissonance

According to dissonance theory, when you are presented with information inconsistent with your current attitudes, beliefs, values, or behavior, you experience a kind of discomfort called **cognitive dissonance**.[2] The word *cognitive* refers to thoughts; *dissonance* means "lack of harmony or agreement." So cognitive dissonance means that you are experiencing a way of thinking that is inconsistent and uncomfortable. Most people seek to avoid feelings of dissonance; thus, creating dissonance with a persuasive speech can be an effective way to change attitudes and behavior.

The first tactic in such a speech is to identify an existing problem or need. Then, the speaker ethically describes the problem to listeners in a way that arouses cognitive dissonance. Finally, the persuasive speaker suggests a solution to the problem that can help listeners reduce dissonance. Listeners can react in several ways to your use of dissonance, only one of which serves your purpose.[3]

> **Listeners may discredit the source (you).** You need to ensure that your audience will perceive you as competent and trustworthy so that they will accept your message.
> **Listeners may reinterpret the message.** They may choose to focus on the parts of your message that are consistent with what they already believe and ignore the unfamiliar or controversial parts. To counter this tendency, make your message as clear as possible.

> **Listeners may seek new information.** Audience members may look for additional information to negate your position. Be sure your own evidence is trustworthy, making it harder to refute.

> **Listeners may stop listening.** Some messages are so much at odds with listeners' current positions that they may decide to stop listening. The principle of selective exposure suggests that we tend to pay attention to messages that are consistent with our points of view and to avoid those that are not. Being aware of listeners' existing attitudes, beliefs, and values can help you ensure they don't tune out.

> **Listeners may change their attitudes, beliefs, values, or behavior—as the speaker wishes them to do.** If listeners change their attitudes, they can reduce their dissonance and restore their sense of balance.

Use Listener Needs

Need is one of the best motivators. The more you understand what your listeners need, the greater the chances are that you can gain and hold their attention and ultimately get them to do what you want.

Abraham Maslow suggested that a hierarchy of needs, as shown in Figure 23.1, motivates everyone's behavior.

FIGURE 23.1 | Maslow's hierarchy of needs.

Maslow suggested that we must meet basic physiological needs (such as food, water, and air) before we can be motivated to respond to higher-level needs.[4] Although research suggests that we are not limited to hierarchical order and can be motivated by several needs at the same time, Maslow's hierarchy provides a useful checklist of potential listener motivations that a persuasive speaker can activate in order to change or reinforce attitudes, beliefs, values, or behavior.

Physiological Needs The most basic needs for all humans are physiological: We all need air, water, and food. According to Maslow's theory, unless those needs are met, it will be difficult to motivate a listener to satisfy other needs. Try to ensure that listeners are physically comfortable before making appeals based on higher-level needs.

Safety Needs Once basic physiological needs are met, listeners are concerned about their safety. We all need to feel safe, secure, and protected. Persuasive speakers often appeal to our need to provide for our own and our loved ones' safety.

Social Needs We all need to feel loved and valued. We need contact with others and reassurance that they care about us. According to Maslow, these social needs translate into our need for a sense of belonging to a group (a fraternity, a religious organization, a circle of friends). Powerful persuasive appeals are based on our need for social contact.

Self-Esteem Needs The need for self-esteem reflects our desire to think well of ourselves. Advertisers often appeal to this need to persuade us to buy products.

Self-Actualization Needs The need for **self-actualization** is the need to fully realize one's highest potential, which Maslow suggested could be addressed only after we met needs at the other four levels. Persuasive calls to be the best at something appeal to this need.

Use Positive Motivation

Positive motivational appeals are suggestions that good things will happen to listeners who heed the speaker's advice. A key to using positive motivational appeals effectively is to know what your listeners value. Knowing what audience members view as desirable, good, and virtuous can help you select the benefits of your persuasive proposal that will best appeal to them. Knowing that your listeners value clean air, for example, may help you persuade them to support your proposal for new limits on emissions.

Use Negative Motivation

The use of a threat to change someone's attitude or behavior is one of the most effective approaches. Negative motivation, also known as a *fear appeal*, takes the form of an "if–then" statement. If you don't do X, then awful things will happen to you. An important need will go unmet unless the desired behavior or attitude change

---

HOW TO

Use Fear Appeals to Persuade

- **Threaten listeners' loved ones.** A strong threat to a loved one tends to be more successful than a fear appeal directed at the audience members themselves.
- **Establish your credibility.** The more credible your audience perceives you to be, the more likely it is that your fear appeal will be effective.
- **Make sure the threat is real.** Fear appeals are more successful if you can convince listeners that the threat will probably occur unless they take the action you are advocating.
- **Make the threat scary.** Increasing the intensity of a fear appeal increases the chances that it will be effective.[5]
- **Empower listeners.** Make sure you tell your listeners what they can do to reduce the threat—take the action you are suggesting.[6]
- **Don't exaggerate.** As an ethical speaker, you must be truthful in fear appeals.

occurs. Ethical and successful fear appeals require careful consideration of your audience. Consider the tips in the How To box.

Developing Your Persuasive Speech

The process of developing a persuasive speech follows the same audience-centered path you would take to develop any speech.

Consider the Audience

Although being audience-centered is important in every speaking situation, it is vital when your objective is to persuade. It would be extremely difficult to persuade someone without knowing something about his or her interests, attitudes, beliefs, values, and behaviors.

Remember that persuasion works differently for different cultural groups. Learn as much as you can about the cultural perspectives of your listeners so that you can ethically adapt your message to use persuasive strategies listeners will find convincing.

Select and Narrow Your Persuasive Topic

The best persuasive-speech topics focus on important rather than frivolous issues. You'll present a better speech if you select a topic you can speak about with sincere conviction. However, the ideal topic speaks to a need, concern, or issue of the audience, as well as to your interests and zeal.

Controversial issues—questions about which people disagree—make excellent sources for persuasive topics. In choosing a controversial topic, you need to be audience-centered. Know the local, state, national, or international issues that interest your listeners.

Determine Your Persuasive Purpose

You know your general purpose is to persuade. To develop your specific purpose, consider your audience. **Social judgment theory** suggests that listeners will come to your speech with one of three positions: (1) a latitude of acceptance, in which they generally agree with you; (2) a latitude of rejection, in which they disagree; or (3) a latitude of noncommitment, in which they are not yet committed.[7] If most of your listeners are in the latitude of rejection, it will be difficult to move them to the latitude of acceptance in a single speech. A more realistic goal might be to make them less certain of their rejection.

Develop Your Central Idea and Main Ideas

When persuading others, most speakers find it useful to state their central idea in the form of a proposition. A **proposition** is a statement with which you want your audience to agree. There are three categories of propositions.

Proposition of Fact A **proposition of fact** focuses on whether something is true or false or on whether it did or did not happen. To be a good speech topic, a proposition of fact must be debatable, such as "Global climate change is (or is not) occurring." It should not be a fact, such as who won the last Super Bowl, that can be easily verified. Most persuasive speeches that focus on a proposition of fact identify and provide evidence for one or more reasons that the proposition is true.

Proposition of Value A **proposition of value** is a statement that calls for the listener to judge the worth or importance of something. Value propositions often directly compare two things, or two courses of action, and suggest that one of the options is better than the other.

Proposition of Policy The third type of proposition, a **proposition of policy**, advocates a specific action—changing a policy, procedure, or behavior. Typically, propositions of policy include the word *should*. For example, "Public schools should encourage more physical activity."

Gather Supporting Material

Keep in mind Aristotle's three "available means" of persuasion as you gather supporting materials: (1) *ethos* includes using credible and ethical supporting material; (2) *logos* requires you to use effective logic and reasoning to support your main ideas; and (3) *pathos* suggests using appropriate emotional support.

Organize Your Speech

Your audience and your specific purpose can help you decide how to begin your message, organize your ideas, and conclude your talk. We'll discuss specific patterns of organization in the next chapter.

Rehearse and Deliver Your Speech

When your goal is to persuade, make a special effort to rehearse your speech in front of another person or to run some of your ideas past others to check the overall clarity and structure of your message.

As you deliver your speech, remember that ELM predicts that the emotional energy of your delivery can, in itself, be persuasive to some of your listeners. From Aristotle's view, your verbal and nonverbal cues reinforce your credibility and logic (ethos and logos), as well as make an emotional connection to listeners (pathos).

STUDY GUIDE

MEET YOUR OBJECTIVES

1. **Describe the goals of persuasive messages.**
   The goals of persuasion are to change or reinforce attitudes, beliefs, values, or behavior.

2. **Explain classic and contemporary theories of how persuasion occurs.**
   Aristotle suggested using ethos, logos, and pathos to persuade. The elaboration likelihood model suggests that listeners either follow a direct route to persuasion, in which they elaborate (think about) the issues and evidence, or an indirect route, in which they don't elaborate.

3. **Describe four ways to motivate listeners to respond to a persuasive message.**
   Persuasive speakers can motivate listeners through cognitive dissonance, satisfying listeners' needs, positive motivational appeals, or fear appeals.

4. **Prepare and present an audience-centered persuasive speech.**
   You can apply principles of persuasion at all steps in the audience-centered speechmaking process.

THINK ABOUT THESE QUESTIONS

1. **Self Assessment** If you were attempting to sell a new computer system to the administration of your school, what persuasive principles would you draw on to develop your message?

2. **Ethics Assessment** Is it ethical to develop a persuasive message that supports an attitude or belief with which you personally disagree?

3. **Critical Assessment** Martha has been asked to speak to the Association for the Preservation of the Environment. What possible persuasive topics and propositions would be appropriate for her audience?

24 Using Persuasive Strategies

OBJECTIVES

1. Identify strategies to improve your initial, derived, and terminal credibility.
2. Use principles of effective logic and evidence to develop a persuasive message.
3. Employ effective techniques of using emotional appeal in a persuasive speech.
4. Adapt your persuasive message to receptive, neutral, and unreceptive audiences.
5. Use strategies for effectively organizing a persuasive speech.

Establishing Your Credibility

Credibility, which Aristotle referred to as *ethos*, is the audience's perception of a speaker's competence, trustworthiness, and dynamism.

> **Competence.** You show **competence** by being informed, skilled, or knowledgeable about your subject. One way to enhance your competence is to cite credible evidence to support your point.
> **Trustworthiness.** While delivering your speech, demonstrate your **trustworthiness** by conveying honesty and sincerity. One way to earn the audience's trust is by demonstrating that you have had experience dealing with the issues you talk about. Your sincerity may be suspect, however, if you advocate something that will result in a direct benefit to you.
> **Dynamism.** You project **dynamism**, or energy, through your delivery. **Charisma** is a form of dynamism. A charismatic person possesses charm, talent,

213

magnetism, and other qualities that make the person attractive and energetic.

The more credible your listeners find you, the more effective you will be as a persuasive communicator. Speakers establish their credibility in three phases.

Initial Credibility

Initial credibility is the impression of your credibility that listeners have even before you speak. Give careful thought to your appearance, and establish eye contact before you begin your talk. Prepare a brief description of your credentials and accomplishments so that the person who introduces you can use it in his or her introductory remarks.

Derived Credibility

Derived credibility is the perception of your credibility that listeners form as you present yourself and your message. These strategies can enhance your derived credibility:

> Establish common ground with listeners by indicating in your opening remarks that you share their values and concerns.
> Support your arguments and conclusions with evidence.
> Present a logically organized, well-delivered message. Using appropriate internal summaries, signposts, and enumeration of key ideas can enhance your credibility as a competent and rational advocate.

Terminal Credibility

The last phase of credibility, called **terminal credibility**, is the perception that listeners have of your credibility when you finish your speech. Continue to make eye contact. Don't leave the lectern or speaking area until you have finished your closing sentence. Even if there is no planned question-and-answer period following your speech, be ready to respond to questions.

Use Logic and Evidence to Persuade

Logic is a formal system of rules for making inferences. Persuasive speakers need to pay careful attention to the way they use logic, or *logos* in Aristotle's wording, to reach a conclusion. Present *evidence* and then use appropriate *reasoning* to lead your listeners to the conclusion you advocate. **Evidence** consists of facts, examples, statistics, and expert opinions that you use to support and prove the points you wish to make. **Reasoning** is the process of drawing a conclusion from evidence. *Proof* consists of the evidence plus the conclusion you draw from it.

Understanding Types of Reasoning

There are three major ways to structure an argument in order to reach a logical conclusion: inductively, deductively, and causally.

Inductive Reasoning Using **inductive reasoning,** you reach a general conclusion based on specific examples, facts, statistics, and opinions. You may not know for certain that the specific instances prove that the conclusion is true, but you decide that, in all probability, the specific instances support the general conclusion.

To judge the validity of a **generalization** arrived at inductively, ask these questions:

> Are there enough specific instances to support the conclusion?
> Are the specific instances typical?
> Are the instances recent?

Reasoning by Analogy *Reasoning by analogy* is a special type of inductive reasoning. An analogy is a comparison. This form of reasoning compares one thing, person, or process with another, to predict how the second thing will perform and respond. You could reason that a law that works in one state would have the same effect if used in another state.

There are questions that you should ask in order to check the validity of conclusions reached via analogy:

› Do the ways in which the two things (such as two states) are alike outweigh the ways in which they are different?
› Is the assertion about the original thing, person, or process true?

Reasoning by Sign *Reasoning by sign,* another special type of inductive reasoning, occurs when the presence of one or more signs leads you to a conclusion that something else has happened or will happen. For example, thunder and dark clouds are signs that rain will happen. When you use or hear reasoning by sign, you must establish that there is a strong, predictive relationship between the sign and the conclusion. Multiple signs improve your ability to predict.

Deductive Reasoning Reasoning from a general statement or principle to reach a specific conclusion is called **deductive reasoning**. This is just the opposite of inductive reasoning.

Deductive reasoning can be structured in the form of a **syllogism**, which includes three elements:

1. A **major premise,** a general statement. A classic example of a major premise is based on mythology: All gods are immortal.
2. A **minor premise,** a more specific statement about an example linked to the major premise. The minor premise in our classic example might be: Zeus is a god.
3. The **conclusion,** based on the major premise and the minor premise. Following our classic example, we could conclude: Zeus is immortal.

You need to ensure that both the major and the minor premises are true and can be supported with evidence. If they are both true, then you can state with certainty—rather than just probability—that your conclusion is also true.

Causal Reasoning   **Causal reasoning** relates two or more events in such a way as to conclude that one or more of the events *caused* the others. Reasoning by sign points out that one thing predicts another, but causal reasoning concludes that one thing actually *causes* another.

> Reasoning from cause to effect, you move from a known fact to a predicted result, or from something that has occurred to something that has not yet occurred. For example, "If we allow the current pollution of the river to continue, townspeople will become ill."
> Reasoning from effect to cause, you move from known effect to unknown cause. You might show that many townspeople have illnesses that are a known effect of polluted water and then point to the river as the likely cause of their illnesses.

QUICK CHECK

Types of Reasoning

- **Inductive reasoning** draws a conclusion based on specific examples. Reasoning by analogy and signs are special types of inductive reasoning.
- **Deductive reasoning** applies a general principle to specific examples. A deductive syllogism contains a major premise, minor premise, and conclusion.
- **Causal reasoning** relates two or more events so as to conclude that one or more events caused the others. Your causal reasoning can proceed from a known cause to an unknown effect, or from a known effect to an unknown cause.

Adapt Reasoning for a Culturally Diverse Audience

Speakers from the United States typically use *factual inductive* reasoning; they identify specific facts and use them to support a general proposition or conclusion. However, not all cultures prefer such a direct, linear approach.[1] Some cultures use a deductive pattern of reasoning, in which a speaker begins with a general premise and then links it to a specific situation. Middle Eastern speakers usually do not use standard inductive or deductive structures. They are more likely to use narrative methods, which persuade listeners by allowing them to draw their own conclusions from stories, extended analogies, and examples.[2]

Supporting Your Reasoning with Evidence

When attempting to persuade listeners, make sure that your evidence logically supports the inductive, deductive, or causal reasoning you are using to reach your conclusion. Evidence in persuasive speeches consists of facts, examples, expert opinions, and statistics.

> A **fact** is something that has been directly observed to be true or can be proved to be true. An **inference** is a conclusion based on available evidence or partial information.
> **Examples** are illustrations that are used to dramatize or clarify a fact. Only valid, true examples can be used to help prove a point. A hypothetical example, one that is fabricated to illustrate a point, should not be used to reach a conclusion. It should be used only to clarify.
> **Opinions** can serve as evidence if they are expressed by an expert. Opinions are usually most persuasive if they are combined with other evidence, such as facts or statistics, that support the expert's position.
> A **statistic** is a number used to summarize several facts or samples.

If you use inductive reasoning (moving from specific examples to a general conclusion), you need to make sure you have enough facts, examples, statistics, and credible opinions to support your conclusion. If you reason deductively (from a generalization to a specific conclusion), you need evidence to document the truth of your initial generalization. When you are developing an argument using causal reasoning, evidence is also vital, as you attempt to establish that one or more events caused something to happen.

Once you have gathered evidence, follow these strategies to use it effectively:[3]

> **Use credible evidence.** Listeners are more likely to respond to your arguments if they determine that your evidence is from a trustworthy, knowledgeable, and unbiased source. **Reluctant testimony,** a statement from someone who has reversed his or her position or a statement that is not in the speaker's best interest, is especially powerful.

> **Use new evidence.** Evidence should not only be up-to-date but also new to listeners—something they have not already heard.

> **Use specific evidence.** Avoid vague terms, such as "many people." Use specific numbers and descriptions whenever possible.

> **Use evidence to tell a story.** Your evidence will be more powerful if the facts, examples, statistics, and opinions fit together to tell a story to make your point.

> **Use culturally appropriate evidence.** Listeners from some cultures will be more persuaded by stories or eyewitness testimony, while others will more likely be swayed by statistics.[4] You may need to ask a sampling of audience members or someone who knows the audience well what kind of evidence will be the most convincing.

Avoid Faulty Reasoning

Many persuaders use inappropriate techniques called *fallacies*. A **fallacy** is false reasoning that occurs when someone attempts to persuade without adequate evidence or with arguments that are irrelevant or inappropriate. You will be a better and more ethical speaker and a better listener if you are aware of the following fallacies.

Causal Fallacy The **causal fallacy** involves making a causal connection without enough evidence to support the cause-and-effect conclusion. Simply because one event follows another does not mean that the two are related.

Bandwagon Fallacy Someone who argues that "everybody thinks it's a good idea, so you should too" is using the **bandwagon fallacy**. Simply saying that "everyone" is "jumping on the bandwagon," or supporting a particular point of view, does not make the point of view correct.

Either/Or Fallacy Someone who argues that there are only two approaches to a problem is trying to oversimplify the issue by using the **either/or fallacy**.

Hasty Generalization A person who reaches a conclusion from little or no evidence is making a **hasty generalization**. Because one person became ill after eating the meat loaf in the cafeteria, everyone eating in the cafeteria will not necessarily develop food poisoning.

Ad Hominem Also known as attacking the person, an **ad hominem** (Latin for "to the man") **argument** involves attacking irrelevant personal characteristics of the person who is proposing an idea, rather than attacking the idea itself.

Red Herring The **red herring fallacy** is used when someone attacks an issue by using irrelevant facts or arguments as distractions. This fallacy gets its name from an old trick of dragging a red herring across a trail to divert any dogs that may be following.

Appeal to Misplaced Authority Ads that use athletes to endorse automobiles make an **appeal to misplaced authority**. Although we have great respect for athletes in their own fields, they are no more expert than we are about the product they are advertising.

Non Sequitur If you argue that a new parking garage should not be built on campus because the grass has not been mowed on the football field for three weeks, you are guilty of a **non sequitur**. Your conclusion simply does not follow from your statement.

Use Emotion to Persuade

As suggested by the two major theories of persuasion described in Chapter 23, we are often persuaded by emotion, which Aristotle called *pathos*, as well as logic.

According to **emotional response theory,** our emotional responses vary along three dimensions: pleasure, arousal, and dominance. If listeners feel pleasure and are also aroused by something, such as a political candidate or a product, they will tend to form a favorable view of the candidate or product. A listener's sense of being dominant has to do with being in control and having permission to behave as he or she wishes. A listener who feels dominant is more likely to respond to the message.

Your key concern as a public speaker is "How can I ethically use emotional appeals to achieve my persuasive purpose?" The How To box provides general strategies.

Another way to arouse listeners' emotions is to reference a **myth,** a belief held in common by a group of people that is based on their values, cultural heritage, or faith. Referring to a shared myth is a way for you to identify and develop a bond with your listeners and to help them see how your ideas support their ideas.

Keep in mind that listeners' cultures influence how receptive they are to emotional expressions and appeals. Some Latin American listeners, for example, expect speakers to express more emotion and passion than

---

HOW TO

Use Emotion to Persuade

- Use concrete examples that help your listeners visualize what you describe.
- Use emotion-arousing words.
- Use nonverbal behavior to communicate your emotional message.
- Use visual images to evoke emotions.
- Use appropriate metaphors and similes.
- Use appropriate fear appeals.
- Consider using appeals to several emotions, including hope, pride, courage, and reverence.

North American listeners expect. To identify listeners' expectations, you can observe other successful speakers addressing similar audiences.

Avoid Misusing Emotional Appeals: Ethical Issues

Regardless of which emotions you use to motivate your audience, you have an obligation to be ethical and forthright. Making false claims, misusing evidence to arouse emotions, or relying only on emotions without supplying any evidence to support a conclusion violates ethical standards of effective public speaking.

Strategies for Adapting Ideas to People and People to Ideas

Audience members may hold differing views of you and your subject. Your task is to find out if there is a prevailing viewpoint held by a majority of your listeners. If they are generally friendly toward you and your ideas, you need to design your speech differently than you would if your listeners were neutral, apathetic, or hostile. We offer some suggestions to help.

Persuading the Receptive Audience

In speaking to a receptive group, you can explore your ideas in depth.

> Identify with your audience. Emphasize the similarities between you and your listeners.
> Clearly state your speaking objective. Provide an overview of your major point or purpose.
> Be explicit in directing your listeners' behavior. Tell your audience exactly what you want them to do and how you expect them to respond to your message.
> Ask listeners for an immediate show of support to help cement the positive response you have developed during your speech.
> Use emotional appeals effectively. You can usually move a favorable audience to action with strong

emotional appeals while also reminding them of the evidence that supports your conclusion.

> Make it easy for your listeners to act. Make sure that what you're asking them to do is clear and simple.

Persuading the Neutral Audience

Many audiences will simply be neutral or indifferent. Your challenge is to make them interested in your message.

> Capture your listeners' attention early in your speech.
> Refer to beliefs that many listeners share.
> Relate your topic not only to your listeners but also to their families, friends, and loved ones.
> Be realistic about what you can accomplish. People who start with an attitude of indifference are probably not going to become enthusiastic after hearing just one speech.

Persuading the Unreceptive Audience

One of the biggest challenges in public speaking is to persuade audience members who are against you or your message. If they are hostile toward you personally, your job is to find ways to enhance your acceptability and persuade them to listen to you. If they are unreceptive to your point of view, there are several approaches that you can use.

> Be realistic about what you can achieve. Don't expect a major shift in attitude from a hostile audience.
> Don't immediately announce that you plan to change their minds.
> Begin your speech by noting areas of agreement before you discuss areas of disagreement.
> Acknowledge the opposing points of view. Your listeners will be more likely to listen to you if they know that you understand their viewpoint.

❯ Establish your credibility. Let your audience know about the experience, interest, knowledge, and skills that give you special insight into the issues at hand.

Sometimes your audience disagrees with you because its members just don't understand your point. Or they may harbor a misconception of you and your message. For such listeners, consider explaining rather than advocating. To enhance accurate understanding or correct a misconception, experienced speakers use a four-part strategy.[5]

1. Summarize the common misconceptions about the issue or idea you are discussing.
2. State why these misconceptions may seem reasonable.
3. Dismiss the misconceptions. Provide evidence to support your point; you need sound and credible data to be persuasive.
4. State the accurate information that you want your audience to remember. With a clear summary statement, reinforce the conclusion you want your listeners to draw from the information you presented.

Strategies for Organizing Persuasive Messages

How you organize your speech has a major effect on your listeners' response to your message. The How To box offers general suggestions for organizing your speech. You can also use or combine the following specific organizational patterns. Visit MySearchLab (**www.mysearchlab.com**) for examples of persuasive speeches that use them.

Problem–Solution

The most basic organizational pattern for a persuasive speech is to make the audience aware of a problem and then to present a solution that clearly solves it. If you are speaking to an apathetic audience or if listeners are not

Organize Your Persuasive Speech

- If you think your audience will be hostile to your point of view, advance your strongest arguments first. If you save your best argument for last, your audience may have already stopped listening.
- Do not bury key arguments and evidence in the middle of your message. Information presented first and last is more likely to be remembered by your listeners.
- If you want your listeners to take some action, it is best to tell them at the end of your speech what you want them to do.
- It is usually better to present both sides of an issue rather than just the advantages of the position you advocate. If you don't acknowledge the counterarguments—arguments against your position—that your listeners have heard, they will probably think about them anyway.
- After you mention counterarguments, refute them with evidence and logic that show how your proposal is better.
- Adapt your organization to your listeners' cultural expectations. North Americans often like a highly structured message, whereas audiences from some other cultures expect a less formal structure.

aware that a problem exists, a problem–solution pattern works nicely.

You must provide ample evidence to document that your perception of the problem is accurate. You'll also need to convince your listeners that the solution you advocate is the most appropriate one to resolve the problem.

Refutation

Another way to persuade an audience to support your point of view is to prove that the arguments against your position are false—that is, to refute them. To use refutation, you first identify objections to your position and then refute or overcome those objections with arguments and evidence. Credible evidence, facts, and data will be more effective than emotional arguments to overcome objections to your position that your listeners hold.

Cause and Effect

As Chapter 11 describes, you can organize your persuasive cause-and-effect speech by discussing an effect, or problem, and then identifying the causes of the problem. You can also organize a message by noting the problem and then spelling out the effects of the problem. With either approach, the goal of using cause-and-effect organization is to convince your listeners that one event *causes* another. Simply because two events occur at the same time or in close succession does not prove that there is a cause-and-effect relationship.

The Motivated Sequence

The motivated sequence is a five-step organizational plan.[6] It uses the *cognitive dissonance* approach: First disturb your listeners, and then point them toward the specific change you want them to adopt.

1. **Attention.** The attention step is, in essence, the introduction to your speech. Grab your listeners' attention with a personal or hypothetical example, a startling statement, an unusual statistic, a rhetorical question, or a well-worded analogy.

2. **Need.** Next, you arouse dissonance. You must establish why your topic should concern your listeners. You must also convince listeners that there is a need for a change and that the need affects them directly.

3. **Satisfaction.** After you present the problem, identify the solution—your plan to satisfy the need. Be brief, but present enough information so that your listeners have a general understanding of how the problem may be solved.

4. **Visualization.** Positive visualization paints a verbal picture of how wonderful the future will be if your solution is adopted. Negative visualization helps

listeners see how awful things will be if your solution is not adopted. Use either type alone, or both together.

5. **Action.** As the basis of your conclusion, tell your audience the specific action they can take to implement your solution. In some high-context cultures, the action step can be stated indirectly; you can imply what you'd like your listeners to do. For audiences from a low-context culture, such as the United States, identify exactly what you want your listeners to do. Give them simple, clear, easy-to-follow steps to achieve your goal.

The motivated sequence is a guide, not an absolute formula. Modify it to suit the needs of your topic and audience. If your audience is neutral, spend time getting their attention and inviting their interest in the problem. If you are speaking to a hostile audience, spend considerable time establishing need; if your listeners are receptive, spend less time on that step. Be audience-centered; adapt your message to your listeners.

STUDY GUIDE

MEET YOUR OBJECTIVES

1. **Identify and use strategies to improve your initial, derived, and terminal credibility.**
   Your competence, trustworthiness, and dynamism contribute to your credibility before, during, and after you speak.

2. **Use principles of effective logic and evidence to develop a persuasive message.**
   Three general types of reasoning are inductive, which includes reasoning by analogy and by sign, deductive, and causal. Evidence includes facts, examples, opinions, and statistics.

Continued

3. **Employ effective techniques of using emotional appeal in a persuasive speech.**
   Speakers can evoke persuasive levels of pleasure, arousal, and dominance among listeners by using examples, emotion-arousing words, nonverbal behavior, shared myths, and selected appeals to fear and other emotions.
4. **Adapt your persuasive message to receptive, neutral, and unreceptive audiences.**
   Explore your ideas in depth when persuading a receptive audience. You must capture the interest of a neutral audience. Look for areas of agreement and choose a realistic goal with an unreceptive audience.
5. **Identify and use strategies for effectively organizing a persuasive speech.**
   Four patterns for organizing a persuasive speech are problem–solution, refutation, cause-and-effect, and the motivated sequence.

THINK ABOUT THESE QUESTIONS

1. **Self Assessment** What specific strategies can you implement to enhance your initial, derived, and final credibility as a public speaker in the minds of your public-speaking classmates?
2. **Ethics Assessment** Does dynamism always contribute to credibility? Should audiences be wary of charismatic speakers?
3. **Critical Assessment** Janice wants to persuade the management of her company to establish a wellness program. Draft outlines for Janice's main ideas according to each of the organizational patterns outlined in this chapter.

25 Speaking on Special Occasions

OBJECTIVES

1. Describe guidelines for effective public-relations speaking.
2. Identify occasions and best practices for ceremonial speeches.
3. List and explain strategies for creating humor in a speech.

Public-Relations Speaking

Public-relations speeches are designed to inform the public and improve relations with them—either in general or because a particular program or situation has raised some questions. If you are called upon to make a public-relations speech, use the following guidelines:

> First, discuss the need or problem that has prompted the speech.
> Go on to explain how the company or organization is working to meet the need or solve the problem, or why it feels there is no problem.
> Anticipate criticism, whether it comes from the audience as a whole or from a minority contingent, and take care not to become unpleasantly defensive.
> Suggest and counter potential problems or objections to the policy or program.
> Emphasize the positive aspects of the policy or program. You want to leave the impression that the company or organization has carefully worked through potential pitfalls and drawbacks.

Ceremonial Speaking

Ceremonial speeches make up a broad class of speeches delivered on many kinds of occasions. Visit MySearchLab (www.mysearchlab.com) to see and hear examples of special-occasion speeches.

Introductions

A **speech of introduction** is much like an informative speech. The speaker provides information about the main speaker to the audience. You also need to make the speaker feel welcome while revealing some of his or her personal qualities to the audience so that they can feel they know the speaker more intimately.

The ultimate purpose of an introduction, however, is to arouse interest in the speaker and his or her topic. Introducing a speaker is similar to introducing your own speech. You need to get the attention of the audience, build the speaker's credibility, and introduce the speaker's general subject.

There are two cardinal rules of introductory speeches:

> **Be brief.** The audience has come to hear the main speaker or to honor the guest, not to listen to you.
> **Be accurate.** Ask the person you are going to introduce to supply you with relevant biographical data beforehand. If someone else provides you with information about the speaker's background, make sure the information is accurate. Be certain that you know how to pronounce the speaker's name and any other names or terms you will need to use.

Keep the needs of your audience in mind at all times. If the person you are introducing truly needs no introduction, do not give one! Just welcome the speaker and step aside. Note that the president of the United States is always introduced simply: "Ladies and gentlemen, the president of the United States."

Toasts

Most people are asked at some time or another to provide a **toast** for some momentous occasion—a wedding, a celebration, a birth, a reunion, or a successful business venture. A toast is a brief salute to such an occasion, usually accompanied by a round of drinks and immediately followed by the raising or clinking together of glasses or goblets.

The modern toast is usually quite short—only a few sentences at most. Some toasts are very personal, as, for example, one given by a best man who is a close friend of both the bride and the groom. In contrast, a toast made by someone who does not know the primary celebrants as intimately may be more generic in nature.

If you are asked to make an impromptu toast, let your audience and the occasion dictate what you say. Sincerity is more important than wit.

Award Presentations

Presenting an award is somewhat like introducing a speaker or a guest: Remember that the audience did not come to hear you, but to see and hear the winner of the award. Delivering a **presentation speech** is an important responsibility—one that has several distinct components.

Refer to the Occasion   Awards are often given to mark the anniversary of a special event, the completion of a long-range task, the accomplishments of a lifetime, or high achievement in some field.

Talk about the History and Significance of the Award   This section of the speech may be fairly long if the audience knows little about the award; it will be brief if the audience already knows the history and purpose of the award. Whatever the award, a discussion of its significance will add to its meaning for the person who receives it.

Name the Person   The longest part of this segment is a glowing description of the achievements that elicited the award. If the name of the person getting the award has already been made public, you may refer to him or her by name throughout your description. If you are going to announce the individual's name for the first time, you will probably want to recite the achievements first and leave the person's name for last. Even though some members of the audience may recognize from your description the person you are talking about, you should still save the drama of the actual announcement until the last moment.

Nominations

Nomination speeches are similar to award presentations. They, too, involve noting the occasion and describing the purpose and significance of, in this case, the office to be filled. The person making the nomination should explain clearly why the nominee's skills, talents, and past achievements serve as qualifications for the position. And the actual nomination should come at the end of the speech.

Acceptances

For every award or nomination, there is usually at least a brief **acceptance speech**. If you ever have to give an acceptance speech, it may be impromptu, because you may not know that you have won until the award is presented. A fairly simple formula should help you compose a good acceptance speech on the spur of the moment.

> First, thank the person making the presentation and the organization that he or she represents. It is also gracious to thank a few people who have contributed greatly to your success—but not a long list of everyone you have ever known, down to the family dog.
> Next, comment on what the award means to you. You may also wish to reflect on the larger significance of the award to the people and ideals it honors.

› Finally, try to find some meaning the award may have for your audience—people who respect your accomplishments and who may themselves aspire to similar achievements.

Keynote Addresses

A **keynote address** is usually presented at or near the beginning of a meeting or conference. It sets the theme and tone for other speakers and events. Your challenge as a keynote speaker is to arouse the interest of the audience and motivate them to learn more or work harder. One way is to incorporate examples and illustrations to which your audience can relate. You should also emphasize the importance of the topic or the purpose of the meeting.

Commencement Addresses

To be audience-centered, a **commencement address** must fulfill two important functions. First, the commencement speaker should praise the graduating class. Because the audience includes the families and friends of the graduates, the commencement speaker can gain their goodwill (as well as that of the graduates themselves) by pointing out the significance of the graduates' accomplishments.

A second function of an audience-centered commencement speech is to turn graduates toward the future. Commencement speakers should suggest new goals and try to inspire the graduates to reach for them.

Commemorative Addresses and Tributes

A **commemorative address**, a speech delivered during special ceremonies held to celebrate some past event, is likely to include a tribute to the person or persons involved.

A commemorative speech is, in part, an informative speech. The speaker needs to present some facts about the event and/or people being celebrated. Then the speaker builds on those facts, urging the audience to let past accomplishments inspire them to achieve new goals.

Eulogies

A **eulogy**—a speech of tribute delivered when someone has died—can be one of the most significant and memorable and also one of the most challenging forms of commemorative address. When you deliver a eulogy, you should mention—indeed, linger on—the unique achievements of the person to whom you are paying tribute and, of course, express a sense of loss.

It is also proper in a eulogy to include personal and even tasteful humorous recollections of the person who has died.

Finally, turn to the living, and encourage them to transcend their sorrow and sense of loss and feel instead gratitude that the dead person had once been alive among them.

QUICK CHECK

Types of Ceremonial Speeches

- Introductions
- Toasts
- Award presentations
- Nominations
- Acceptances
- Keynote addresses
- Commencement addresses
- Commemorative addresses and tributes
- Eulogies

After-Dinner Speaking: Using Humor Effectively

After-dinner speeches may present information or persuade, but their primary purpose is to entertain, to make people laugh. Speakers, actors, and comedians frequently employ the following strategies to make audiences laugh.

Humorous Stories

Humorous stories should be simple. Complicated stories and jokes are rarely perceived by audiences as funny. Successful humorous speakers also need a broad repertoire. And it is important to know one's anecdotes very well. Only if you know the material can you hope to deliver it with the intonation and timing that will make it funny.

Humorous Verbal Strategies

Either a humorous anecdote or a shorter "one-liner" may rely on one of the following verbal strategies for humorous effect.

Play on Words **Puns** rely on double meanings to create humor. **Spoonerisms** occur when someone switches

---

HOW TO Choose Humorous Speech Topics

Your audience "gives attempts at humor their success or failure."[1] The following ideas can help you choose a topic that your audience will agree is funny.

- **Use what makes you laugh.** Chances are that if you have found an experience funny, an audience will, too.
- **Make fun of yourself.** Audiences almost always enjoy hearing self-deprecating humor.
- **Find humor in serious subjects.** Although your speech, as a whole, may be serious, you can often find humor in certain aspects of your topic. In his documentary film *Sicko*, Michael Moore showed a scrolling text of medical conditions that health insurance companies use to deny clients coverage against an outer-space backdrop while playing the *Star Wars* theme music.[2]
- **Avoid inappropriate subjects.** Topics that create a great deal of emotional noise for your audience (such as grief or anger) are not good subjects for humorous speeches.

the initial sounds of words in a single phrase—for example, "sublic peaking" instead of "public speaking." **Malapropism** is the mistaken use of a word that sounds much like the intended word—*destruction* for *instruction,* for example.

Hyperbole Hyperbole, or exaggeration, is often funny. In an after-dinner speech on "The Alphabet and Simplified Spelling," Mark Twain claimed,

> Simplified spelling brought about sun-spots, the San Francisco earthquake, and the recent business depression, which we would never have had if spelling had been left all alone.[3]

Of course, spelling could not have caused such catastrophes, but by using hyperbole, Twain makes his point in a humorous way.

Understatement The opposite of hyperbole, **understatement** involves downplaying a fact or event.

Verbal Irony A speaker who employs **verbal irony** says just the opposite of what he or she really means. Student Chris O'Keefe opens his speech on reading Shakespeare with the following statement:

> At a certain point in my life, I came to the realization that I wanted to spend my life's effort to become a great playwright.[4]

Chris reveals the irony of the statement when he continues:

> It has been about an hour and a half now and the feeling is still going strong.

Wit One of the most frequently used verbal strategies for achieving humor is the use of **wit**: relating an incident that takes an unexpected turn at the end. Accepting the 2007 Oscar for Best Actress, Helen Mirren paid tribute to the monarch she had portrayed on screen in *The Queen*:

For 50 years and more, Elizabeth Windsor has maintained her dignity, her sense of duty and her hairstyle.[5]

The wit occurs in the final phrase "her hairstyle," which catches off-guard the audience anticipating another majestic attribute.

Humorous Nonverbal Strategies

After-dinner speakers often create humor through nonverbal cues such as posture, gesture, and voice, which are discussed in detail in Chapters 17 and 18. Well-timed pauses are especially crucial delivery cues for after-dinner speakers to master.

Even if you are a person who is not naturally funny, you can use the strategies outlined above to prepare and deliver an after-dinner speech that is lighthearted and clever. Such a speech can still be a success.

STUDY GUIDE

MEET YOUR OBJECTIVES

1. **Describe guidelines for effective public-relations speaking.**

   A public-relations speaker describes the problem or program that prompted the speech, anticipating and countering criticisms.

2. **Identify occasions and best practices for ceremonial speeches.**

   Chances are that at some time you will be called on to apply your speaking skills to make an introduction, toast, award presentation, nomination, acceptance speech, keynote, commencement, or commemorative address, or a eulogy.

3. **List and explain strategies for creating humor in a speech.**

   After-dinner speakers entertain through the use of humorous topics and stories, humorous verbal strategies, and humorous nonverbal strategies.

THINK ABOUT THESE QUESTIONS

1. **Self Assessment** You will be introducing a Pulitzer Prize–winning poet before her reading on your campus. How do you follow the cardinal rules of introductory speeches?

2. **Ethics Assessment** Several Web sites offer eulogy-writing services or prewritten generic eulogies. If you were asked to deliver a eulogy, would it be ethical to buy such a speech?

3. **Critical Assessment** A friend has been invited to give an after-dinner speech to a local service group but has no idea what to talk about. What advice can you offer?

26 Speaking in Small Groups

OBJECTIVES

1. Detail the steps that groups use to solve problems with reflective thinking.
2. Explain how to participate effectively in a group.
3. Describe common roles and styles of leadership.
4. Identify key steps in planning and making a group presentation.

Small group communication is interaction among three to around a dozen people who share a common purpose, feel a sense of belonging to the group, and influence one another.[1] Groups typically make better-quality decisions than do individuals because they have more information available, spark creativity among members, and can better recall and more actively process information. Group members are also usually more satisfied with participatory decisions than if someone just told them what to do. However, group members may also feel pressure to conform to the view of the group or of one dominant member. Some members shirk their responsibilities.[2] To learn more about small group communication, visit MySearchLab (**www.mysearchlab.com**).

Solving Problems in Groups and Teams

A central purpose of many groups is solving problems—finding ways of overcoming obstacles to achieve a desired goal.

John Dewey, a philosopher and educator, suggested using **reflective thinking,** a series of steps to solve problems:[3]

1. Identify and define the problem.
2. Analyze the problem.
3. Generate possible solutions.
4. Select the best solution.
5. Test and implement the solution.

Although not every problem-solving discussion has to follow these steps, you can use them as a blueprint to relieve uncertainty when groups try to solve problems.

Identify and Define the Problem

Groups work best when they define their problem clearly and early in the problem-solving process. To reach a clear definition, the group should consider the following questions:

> What is the specific problem that concerns us?
> What terms, concepts, or ideas do we need to understand in order to solve the problem?
> Who is harmed by the problem?
> When do the harmful effects occur?

Policy questions can help define a problem and identify a course of action to solve it. Policy questions begin with phrases such as, "What should be done about . . .?" or "What could be done to improve. . . .?" For example, "What could be done to improve security at U.S. airports?" "What can we do to improve nutrition in school cafeterias?"

Analyze the Problem

Once the group understands the problem and has a well-worded question, the next step is to analyze the problem. **Analysis** is a process of examining the causes, effects, symptoms, history, and other background information that will help a group eventually reach a solution. When analyzing a problem, a group should consider the following questions:

> What is the history of the problem?
> What are the symptoms and extent of the problem?
> What are the causes and effects of the problem?

> Can the problem be subdivided for further definition and analysis?
> What methods do we already have for solving the problem, and what are their limitations?
> What obstacles might prevent a solution?

As part of the process of analyzing the problem, a group should identify **criteria**, standards for identifying an acceptable solution. Criteria not only help you recognize a good solution when you discover one but also help the group stay focused on its goal. Typical criteria for an acceptable solution specify that the solution should be agreed to by all group members, implemented on schedule and within a given budget, and remove the obstacles causing the problem.

Generate Possible Solutions

When your group has identified, defined, and analyzed the problem, you will be ready to generate possible solutions using group brainstorming, as described in the How To box:

HOW TO

Brainstorm with a Group

- **Set aside judgment and criticism.** Criticism and faultfinding stifle creativity.
- **Consider anonymous brainstorming.** If group members find withholding judgment difficult, have members write suggestions and then share the ideas with the group on paper or via an electronic method that allows users to submit ideas anonymously.
- **Think of as many possible solutions to the problem as you can.** All ideas are acceptable, even wild and crazy ones. Piggyback off one another's ideas.
- **Record all the ideas that are mentioned.** Use a flipchart, chalkboard, electronic whiteboard, or other device so that all group members can see and respond to all the ideas.
- **After a set time has elapsed, evaluate the ideas.** Use the criteria the group has established. Approach the solutions positively. Do not be quick to dismiss an idea, but do voice any concerns or questions you might have. The group can brainstorm again later if it needs more creative ideas.

Select the Best Solution

Next, the group needs to select the solution that best meets the criteria and solves the problem. At this point, the group may need to modify its criteria or even its definition of the problem.

In evaluating the solution, consider the following questions:

> Which solution deals best with the obstacles?
> Is the solution effective in both the short term and the long term?
> What are the advantages and disadvantages?
> Does the solution meet the established criteria?
> Should the group revise its criteria?
> What is required to implement the solution?
> When can the group implement the solution?
> What result will indicate success?

To achieve **consensus**—all members supporting the final decision—it helps to summarize frequently and keep the group oriented toward its goal. Emphasizing areas of group agreement, clarifying misunderstandings, writing down known facts for all members to see, and keeping the discussion focused on issues rather than on emotions are also strategies that facilitate group consensus.[4]

Test and Implement the Solution

The group may want to develop a step-by-step plan for implementing the solution, a time frame for implementation, and a list of individuals who will be responsible for carrying out specific tasks.

Participating in Small Groups

To be an effective group participant, you have to understand how to manage the problem-solving process. You also need to prepare for meetings, evaluate evidence, effectively summarize the group's progress, listen courteously, and be sensitive to conflict.

Come Prepared for Group Discussions

Prepare for group discussions by researching the issues, using the library or Internet. Bring your research notes to help the group analyze the problem.

Do Not Suggest Solutions before Analyzing the Problem

Resist the temptation to settle quickly on one solution before your group has systematically examined the causes, effects, history, and symptoms of a problem.

Evaluate Evidence

To make a successful decision, examine and evaluate evidence. Ineffective groups are more likely to reach decisions quickly without considering the validity of evidence (or sometimes without any evidence at all). Such groups usually reach flawed conclusions.

Help Summarize the Group's Progress

It is easy for groups to get off the subject. Frequently summarize what the group has achieved, and point group discussion toward the goal or task at hand. Ask questions about the discussion process rather than about the topic: "Where are we now?" "Could someone summarize what we have accomplished?" and "Aren't we getting off the subject?"

Listen and Respond Courteously to Others

Understanding what others say is not enough. You also need to respect their points of view. Even if you disagree with someone's ideas, keep your emotions in check and respond courteously. Being closed-minded and defensive usually breeds group conflict.

Help Manage Conflict

In the course of exchanging ideas and opinions about controversial issues, disagreements are bound to occur.[5] You can help prevent conflicts from derailing the problem-solving process by doing the following:

> Keep the discussion focused on issues, not on personalities.
> Rely on facts rather than on personal opinions for evidence.
> Seek ways to compromise; don't assume that there must be a winner and a loser.
> Try to clarify misunderstandings in meaning.
> Be descriptive rather than evaluative and judgmental.
> Keep emotions in check.

Visit MySearchLab (**www.mysearchlab.com**) to learn more about managing conflict.

Leading Small Groups

To lead is to influence others. Some think of a leader as one individual empowered to delegate work and direct the group. In reality, however, group leadership is often shared.

Leadership Responsibilities

Leaders help groups accomplish their tasks and help them to maintain healthy social relationships. Rarely does one person perform all leadership responsibilities, even if a leader is formally appointed or elected. Most often, individual group members assume some specific leadership task, based on their personalities, skills, sensitivity, and the group's needs.

If you determine that the group needs a clearer focus on the task or more attention to social comfort, be ready to influence the group appropriately to help get the job done in a positive, productive way.

Leadership Styles

Leaders can be described by the patterns of behavior, or leadership styles, they exhibit. The following describe general leadership styles.[6]

> **Authoritarian leaders** assume positions of superiority, giving orders and taking control of the group's activity. Although authoritarian leaders can usually

organize group activities with a high degree of efficiency and virtually eliminate uncertainty about who should do what, most problem-solving groups prefer democratic leaders.

› **Democratic leaders** involve group members in the decision-making process, rather than dictate what should be done. Democratic leaders focus more on guiding discussion than on issuing commands.

› **Laissez-faire leaders** allow group members complete freedom in all aspects of the decision-making process. They do little to help the group achieve its goal. This style of "nonleadership" often leaves a group frustrated because it lacks guidance and has to struggle with organizing the work.

› **Transformational leaders** influence others by building a shared vision of the future, inspiring others to achieve, developing high-quality individual relationships with others, and helping people see how what they do is related to a larger framework or system. Transformational leaders are good communicators who support and encourage rather than demean or demand.

What is the most effective leadership style? No single style is effective in every group situation. The best leadership style depends on the nature of the group task, the power of the leader, and the relationship between leader and group members.

Group Presentations

After a group has solved a problem or uncovered new information, group members often present their findings to others. Groups should use the same audience-centered principles as individual speakers. The central and most important step is to analyze the audience that will listen to the presentation. In addition, consider these suggestions for enhancing teamwork:

› **Make sure group members understand the task or assignment, and work together to identify a topic.**

Take a few moments to verbalize the goals and objectives of the assignment.

> **Try brainstorming to develop a topic or solve a problem.** Use your audience analysis, as well as group members' interests and talents, to help you choose among your ideas.

> **Give group members individual assignments.** After you decide on your group's presentation topic, divide up the tasks involved in investigating the issues. Devise a plan for keeping in touch with one another to share information and ideas.

> **Develop a group outline.** After group members have researched key issues, begin drafting an outline of your group presentation. Your presentation should have an introduction and a conclusion that reflect your group's work as an integrated problem-solving team. Decide who will present which portions of your outline.

> **Decide on your presentation format.** Choose from a *symposium*, in which the group presents a short speech to the audience, a *forum*, in which the group answers audience questions with short impromptu speeches, or a *panel* discussion, in which individuals from the group give information and answer questions. You could also use some combination of approaches.

QUICK CHECK

Plan a Group Presentation

- Make sure each group member understands the task or assignment.
- Work together to identify a topic.
- Try brainstorming to develop a topic or problem question.
- Give group members individual assignments.
- Develop a group outline.
- Decide on your presentation approach.
- Rehearse the presentation.

> **Rehearse the presentation.** If you are using visual aids, be sure to incorporate them in your rehearsal. Also be sure to time your presentation when you rehearse.

The skills needed to give a group presentation are the same audience-centered speaking skills presented throughout this book. In addition, keep the following tips in mind for coordinating efforts among group members.

> **Clarify your purpose.** The first speaker can let listeners know what your speaking goal is and explain why you are presenting the information to them. If your group is responding to a specific question, it may be helpful to visually display the question or purpose of the presentation.
> **Use presentation aids effectively.** Visual aids can help to unify your group presentation. Consider having each group member use the same template and font style to add to the coordinated look and feel of your presentation.
> **Assign someone to serve as coordinator or moderator.** A moderator can provide needed structure to a group presentation by introducing both the topic and the group members, keeping track of time, and ensuring that one or more people don't dominate the discussion or speak too little.
> **Armed with a well-planned outline, present your findings to your audience.** If you are using a symposium format, each group presentation is essentially a mini-speech. A panel or forum presentation is more extemporaneous and may even have an impromptu quality, but your delivery and comments should still be well organized.
> **Be ready to answer questions.** Besides being informed about your topic, you should have thoroughly read any written report the group has distributed.

HOW TO

Answer Questions after a Group Presentation

Use these tips, as well as the ones in Chapter 19, to help you and your group manage a question-and-answer session:

- **Be prepared for pointed or hostile questions.** First, keep your composure. Second, try to rephrase a negative question. For example, if someone asks, "Why did you make such a mess of things by recommending a budget increase?" you could rephrase by saying, "Why did we recommend a controversial budget increase?"
- **If you don't understand a question, ask for more clarification.**
- **Don't criticize questioners.** If someone asks a question that has just been asked and answered, or asks an irrelevant or poorly worded question, be polite, tactful, and gracious. Calmly provide an answer and move on.
- **Don't let a questioner make a speech.** If it looks as if a questioner is using the question-and-answer period to give an oration, gently ask, "And what is your question?" or "How can we help you?" Such questions should result in a question that you can address and then return the communication process to the control of the group.

STUDY GUIDE

MEET YOUR OBJECTIVES

1. **Detail the steps that groups use to solve problems with reflective thinking.**
   To solve problems, groups must (1) identify and define the problem, (2) analyze the problem, (3) generate possible solutions, (4) select the best solution, and (5) test and implement the solution.

2. **Explain how to participate effectively in a group.**
   Effective group members prepare for meetings, evaluate evidence, effectively summarize the group's progress, listen courteously, and help manage conflict.

3. **Describe common roles and styles of leadership.**
   Group members often share leadership responsibility to help groups accomplish tasks and maintain a healthy social climate. Styles of leadership include authoritarian, democratic, laissez-faire, and transformational.

4. **Identify key steps in planning and making a group presentation.**
   Group presentations rely on the same principles of audience-centered speaking as individual speeches, but also require a coordinated team effort.

THINK ABOUT THESE QUESTIONS

1. **Self Assessment** Your work team has been assigned to develop a new process for filling orders. What process should the team follow to solve its problem?

2. **Ethics Assessment** One member of Corey's group is not doing a fair share of the work. Is it ethical for other group members to do extra work to make up for the slacker?

3. **Critical Assessment** Karl seems to have taken charge of his group and is making assignments to other group members. Although Karl is helping to get a lot accomplished, José resents Karl's overly zealous efforts. Should José keep quiet and just go along with Karl, or speak up and express his concerns about Karl's actions? Why?

Notes

CHAPTER 1 Speaking in Public

1. Dee-Ann Durbin, "Study: Plenty of Jobs for Graduates in 2000," *Austin American-Statesman* 5 (December 1999): A28.
2. Valueinvestorsportal. "Warren Buffet on Communication Skills." YouTube. December 6, 2010. Web. http://www.youtube.com/watch?v=tpgcEYpLzP0. Accessed May 14, 2013.
3. Jerry L. Winsor, Dan B. Curtis, and Ronald D. Stephens, "National Preferences in Business and Communication Education: A Survey Update," *Journal of the Association for Communication Administration* (September 3, 1997): 174.
4. University of Wisconsin—River Falls, Career Services, "What Skills and Attributes Employers Seek When Hiring Students," June 4, 2007 http://www.uwrf.edu/ccs/skills/htm.
5. Camille Luckenbaugh and Kevin Gray, "Employers Describe Perfect Job Candidate," National Association of Colleges and Employers Survey, June 4, 2007 http://www.naceweb.org/press/display.asp?year=2003&prid+ 169?
6. Randall S. Hansen and Katharine Handson, "What Do Employers Really Want? Top Skills and Values Employers Seek from Job-Seekers," June 4, 2007 http://www.quintcareers.com/job_skills_values.html.

CHAPTER 2 Improving Your Confidence

1. G. D. Bodie, "A Racing Heart, Rattling Knees, and Ruminative Thoughts: Defining and Explaining Public Speaking Anxiety," *Communication Education* 59 (2010): 70–105; K. K. Dwyer and M. M. Davidson, "Is Public Speaking Really More Feared Than Death?" *Communication Research Reports* 29, 2 (April-June 2012): 99–107.
2. Survey conducted by R. H. Bruskin and Associates, *Spectra* 9 (December 1973): 4; D. Wallechinsky, Irving Wallace, and Amy Wallace, *The People's Almanac Presents the Book of Lists* (New York: Morrow, 1977).
3. Steven Booth Butterfield, "Instructional Interventions for Reducing Situational Anxiety and Avoidance," *Communication Education* 37 (1988): 214–23; also see Michael Motley, *Overcoming Your Fear of Public Speaking: A Proven Method* (New York: McGraw-Hill, 1995).
4. Joe Ayres and Theodore S. Hopf, "The Long-Term Effect of Visualization in the Classroom: A Brief Research Report," *Communication Education* 39 (1990): 75–78.
5. Amber N. Finn, Chris R. Sawyer, and Ralph R. Behnke, "A Model of Anxious Arousal for Public Speaking," *Communication Education* 58 (2009): 417–32.
6. Amy M. Bippus and John A. Daly, "What Do People Think Causes Stage Fright? Naïve Attributions About the Reasons for Public-Speaking Anxiety," *Communication Education* 48 (1999): 63–72.
7. Yang Lin and Andrew S. Rancer, "Sex Differences in Intercultural Communication Apprehension, Ethnocentrism, and Intercultural Willingness to Communicate," *Psychological Reports* 92 (2003): 195–200.
8. S. Shimotsu and T. P. Mottet, "The Relationships Among Perfectionism, Communication Apprehension, and Temperament," *Communication Research Reports* 26, 3 (2009): 188–97.

9. Kay B. Harris, Chris R. Sawyer, and Ralph R. Behnke, "Predicting Speech State Anxiety from Trait Anxiety, Reactivity, and Situational Influences," *Communication Quarterly* 54 (2006): 213–26; M. J. Beatty, A. D. Heisel, R. J. Lewis, M. E. Pence, A. Reinhart, and Y. Tian, "Communication Apprehension and Resting Alpha Range Asymmetry in the Anterior Cortex," *Communication Education* 60, 4 (2011): 441–60; Valerie A. MacIntyre, P. D. MacIntyre, and G. Carre, "Heart Rate as a Predictor of Speaking Anxiety," *Communication Research Reports*, 27, 4 (2010): 286–97.

10. Kay B. Harris, Chris R. Sawyer, and Ralph R. Behnke, "Predicting Speech State Anxiety from Trait Anxiety, Reactivity, and Situational Influences," *Communication Quarterly* 54 (2006): 213–26.

11. Graham D. Bodie, "A Racing Heart, Rattling Knees, and Ruminative Thoughts: Defining, Explaining, and Treating Public Speaking Anxiety," *Communication Education* 59, 1 (January 2010): 70–105.

12. Shannon C. McCullough, Shelly G. Russell, Ralph R. Behnke, Chris R. Sawyer, and Paul L. Witt, "Anticipatory Public Speaking State Anxiety as a Function of Body Sensations and State of Mind," *Communication Quarterly* 54 (2006): 101–09.

13. Chad Edwards and Suzanne Walker, "Using Public Speaking Learning Communities to Reduce Communication Apprehension," *Texas Speech Communication Journal* 32 (2007): 65–71.

CHAPTER 3 Presenting Your First Speech

1. J. C. Pearson, J. T. Child, and D. H. Kahl, Jr., "Preparation Meeting Opportunity: How Do College Students Prepare for Public Speeches?" *Communication Quarterly* 54:3 (August 2006): 351–66.

2. Greg Winter, "The Chips Are Down: Frito-Lay Cuts Costs with Smaller Servings," *Austin American-Statesman* 2 (January 2001): A6.

CHAPTER 4 Ethics and Free Speech

1. National Communication Association, "NCA Credo for Communication Ethics," 1999, June 27, 2001 http://www.natcom.org/conferences/Ethics/ethicsconfcredo99.htm.

2. Samuel Walker, *Hate Speech* (Lincoln: University of Nebraska Press, 1994) 162.

3. "Libel and Slander," *The Ethical Spectacle*, June 1, 1998 http://www.spectacle.org/freespch/musm/libel.html.

4. "Supreme Court Rules: Cyberspace Will Be Free! ACLU Hails Victory in Internet Censorship Challenge," American Civil Liberties Union Freedom Network, June 1, 1998 http://www.aclu.org/news/no62697a.html.

5. Associated Press, "Free-Speech, Other Groups File Briefs Opposing Patriot Act." November 4, 2003.

6. Free Speech Debate. FreeSpeechDebate.com.

7. Michele Eodice, "Plagiarism, Pedagogy, and Controversy: A Conversation with Rebecca Moore Howard," *Issues in Writing* 13.1 (Fall/Winter 2002).

8. "Bed Bugs." Centers for Disease Control and Prevention, Web. June 9, 2013 http://www.cdc.gov/parasites/bedbugs/.

CHAPTER 5 Listening

1. Laura Ann Janusik, "Building Listening Theory: The Validation of the Conversational Listening Span," *Communication Studies* 58, 2 (June 2007): 139–56.

2. Ralph G. Nichols and Leonard A. Stevens, "Six Bad Listening Habits," in *Are You Listening?* (New York: McGraw-Hill, 1957).

3. K. K. Halone and L. L. Pecchioni, "Relational Listening: A Grounded Theoretical Model," *Communication Reports* 14 (2001): 59–71.

4. G. D. Bodie, D. L. Worthington, and C. C. Gearhart, "The Listening Styles Profile-Revised (LSP-R): A Scale Revision and Evidence for Validity," *Communication Quarterly* 16 (2013); 72–90; see Larry L. Barker and Kittie W. Watson, *Listen Up* (New York: St. Martin's Press, 2000); also see M. Imhof, "Who Are We as We Listen? Individual Listening Profiles in Varying Contexts," *International Journal of Listening* 18 (2004): 36–45.

5. Harold Barrett, *Rhetoric and Civility: Human Development, Narcissism, and the Good Audience* (Albany: SUNY, 1991) 154.

6. John T. Masterson, Steven A. Beebe, and Norman H. Watson, *Invitation to Effective Speech Communication* (Glenview, IL: Scott, Foresman, 1989) 4.

7. Robert Rowland, *Analyzing Rhetoric: A Handbook for the Informed Citizen in a New Millennium* (Dubuque, IA: Kendall/Hunt Publishing Company, 2002) 17–28.

CHAPTER 6 Analyzing Your Audience

1. For an excellent discussion of how to adapt to specific audience situations, see Jo Sprague and Douglas Stuart, *The Speaker's Handbook* (Belmont, CA: Wadsworth and Thompson, 2005) 345.

2. Devorah Lieberman, *Public Speaking in the Multicultural Environment* (Boston: Allyn & Bacon, 2000). Also see Edward T. Hall, *The Silent Language* (Greenwich, CT: Fawcett, 1959); and Edward T. Hall, *The Hidden Dimension* (Garden City, NY: Doubleday, 1966).

CHAPTER 7 Adapting to Your Audience as You Speak

1. Devorah Lieberman, *Public Speaking in the Multicultural Environment* (Boston: Allyn and Bacon, 2000). Also see Edward T. Hall, *The Silent Language* (Greenwich, CT: Fawcett, 1959); and Edward T. Hall, *The Hidden Dimension* (Garden City, NY: Doubleday, 1966).

2. The research summarized here is based on pioneering work by Geert Hofstede, *Culture's Consequences: International Differences in Work-Related Values* (Beverly Hills, CA: Sage, 1984). Also see Edward T. Hall, *Beyond Culture* (New York: Doubleday, 1976).

CHAPTER 8 Developing Your Speech

1. Alex F. Osborn, *Applied Imagination* (New York: Scribner's, 1962).

CHAPTER 9 Gathering Supporting Material

1. "Types of Web Sites," Xavier University Library, 2010.

2. Elizabeth Kirk, "Practical Steps in Evaluating Internet Resources," May 7, 2001 http://milton.mse.jhu.edu:8001/research/education/practical.html.

3. Paul Gorski, "A Multicultural Model for Evaluating Educational Web Sites," December 1999 http://curry.edschool.virginia.edu/go/multicultural/net/comps/model.html.

CHAPTER 10 Supporting Your Speech

1. James Stanfill, "Entomophagy: The Other Other White Meat," *Winning Orations 2009* (Mankato, MN: Interstate Oratorical Association, 2009) 24.

2. Michael Blastland and David Spiegelhalter, *The Norm Chronicles: Stories and Numbers about Danger* (London: Profile Books, 2013) 47.

3. Daniel Hinderliter, "Collaborative Consumption," *Winning Orations 2012* (Mankato, MN: Interstate Oratorical Association, 2012) 140.

CHAPTER 11 Organizing Your Speech

1. The following information is adapted from Devorah A. Lieberman, *Public Speaking in the Multicultural Environment* (Englewood Cliffs, NJ: Prentice Hall, 1994).
2. Martin Medhurst, "The Text(ure) of the World in Presidential Rhetoric," *Vital Speeches of the Day* (June 2012).
3. Molly A. Lovell, "Hotel Security: The Hidden Crisis," *Winning Orations 1994* (Mankato, MN: Interstate Oratorical Association, 1994) 18.

CHAPTER 13 Developing a Conclusion

1. "Give Me Liberty or Give Me Death!" *Colonial Williamsburg*, August 22, 2013 http://www.history.org/almanack/life/politics/giveme.cfm.
2. K. Phillip Táylor, "Speech Teachers' Pet Peeves: Student Behaviors That Public Instructors Find Annoying, Irritating, and Unwanted in Student Speeches," *Florida Communication Journal* 33, 2 (2005): 56.

CHAPTER 15 Using Words Well

1. David Crystal, "Speaking of Writing and Writing of Speaking," *Longman Dictionaries: Express Yourself with Confidence!* (Pearson Education, 2005). Available online at www.pearsonlongman.com/dictionaries/pdfs/speaking-writing-crystal.pdf
[Also available at http://www.pearsonelt.com/professionaldevelopment/articles/Speaking+of+writing+and+writing+of+speaking+Crystal]
2. Michael M. Klepper, *I'd Rather Die Than Give a Speech* (New York: Carol Publishing Group, 1994) 45.
3. Michiko Kakutani, "Struggling to Find Words for a Horror Beyond Words," *New York Times*, September 13, 2001: E1.
4. John F. Kennedy, "Inaugural Address (January 20, 1961)" in *Speeches in English*, ed. Bower Aly and Lucille F. Aly (New York: Random House, 1968) 272.
5. Barack Obama, "Look at the World Through Their Eyes," *Vital Speeches of the Day* (May 2013): 138–42.
6. Franklin Roosevelt, Inaugural Address of 1933 (Washington, DC: National Archives and Records Administration, 1988) 13–14.

CHAPTER 16 Methods of Delivery

1. Roger Ailes, *You Are the Message* (New York: Doubleday, 1989) 37–38; Gellis Communications, "Top Tips for Preparing and Delivering a Manuscript Speech." November 4, 2011. http://www.gellis.com/blog/top-tips-preparing-and-delivering-manuscript-speech; David W. Richardson, "Delivering a Manuscript Speech." 2013. http://www.richspeaking.com/articles/manuscript_speech.html.

CHAPTER 17 Nonverbal Communication

1. Steven A. Beebe, "Eye Contact: A Nonverbal Determinant of Speaker Credibility," *Speech Teacher* 23 (January 1974): 21–25; Steven A. Beebe, "Effects of Eye Contact, Posture, and Vocal Inflection upon Credibility and Comprehension," *Australian Scan Journal of Nonverbal Communication*

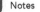

7–8 (1979–1980): 57–70; Martin Cobin, "Response to Eye Contact," *Quarterly Journal of Speech* 48 (1963): 415–19.

2. For a comprehensive review of immediacy in an instructional context, see Virginia P. Richmond, Derek R. Lange, and James C. McCroskey, "Teacher Immediacy and the Teacher-Student Relationship," in Timothy P. Mottet, Virginia P. Richmond, and James C. McCroskey, *Handbook of Instructional Communication: Rhetorical and Relational Perspectives* (Boston: Allyn & Bacon, 2006) 167–93.

3. Michael J. Beatty, "Some Effects of Posture on Speaker Credibility," library paper, University of Central Missouri, 1973.

4. Paul Ekman and Wallace Friesen, *Unmasking the Face* (Englewood Cliffs, NJ: Prentice Hall, 1975); D. Keltner and P. Ekman, "Facial Expression of Emotion," in M. Lewis and J. M. Haviland-Jones, eds., *Handbook of Emotions* (New York: Gilford, 2000) 236–49; D. Keltner, P. Ekman, G. S. Gonzaga, and J. Beer, "Facial Expression of Emotion," in R. J. Davidson, K. R. Scherer, and H. H. Goldsmith, eds., *Handbook of Affective Sciences* (New York: Oxford University Press, 2003) 415–32.

CHAPTER 18 Verbal Communication

1. Adapted from Lester Schilling, *Voice and Diction for the Speech Arts* (San Marcos: Southwest Texas State University Press, 1979).

2. Mary M. Gill, "Accent and Stereotypes: Their Effect on Perceptions of Teachers and Lecture Comprehension," *Journal of Applied Communication* 22 (1994): 348–61.

3. These suggestions were made by Jo Sprague and Douglas Stuart, *The Speaker's Handbook* (Fort Worth, TX: Harcourt Brace Jovanovich, 1992) 331, and were based on research by Patricia A. Porter, Margaret Grant, and Mary Draper, *Communicating Effectively in English: Oral Communication for Non-Native Speakers* (Belmont, CA: Wadsworth, 1985).

4. James W. Neuliep, *Intercultural Communication: A Contextual Approach* (Boston: Houghton Mifflin, 2000) 247.

CHAPTER 19 Adapting and Delivering Your Speech

1. Virginia P. Richmond, Derek R. Lane, and James C. McCroskey, "Teacher Immediacy and the Teacher-Student Relationship," in Timothy P. Mottet, Virginia P. Richmond, and James C. McCroskey, *Handbook of Instructional Communication: Rhetorical and Relational Perspectives* (Boston: Allyn & Bacon, 2006) 167.

2. James C. McCroskey, Aino Sallinen, Joan M. Fayer, Virginia P. Richmond, and Robert A. Barraclough, "Non-verbal Immediacy and Cognitive Learning: A Cross-Cultural Investigation," *Communication Education* 45 (1996): 200–11.

3. Larry A. Samovar and Richard E. Porter, *Communication between Cultures* (Belmont, CA: Wadsworth, 2001) 166.

4. William B. Gudykunst, *Bridging Differences: Effective Intergroup Communication* (Thousand Oaks, CA: Sage, 1998) 12.

5. Brent Filson, *Executive Speeches: Tips on How to Write and Deliver Speeches from 51 CEOs* (New York: Wiley, 1994) 144–45.

CHAPTER 20 Selecting Presentation Aids

1. Emil Bohn and David Jabusch, "The Effect of Four Methods of Instruction on the Use of Visual Aids in Speeches," *The Western Journal of Speech Communication* 46 (Summer 1982): 253–65.

2. J. S. Wilentz, *The Senses of Man* (New York: Crowell, 1968).

3. Michael E. Patterson, Donald F. Dansereau, and Dianna Newbern, "Effects of Communication Aids and Strategies on Cooperative Teaching," *Journal of Educational Psychology* 84 (1992): 453–61.

4. Richard E. Mayer and Valerie K. Sims, "For Whom Is a Picture Worth a Thousand Words? Extensions of a Dual-Coding Theory of Multimedia Learning," *Journal of Educational Psychology* 86 (1994): 389–401.

5. Rebecca B. Worley and Marilyn A. Dyrud, "Presentations and the PowerPoint Problem," *Business Communication Quarterly* 67 (March 2004): 78–80; Elizabeth Bumiller, "We Have Met the Enemy and He Is PowerPoint," *New York Times* (April 26, 2010; May 6, 2010) www.nytimes.com.

6. We acknowledge Dan Cavanaugh's excellent supplement *Preparing Visual Aids for Presentations* (Boston: Allyn & Bacon/Longman, 2001) as a source for many of our tips and suggestions.

CHAPTER 22 Informative Speaking

1. Joseph L. Chesebro, "Effects of Teacher Clarity and Nonverbal Immediacy on Student Learning, Receiver Apprehension, and Affect," *Communication Education* 52 (April 2003): 135–47.

2. Steven A. Beebe, Timothy P. Mottet, and K. David Roach, *Training and Development: Communicating for Success* (Boston: Pearson, 2013).

3. Katherine E. Rowan, "A New Pedagogy for Explanatory Public Speaking: Why Arrangement Should Not Substitute for Invention," *Communication Education* 44 (1995): 236–50.

4. Michael A. Boerger and Tracy B. Henley, "The Use of Analogy in Giving Instructions," *Psychological Record* 49 (1999): 193–209.

5. Marcie Groover, "Learning to Communicate: The Importance of Speech Education in Public Schools," *In Winning Orations 1984* (Mankato, MN: Interstate Oratorical Association, 1984) 7.

6. See Bruce W. A. Whittlesea and Lisa D. Williams, "The Discrepancy-Attribution Hypothesis II: Expectation, Uncertainty, Surprise, and Feelings of Familiarity," *Journal of Experimental Psychology: Learning, Memory, and Cognition* 2 (2001): 14–33; also see Suzanne Hidi, "Interest and Its Contribution as a Mental Resource for Learning," *Review of Educational Research* 60 (1990): 549–71; Mark Sadoski, Ernest T. Goetz, and Maximo Rodriguez, "Engaging Texts: Effects of Concreteness of Comprehensibility, Interest, and Recall in Four Text Types," *Journal of Educational Psychology* 92 (2000): 85–95.

7. George Miller, "The Magical Number Seven, Plus or Minus Two," *Psychological Review* 63 (1956): 81–97.

8. D. K. Cruickshank and J. J. Kennedy, "Teacher Clarity," *Teaching & Teacher Education* 2 (1986): 43–67.

CHAPTER 23 Understanding Principles of Persuasive Speaking

1. For a discussion of the elaboration likelihood model, see R. Petty and D. Wegener, "The Elaboration Likelihood Model: Current Status and Controversies," in S. Chaiken and Y. Trope, eds., *Dual Process Theories in Social Psychology* (New York: Guilford, 1999) 41–72; also see R. Petty and J. T. Cacioppo, *Communication and Persuasion: Central and Peripheral Routes to Attitude Change* (New York: Springer-Verlag, 1986).

2. Leon Festinger, *A Theory of Cognitive Dissonance* (Evanston, IL: Row, Peterson, 1957).

3. For additional discussion, see Wayne C. Minnick, *The Art of Persuasion* (Boston: Houghton Mifflin, 1967).

4. Abraham H. Maslow, "A Theory of Human Motivation," in *Motivation and Personality* (New York: Harper & Row, 1954) chap. 5.

5. Paul A. Mongeau, "Another Look at Fear-Arousing Persuasive Appeals," in Mike Allen and Raymond W. Preiss, eds., *Persuasion: Advances through Meta-Analysis* (Cresskill, NJ: Hampton Press, 1998) 65.

6. K. Witte, "Putting the Fear Back into Fear Appeals: The Extended Parallel Process Model," *Communication Monographs* 59 (1992): 329–47.

7. C. W. Sherif, M. Sherif, and R. E. Nebergall, *Attitudes and Attitude Change: The Social Judgment-Involvement Approach* (Philadelphia: Saunders, 1965).

CHAPTER 24 Using Persuasive Strategies

1. For an excellent discussion of the influence of culture on public speaking, see Devorah A. Lieberman, *Public Speaking in the Multicultural Environment* (Boston: Allyn and Bacon, 2000).

2. Devorah A. Lieberman and G. Fisher, "International Negotiation," in Larry A. Samovar and Richard E. Porter, eds., *Intercultural Communication: A Reader* (Belmont, CA: Wadsworth, 1991) 193–200.

3. J. C. Reinard, "The Empirical Study of the Persuasive Effects of Evidence: The Status after Fifty Years of Research," *Human Communication Research* 15 (1988): 37–38.

4. Myron W. Lustig and Jolene Koester, *Intercultural Competence: Interpersonal Communication across Cultures* (Boston: Allyn & Bacon, 2009).

5. K. Rowan, "A New Pedagogy for Explanatory Public Speaking: Why Arrangement Should Not Substitute for Invention," *Communication Education* 44 (1995): 236–50.

6. Douglas Ehninger, Bruce E. Gronbeck, Ray E. McKerrow, and Alan H. Monroe, *Principles and Types of Speech Communication* (Glenview, IL: Scott, Foresman, 1986) 15.

CHAPTER 25 Speaking on Special Occasions

1. John C. Meyer, "Humor as a Double-Edged Sword: Four Functions of Humor in Communication," *Communication Theory* 10, 3 (August 2000): 311.

2. Michael Koresky, "Prognosis: Dire, Michael Moore's 'Sicko'." *indiWIRE* June 22, 2007, www.indiewire.com/movies.

3. Mark Twain, "The Alphabet and Simplified Spelling," address at the dedication of the New York Engineers' Club, December 9, 1907, *Mark Twain's Speeches; with an Introduction by William Dean Howells*, Electronic Text Center, University of Virginia Library, June 4, 2004, etext.lib.Virginia.edu.

4. Chris O'Keefe, untitled speech, in *Championship Debates and Speeches*, John K. Boaz and James Brey, eds., (Speech Communication Association and American Forensic Association, 1987) 99.

5. "Mirren 'Too Busy' to Meet Queen," *BBC News* May 10, 2007.

CHAPTER 26 Speaking in Small Groups

1. Our definition of *team* is based on a discussion in Steven A. Beebe and John T. Masterson, *Communicating in Small Groups: Principles and Practices*, 11th ed. (Boston: Pearson, 2015); and in Steven A. Beebe, Susan J. Beebe, and Diana K. Ivy, *Communication Principles for a Lifetime* (Boston: Pearson, 2013): 240–41.

2. For discussions of the advantages and disadvantages of working in small groups, see Norman R. F. Maier, "Assets and Liabilities in Group Problem Solving: The Need for an Integrative Function," *Psychological Review* 74 (1967): 239–49; Michael Argyle, *Cooperation: The Basis of Sociability* (London: Routledge, 1991); J. Surowiecki, *The Wisdom of Crowds* (New York: Anchor, 2005); P. R. Laughlin, E. C. Hatch, J. Silver, and L. Boh, "Groups Perform Better Than the Best Individuals on Letters-to-Numbers Problems: Effects on Group Size," *Journal of Personality and Social Psychology* 90 (2006): 644–51. J. S. Mueller, "Why Individuals in Larger Teams Perform Worse," *Organizational Behavior and Human Decision Processes* 117 (2012): 111–24; B. R. Staats, K. L. Milkman, and C. R. Fox, "The Team Scaling Fallacy: Underestimating the Declining Efficiency of Larger Teams," *Organizational Behavior and Human Decision Processes* 118 (2012): 132–42; B. M. Waller, L. Hope, N. Burrowes, and E. R. Morrison, "Twelve (Not So) Angry Men: Managing Conversational Group Size Increases Perceived Contribution by Decision Makers," *Group Processes & Intergroup Relations* 14, 6 (2011): 835–43.

3. John Dewey, *How We Think* (Boston: Heath, 1910).

4. C. A. VanLear and E. A. Mabry, "Testing Contrasting Interaction Models for Discriminating between Consensual and Dissentient Decision-Making Groups," *Small Group Research* 30 (1999): 29–58; also see T. J. Saine and D. G. Bock, "A Comparison of the Distributional and Sequential Structures of Interaction in High and Low Consensus Groups," *Central States Speech Journal* 24 (1973): 125–39.

5. For a summary of research about conflict management in small groups, see S. M. Farmer and J. Roth, "Conflict-Handling Behavior in Work Groups: Effects of Group Structure, Decision Processes, and Time," *Small Group Research* 29 (1998): 669–713; also see Beebe and Masterson, *Communicating in Small Groups*.

6. Ralph White and Ronald Lippitt, "Leader Behavior and Member Reaction in Three 'Social Climates'," *in Group Dynamics*, 3rd ed., Darwin Cartwright and Alvin Zander eds. (New York: Harper & Row, 1968) 319; Francis J. Yammarino and Alan J. Dubinsky, "Transformational Leadership Theory: Using Levels of Analysis to Determine Boundary Conditions," *Personnel Psychology* 47 (1994): 787–809.

Glossary

acceptance speech: A speech of thanks for an award, nomination, or other honor

accommodation: Sensitivity to the feelings, needs, interests, and backgrounds of other people

ad hominem argument: An attack on irrelevant personal characteristics of the person who is proposing an idea rather than on the idea itself

after-dinner speech: An entertaining speech, usually delivered in conjunction with a mealtime meeting or banquet

alliteration: The repetition of a consonant sound (usually the first consonant) several times in a phrase, clause, or sentence

analogy: A comparison between two things; also, a special type of inductive reasoning that compares one thing, person, or process with another to predict how something will perform and respond

analysis: Examination of the causes, effects, and history of a problem to understand it better

andragogy: The art and science of teaching adults

anecdote: An illustration or brief story

antithesis: Opposition, such as that used in two-part sentences in which the second part contrasts in meaning with the first

appeal to misplaced authority: Use of the testimony of an expert in a given field to endorse an idea or product for which the expert does not have the appropriate credentials or expertise

articulation: The production of clear and distinct speech sounds

attend: To focus on incoming information

attitude: A learned predisposition to respond favorably or unfavorably toward something; a like or dislike

audience adaptation: The process of ethically using information about an audience in order to adapt one's message so that it is clear and achieves the speaking objective

audience analysis: The process of examining information about those who are expected to listen to a speech

authoritarian leader: A leader who assumes a position of superiority, giving orders and assuming control of the group's activity

bandwagon fallacy: Reasoning that suggests that because everyone else believes something or is doing something, then it must be valid or correct

bar graph: A graph in which bars of various lengths represent information

behavioral objective: Statement of the specific purpose of a speech, expressed in terms of desired audience behavior at the end of the speech

belief: An individual's perception of what is true or false

blueprint: The central idea of a speech plus a preview of main ideas

Boolean search: An advanced Web-searching technique that allows a user to narrow a subject or keyword search by adding various requirements

boom microphone: A microphone that is suspended from a bar and moved to follow the speaker; often used in movies and TV

brainstorming: A problem-solving technique used to generate many ideas

brief illustration: An unelaborated example, often only a sentence or two long

causal fallacy: A faulty cause-and-effect connection between two things or events

causal reasoning: Reasoning in which the relationship between two or more events leads you to conclude that one or more of the events caused the others

cause-and-effect organization: Organization that focuses on a situation and its causes or a situation and its effects

central idea: A one-sentence summary of a speech

channels: The visual and auditory means by which a message is transmitted from sender to receiver

charisma: Characteristic of a talented, charming, attractive speaker

chart: A display that summarizes information by using words, numbers, or images

chronological organization: Organization by time or sequence

clip art: Images, in printed form or stored in a computer file, that can be used in presentation aids

closed-ended questions: Questions that offer alternatives from which to choose, such as true/false, agree/disagree, or multiple-choice

closure: The quality of a conclusion that makes a speech sound "finished"

code: A verbal or nonverbal symbol for an idea or image

cognitive dissonance: The sense of mental discomfort that prompts a person to change when new information conflicts with previously organized thought patterns

commemorative address: A speech delivered during ceremonies held in memory of some past event and often the person or persons involved

commencement address: A speech delivered at a graduation or commencement ceremony

common ground: Ways in which you and your listeners are alike

competence: An aspect of a speaker's credibility that reflects whether the speaker is perceived as informed, skilled, or knowledgeable

complexity, organization by: Arrangement of the ideas in a speech from the simplest to the most complex

conclusion: The logical outcome of a deductive argument, which stems from the major premise and the minor premise

connotation: The meaning listeners associate with a word, based on past experience

consensus: The support and commitment of all group members to the decision of the group

context: The environment or situation in which a speech occurs

credibility: An audience's perception of a speaker as competent, trustworthy, knowledgeable, and dynamic

criteria: Standards for identifying an acceptable solution to a problem

critical listening: Evaluating the quality, appropriateness, value, and importance of the information put forth by a speaker

critical thinking: Making judgments about the conclusions presented in what you see, hear, and read

culture: A learned system of knowledge, behavior, attitudes, beliefs, values, and norms that is shared by a group of people

declamation: The delivery of an already famous speech

decode: To translate verbal or nonverbal symbols into ideas and images that constitute a message

decorative fonts: Typefaces in which the letters are stylized and convey a feeling or tone

deductive reasoning: Reasoning that moves from a general statement or principle to a specific, certain conclusion

definition: A statement of what a term means or how it is applied in a specific instance

democratic leader: A leader who involves group members in the decision-making process rather than dictating what should be done

demographics: Statistics on population characteristics, such as age, sexual orientation, race, gender, educational level, and religious views

denotation: The literal meaning of a word

derived credibility: The perception of a speaker's credibility that is formed during a speech

description: A word picture of something

dialect: A consistent style of pronouncing words that is common to an ethnic group or geographic region

direct persuasion route: When listeners are persuaded by their crucial evaluation of the logic and evidence of an argument

domain: A type of Web site, indicated by the last three letters of the site's URL

dynamism: An aspect of a speaker's credibility that reflects whether the speaker is perceived as energetic

either/or fallacy: The oversimplification of an issue into a choice between only two outcomes or possibilities

elaborate: From the standpoint of the elaboration likelihood model (ELM) of persuasion, to think about information, ideas, and issues related to the content of a message

elaboration likelihood model (ELM) of persuasion: The theory that listeners can be persuaded directly, by logic, reasoning, and evidence, or indirectly, by the overall emotional impact of the message

elocution: The expression of emotion through posture, movement, gestures, facial expression, and voice

emotional response theory: Theory stating that human emotional responses can be classified as eliciting feelings of pleasure, arousal, or dominance

empowerment: Influence and potential leadership, gained in part by speaking with competence and confidence

encode: To translate ideas and images into verbal or nonverbal symbols

ethical speech: Speech that is responsible, honest, and tolerant

ethics: The beliefs, values, and moral principles by which people determine what is right or wrong

ethnic vernacular: A variety of English that includes words and phrases used by a specific ethnic group

ethnicity: That portion of a person's cultural background that relates to a national or religious heritage

ethnocentrism: The attitude that one's own culture and cultural perspectives and methods are superior to those of others

ethos: The term Aristotle used to refer to a speaker's credibility

eulogy: A speech of tribute about someone who has died

evidence: The facts, examples, opinions, and statistics that a speaker uses to support a conclusion

example: An illustration used to dramatize or clarify a fact

expert testimony: An opinion offered by someone who is an authority on the subject under discussion

explanation: A statement of how something is done or why it exists in its present form or existed in its past form

extemporaneous speaking: Speaking from a written or memorized speech outline without having memorized the exact wording of the speech

extended illustration: A detailed example that resembles a story

external noise: Physical sounds that interfere with communication

fact: Information that direct observation has proven to be true or that can be proved to be true

fallacy: False reasoning that occurs when someone attempts to persuade without adequate evidence or with arguments that are irrelevant or inappropriate

feedback: Verbal and nonverbal responses provided by an audience to a speaker

figurative analogy: A comparison between two essentially dissimilar things that share some common feature on which the comparison depends

figure of speech: Language that deviates from the ordinary, expected meaning of words to make a description or comparison unique, vivid, and memorable

First Amendment: The amendment to the U.S. Constitution that guarantees free speech; the first of the ten amendments to the U.S. Constitution known collectively as the Bill of Rights font: A typeface of a particular style and design

free speech: Legally protected speech or speech acts

gender: The culturally constructed and psychologically based perception of one's self as feminine or masculine

general purpose: The overarching goal of a speech—to inform, persuade, or entertain

generalization: An all-encompassing statement

graph: A pictorial representation of statistical data

hard evidence: Factual examples and statistics

hasty generalization: A conclusion reached without adequate evidence

hyperbole: Exaggeration

hypothetical illustration: An example that might happen but that has not actually occurred

illustration: A story or anecdote that provides an example of an idea, issue, or problem the speaker is discussing

immediacy: Nonverbal expressions of closeness to and liking for an audience, made through such means as physical approach or eye contact

impromptu speaking: Delivering a speech without advance preparation

indirect persuasion route: When listeners are persuaded by factors other than the logic and evidence of a speech, such as the speaker's charisma or appeal to emotions

inductive reasoning: Reasoning that uses specific instances or examples to reach a general, probable conclusion

inference: A conclusion based on available evidence or partial information; an evaluation that has not been directly observed

inflection: The variation in the pitch of the voice

initial credibility: The impression of a speaker's credibility that listeners have before the speaker starts a speech

internal noise: Anything physiological or psychological that interferes with communication

inversion: Reversal of the normal word order of a phrase or sentence

jargon: The specialized language of a profession

keynote address: A speech that sets the theme and tone for a meeting or conference

laissez-faire leader: A leader who allows group members complete freedom in all aspects of the decision-making process

lavaliere microphone: A microphone that can be clipped to an article of clothing or worn on a cord around the neck

lay testimony: An opinion or description offered by a nonexpert who has firsthand experience

learning style: A person's preferred method for aquiring new knowledge

line graph: A graph that uses lines or curves to show relationships between two or more variables

literal analogy: A comparison between two similar things

literary quotation: An opinion or description by a writer, expressed in a memorable and often poetic way

logic: A formal system of rules used to reach a conclusion

logos: The term Aristotle used to refer to logic

main ideas: The key points of a speech; subdivisions of the central idea

major premise: A general statement that is the first element of a syllogism

malapropism: The mistaken use of a word that sounds like the intended word

manuscript speaking: Reading a speech from a written text

mapping: Use of geometric shapes to sketch how all the main ideas, subpoints, and supporting material of a speech relate to the central idea and to one another

memorized speaking: Delivering a speech word for word from memory without using notes

message: The content of a speech plus the way it is said

metaphor: An implied comparison between two things or concepts

minor premise: A specific statement about an example that is linked to the major premise; the second element of a syllogism

model: A small object that represents a larger object

motivation: The underlying internal force that drives people to achieve their goals

myth: A shared belief based on the underlying values, cultural heritage, and faith of a group of people

nomination speech: A speech that officially recommends someone as a candidate for an office or position

non sequitur: Latin for "it does not follow"; an idea or conclusion that does not logically relate to or follow from the previous idea or conclusion omission: Leaving out a word or phrase that the listener expects to hear

online database: A subscription-based electronic resource that may offer access to abstracts and/or the full texts of entries, in addition to bibliographic data

open-ended questions: Questions that allow for unrestricted answers by not limiting answers to choices or alternatives

opinion: Testimony or a quotation that expresses someone's attitudes, beliefs, or values

oral citation: The oral presentation of such information about a source as the author, title, and year of publication

parallelism: Use of the same grammatical pattern for two or more clauses or sentences

patchwriting: Failure to give credit for compelling phrases taken from another source

pathos: Term used by Aristotle to refer to appeals to emotion

personification: The attribution of human qualities to inanimate things or ideas

persuasion: The process of changing or reinforcing a listener's attitudes, beliefs, values, or behavior

picture graph: A graph that uses images or pictures to symbolize data

pie graph: A circular graph divided into wedges that show the distribution of data

pitch: How high or low a voice sounds

plagiarism: Presenting someone else's words or ideas as though they were one's own

prejudice: Preconceived opinions, attitudes, and beliefs about a person, place, or thing

preliminary bibliography: A list of potential resources to be used in the preparation of a speech

preparation outline: A detailed outline that includes main ideas, subpoints, and supporting material and that may also include a speech's specific purpose, introduction, blueprint, internal previews and summaries, transitions, and conclusion

presentation aid: Anything tangible (drawings, charts, graphs, video images, photographs, music) that helps communicate an idea to an audience

presentation speech: A speech that accompanies the presentation of an award

preview: A statement of what is to come

primacy, organization by: Arrangement of the ideas in a speech from the most important to the least important

primary source: The original collector and interpreter of information or data

problem–solution pattern: Organization that focuses on a problem and various solutions or a solution and the problems it would solve

pronunciation: The proper use of sounds to form words clearly and accurately

proposition: A statement with which a speaker wants an audience to agree

proposition of fact: A proposition that focuses on whether something is true or false or whether it did or did not happen

proposition of policy: A proposition that advocates a change in a policy, procedure, or behavior

proposition of value: A proposition that calls for a listener to judge the worth or importance of something

psychological audience analysis: Analyzing the attitudes, beliefs, values, and other psychological information about an audience in order to develop a clear and effective message

public-relations speech: A speech designed to inform the public, to strengthen alliances with them, and in some cases to recommend policy

pun: A verbal device that uses double meanings to create humor

race: A person's biological heritage

reasoning: The process of drawing a conclusion from evidence

receiver: A listener or an audience member

recency, organization by: Arrangement of the ideas in a speech from the least to the most important

red herring fallacy: Irrelevant facts or information used to distract someone from the issue under discussion

reflective thinking: A method of structuring a problem-solving discussion that involves (1) identifying and defining the problem, (2) analyzing the problem, (3) generating possible solutions, (4) selecting the best solution, and (5) testing and implementing the solution

regionalism: A word or phrase used uniquely by speakers in one part of a country

relationship: An ongoing connection you have with another person reluctant testimony: A statement by someone who has reversed his or her position on a given issue

remember: To recall ideas and information

repetition: Use of a key word or phrase more than once for emphasis

respond: To react to a message with behavior

rhetorical criticism: The process of using a method or standards to evaluate the effectiveness and appropriateness of messages

rhetorical question: A question intended to provoke thought rather than elicit an answer

rhetorical strategies: Methods and techniques used by speakers to achieve their goals

sans serif fonts: Typefaces in which the letters do not have serifs (small lines at the tops and bottoms)

script fonts: Typefaces that imitate handwriting

secondary source: An individual, organization, or publication that reports information or data gathered by another entity

select: To single out a message from several competing ones

self-actualization needs: The need to realize one's highest potential

serif fonts: Typefaces in which the letters have small lines (serifs) at the tops and bottoms

sex: A person's biological status as male or female, as reflected in his or her anatomy and reproductive system

signpost: A cue about the relationships between a speaker's ideas

simile: A comparison between two things that uses the word *like* or *as*

situational audience analysis: Examining the time and place of a speech, the audience size, and the speaking occasion in order to develop a clear and effective message

small group communication: Interaction among three to twelve people who share a common purpose, feel a sense of belonging to the group, and influence one another

social judgment theory: A theory that categorizes listener responses to a persuasive message according to the latitude of acceptance, the latitude of rejection, or the latitude of noncommitment

socioeconomic status: A person's perceived importance and influence based on factors such as income, occupation, and educational level

soft evidence: Supporting material based mainly on opinion or inference, including hypothetical illustrations, descriptions, explanations, definitions, analogies, and opinions

source: The public speaker

spatial organization: Arrangement of the ideas in a speech according to location or direction

speaking notes: A brief outline from which a speech is delivered

specific purpose: A concise statement indicating what you want your listeners to know, feel, or be able to do when you finish speaking

speech act: A behavior, such as flag burning, that is viewed by law as nonverbal communication and is subject to the same protections and limitations as verbal speech

speech of introduction: A speech that provides information about another speaker

speech to inform: A speech that teaches others new information, ideas, concepts, principles, or processes in order to enhance their knowledge or understanding about something

spoonerism: A play on words involving the switching of the initial sounds of the words in a phrase

stacks: The collection of books in a library

standard outline form: Numbered and lettered headings and subheadings arranged hierarchically to indicate the relationships among parts of a speech

standard U.S. English: The English taught by schools and used in the media, business, and government in the United States

stationary microphone: A microphone attached to a podium, sitting on a desk, or standing on the floor

statistics: Numerical data that summarize facts or samples

summary: A recap of what has been said

suspension: Withholding a key word or phrase until the end of a sentence

syllogism: A three-part way of developing an argument, using a major premise, a minor premise, and a conclusion

symbols: Words, images, and behaviors that create meaning for someone

target audience: A specific segment of an audience that you most want to influence

terminal credibility: The final impression listeners have of a speaker's credibility after a speech concludes toast: A brief salute to a momentous occasion, usually accompanied by a round of drinks and immediately followed by the raising or clinking together of glasses or goblets

topical organization: Organization of the natural divisions in a central idea on the basis of recency, primacy, complexity, or the speaker's preference

transformational leader: A leader who influences others by building a shared vision of the future, inspiring others to achieve, developing high-quality individual relationships with others, and helping people see how what they do is related to a larger framework or system

transition: A verbal or nonverbal signal that a speaker has finished discussing one idea and is moving to another

trustworthiness: An aspect of a speaker's credibility that reflects whether the speaker is perceived as believable and honest

understand: To assign meaning to the stimuli to which you attend

understatement: A statement downplaying a fact or event

value: An enduring conception of right and wrong, good and bad

verbal irony: A statement that expresses the exact opposite of the intended meaning

vertical search engine: A site that indexes World Wide Web information in a specific field

visual rhetoric: The use of images as an integrated element in the total communication effort that a speaker makes to achieve the speaking goal

volume: The softness or loudness of a speaker's voice

wit: Verbal means of relating an incident or a statement so that it concludes in an unexpected way

word picture: A vivid description that appeals to the senses

working memory theory: Theory stating that when the capacity of listeners' working memory becomes full, they start to have trouble concentrating on and remembering messages

written citation: The written presentation of such information about a source as the author, title, and year of publication, usually formatted according to a conventional style guide

Credits

p. 2: Table 1.1, Copyrighted by Pearson Education, Upper Saddle River, NJ.
p. 4: Figure 1.1, Copyrighted by Pearson Education, Upper Saddle River, NJ.
p. 8: Survey conducted by R. H. Bruskin and Associates, Spectra 9 (December 1973): 4; D. Wallechinsky, Irving Wallace, and Amy Wallace, *The People's Almanac Presents the Book of Lists* (New York: Morrow, 1977). p. 11: quotation, George Jessel. p. 17: Figure 3.1: Copyrighted by Pearson Education, Upper Saddle River, NJ. p. 25: quotation, Franklin D. Roosevelt. p. 27: National Communication Association, "NCA Credo for Communication Ethics," 1999, 27 June 2001 http://www.natcom.org/conferences/Ethics/ ethicsconfcredo99.htm. p. 28: United States Constitution. p. 28: Samuel Walker, *Hate Speech* (Lincoln: University of Nebraska Press, 1994) 162.
p. 29: "Supreme Court Rules: Cyberspace Will Be Free! ACLU Hails Victory in Internet Censorship Challenge," American Civil Liberties Union Freedom Network, 26 June 1997, 1 June 1998 http://https://www.aclu.org/technology-and-liberty/aclu-hails-supreme-court-victory-internet-censorship-challenge.
p. 32: "Bed Bugs." Centers for Disease Control and Prevention, 13 January 2013. Web. 9 June 2013. p. 101: Martin Medhurst, "The Text(ure) of the World in Presidential Rhetoric," *Vital Speeches of the Day* (June 2012). p. 104: Molly A. Lovell, "Hotel Security: The Hidden Crisis," *Winning Orations* 1994 (Mankato, MN: Interstate Oratorical Association, 1994) 18. p. 129: David Crystal, "Speaking of Writing and Writing of Speaking," *Longman Dictionaries: Express Yourself with Confidence!* (Pearson Education, 2005). p. 134: Michael M. Klepper, *I'd Rather Die Than Give a Speech* (New York: Carol Publishing Group, 1994) 45. p. 135: Michiko Kakutani, "Struggling to Find Words for a Horror Beyond Words," *New York Times* 13 Sept. 2001: E1. p. 135: John F. Kennedy, Inaugural Address (20 Jan. 1961), *Speeches in English*, ed. Bower Aly and Lucille F. Aly (New York: Random House, 1968) 272. p. 136: Barack Obama, "Look at the World Through Their Eyes," *Vital Speeches of the Day* (May 2013): 138-42. p. 137: Franklin Roosevelt, Inaugural Address of 1933 (Washington, DC: National Archives and Records Administration, 1988) 13–14. p. 159: Kennedy, inaugural address. p. 192: Marcie Groover, "Learning to Communicate: The Importance of Speech Education in Public Schools," *Winning Orations* 1984 (Mankato, MN: Interstate Oratorical Association, 1984) 7. p. 206: Maslow, Abraham H.; Frager, Robert D.; Fadiman, James, *Motivation and Personality*, 3rd ed., © 1987. Reprinted and electronically reproduced by permission of Pearson Education, Upper Saddle River, New Jersey. p. 235: John C. Meyer, "Humor as a Double-Edged Sword: Four Functions of Humor in Communication," *Communication Theory* 10(3) (August 2000): 311. p. 236: Mark Twain, "The Alphabet and Simplified Spelling," address at the dedication of the New York Engineers' Club, December 9, 1907, Mark Twain's Speeches; with an Introduction by William Dean Howells, Electronic Text Center, University of Virginia Library, 4 June 2004 etext.lib.Virginia.edu. p. 236: Chris O'Keefe, untitled speech, in John K. Boaz and James Brey, eds., *1987 Championship Debates and Speeches* (Speech Communication Association and American Forensic Association, 1987) 99.
p. 237: "Mirren 'Too Busy' to Meet Queen," BBC News 10 May 2007. p. 239: John Dewey, *How We Think* (Boston: Heath, 1910).

Index

CONTENTS

PREFACE

One component common to all educational endeavors is the ability to express ideas, research, and stories in a format that can be understood. Many students have come to realize that this means more than putting lines on a page. In the social sciences, a formal writing format is required. The writing format that has been accepted as the standard in the social sciences is from the American Psychological Association (APA).

Many students dread the inference and imposition of any writing format but eventually understand the need for consistency in formal writing. This guide, which we have written to be "user friendly," is meant to assist students in their writing. We believe that this guide will also be useful to faculty instructing students in the use of the APA format, but we also believe that the guide can stand alone for use by students not enrolled in a research-writing course.

It is our hope that this guide will help ease the worries of correct citations and proper referencing and enable students to focus on the research and writing of excellent papers.

Chalon E. Anderson
Amy Carrell

1

THE BASICS: APA RULES

The APA has determined that manuscripts written using this format should follow specific guidelines. The basic essentials of APA style follow:

- The manuscript should be printed on white bond paper, 8 1/2 by 11 inches. Pages should be printed on only one side of the paper.
- Standard margins are 1 inch on all four sides.
- The manuscript is double-spaced.
- Use 12-point Times New Roman font.
- The pages of the manuscript should appear in the following sequence: title page (including author note), abstract, text pages (introduction, method, results, and discussion), references, footnotes (if applicable), tables and figures (the tables and figures appear on separate pages, one per page; include a double-spaced caption below the figure), and appendices.
- Beginning with the title page, all pages are numbered and should include the running head. The running head, which can be no more than 50 characters, should appear at the top of each page, flush left in all uppercase letters.
- The abstract starts on page 2 of the paper. The word *Abstract* is typed and centered 1 inch from the top of the page. Word limits for abstracts vary by journal but are typically 150 to 250 words.

- The actual text of the manuscript begins on page 3. The title of the manuscript should be centered at the top of the page. All principal words in the title should begin with capital letters.

- Use words to spell out numbers one through nine and Arabic numerals to express numbers starting at 10 and continuing forward.

- When beginning a sentence, spell out the number regardless of the value.

- If two numbers are grouped for comparison, use Arabic numerals regardless of the values of the numbers.

- Use Arabic numerals to express exact measurements.

- The Method, Results, and Discussion headings should be continuous and should not purposely start a new page.

- The references follow the discussion section. The word *References* should be typed in sentence case and centered at the top of the page.

- The first line of each reference is set flush left and subsequent lines are indented five spaces, or 1/2 inch.

- Footnotes, such as content and copyright notes, belong in one of two places: on a separate page following the references, or at the bottom of the manuscript page where the related information is introduced. If included on a page following the references, the title *Footnotes* should be centered at the top of the page in sentence case.

- The tables and figures are placed after the footnotes (or the references if there are no footnotes), and each table and figure appears on a separate page.

- Tables and figures are numbered sequentially but separately; that is, there will be Table 1 and Figure 1.

- All basic formatting rules apply to tables.

- The principle words of table and figure titles—such as nouns, pronouns, verbs, and adjectives—are capitalized. Do not capitalize connecting words and prepositions.

- The appendix follows the tables and figures. The word *Appendix* appears typed in sentence case, centered 1 inch from the top of the page. If there is more than one appendix, use capital letters (beginning with *A*) to identify each appendix (e.g., Appendix A, Appendix B, etc.).
- Begin the text of the appendix flush left, followed by indented paragraphs.
- If figures and tables are included in the appendix, their titles must reflect the fact that they are part of the appendix; use the words *Table* and *Figure* with their numerical correspondence. (e.g., Appendix Table A1). This text should be left justified.

2

WHY DOCUMENT?

When using the words or ideas of someone else, you must give credit to your source. If you fail to identify the source of the words or ideas of someone else, you are plagiarizing. Plagiarism is a form of theft—the plagiarist steals the words or ideas of someone else and claims them for his or her own. To avoid such theft, you have three options: direct quotation, paraphrase, or summary.

Direct Quotation

A direct quotation is reproduced verbatim from an original source and needs to include an in-text citation and a reference in the reference list.

Paraphrase

A paraphrase involves restating someone else's ideas using your own words, your own style, and your own sentence structure. It is approximately the same length as the material that you are paraphrasing.

Summary

A summary involves condensing someone else's ideas using your own words, style, and sentence structure.

3

SECTIONS OF THE APA MANUSCRIPT

A manuscript written in APA style should include the following sections in the following order: title page, abstract, introduction, method, results, discussion, references, footnotes (if applicable), tables, figures, and appendix. The following is a brief description of each section.

Title Page

The title page contains these elements in the following order:

1. *Page number*. The page number appears in the upper right corner of every page in the manuscript.
2. *Running head*. An abbreviation of the title, typed in ALL CAPS and no longer than 50 characters, appears on all pages of the manuscript. The running head is left justified and 1 inch from the top of the page (see section on running heads and headers).
3. *Title of manuscript*. Capitalize the first letter of each of the principal words in the title. Double-space the title if it is two or more lines in length. The title should be aesthetically pleasing in that multiple title lines should be approximately equal in length, and it should be centered on the page.
4. *Full name(s) of the author(s)*. Each author's full name—first, middle, and last—is listed without professional titles or degrees.

The departmental and institutional affiliations of each author should also be included. This information should be centered on the page.

5. *Author note.* The manuscript's author note should appear on the title page below the title and author's name and affiliation. It should be placed under a centered heading labeled *Author Note*. These notes have several functions. Most importantly, author notes identify author affiliation. Author notes also reveal sources of financial support and acknowledge the professional contributions of colleagues. They also provide contact information for those who have further interest in the research.

Abstract

The abstract should start on page 2 of the manuscript. Center the heading *Abstract* in sentence case (no boldface, italics, or underlining) at the top of the page. The abstract is a concise overview of the manuscript, containing the hypothesis/hypotheses and summaries of the method, results, and discussion sections of the manuscript. The abstract is not indented, and should be roughly 150 to 250 words, depending on the journal. All numbers included in the abstract should be in Arabic numerals; written numbers are used only to begin a sentence.

Introduction

Overall, the introduction section of the manuscript sets the stage for the reader. It should present the problem being studied and explain the research strategy used. In a few short pages, it should identify why the problem is important, clearly state the hypothesis/hypotheses, define the variables, and discuss the implications of the study.

The introduction does not receive a label. Instead, the title of the manuscript should be typed and centered at the top of the page, with the actual text beginning after it. The introduction section should start a new page. The method, results, and discussion sections do not start new pages and should immediately follow from the previous section.

Method

The method section of the manuscript should be a detailed account of the actual research being done and should enable other researchers to replicate the study without difficulty. The method section follows the centered heading **Method** (boldfaced, but no italics or underlining). The method section may contain any or all of the following subheadings in sentence case, boldfaced, and left justified: **Participants**, **Materials** (or **Apparatus**), and **Procedure**.

Participants

The participants subsection should include the sample size and pertinent demographic information (e.g., race, sex, age, etc.). Be sure to describe how the participants were recruited or selected for the research, including agreements and payments made. If using nonhuman subjects, include the genus and species or any other specific identification information. Always include a statement reporting that treatment of the participants (whether human or nonhuman) was in accordance with the ethical standards set forth by the APA.

Materials (or Apparatus)

The materials or apparatus subsection includes a brief but detailed description and explanation of the materials (or apparatuses, if any) used in the actual research.

Procedure

Because the purpose of the procedure section is to enable the reader to replicate the study, this section should be a brief but concise step-by-step account of how the research was carried out. All instructions should be summarized in a reasonable fashion. Describe how participants were selected, how variables were manipulated, and so forth.

Results

The results section is the component of the manuscript that provides a summary of the data collected and the analysis and outcome of that data. The results section is prefaced with the heading **Results**, which is bold and centered. The following is what you need to do to complete the results section:

- Summarize the main finding and results of the statistical data.
- In specific research designs (i.e., experimental studies, descriptive studies), be sure that the summary of the data supports the conclusions stated in the paper.
- Include all relevant results, even those that are uncomfortable or were not expected.
- Do not include individual scores from the dependant variable(s) unless, for example, they are associated with a case study. Raw data can be shared via supplemental online archives.
- Indicate the significance or lack of significance regarding the hypothesis.
- Use tables and figures to add clarity to results, and refer to them in the text of the paper.
- Be very specific in the explanations associated with tables and figures.
- In the statistical presentation report, include the following:
    1. Inferential statistics
    2. Value of the inferential test
    3. Degrees of freedom and probability
    4. Direction of the effect
    5. Descriptive data, including measures of variability
    6. Justification of design and use of statistical test
    7. All supportive information for parametric tests, randomized-block layouts, correlational analyses, and/or nonparametric analyses
    8. Pertinent statistical power

9. Statistical significance

10. Effect size

Discussion

The discussion section, which is prefaced by a bold and centered **Discussion** heading, is where you evaluate and interpret your results. The discussion should begin by stating the findings of the research and whether they support the hypotheses. Implications of the findings should be discussed in relation to the hypotheses as well as to previous studies done. Problems, or potential problems, with the research should also be discussed. The discussion section should end with a more general presentation and indicate the direction of future research.

References

The reference section provides documentation of works cited in your manuscript. The word *References* should be centered at the top of a new page. Entries in the reference list are alphabetized and should be typed as a hanging indent (the first line of the reference not indented and each succeeding line indented 1/2 inch or approximately five spaces).

Footnotes

Footnotes should be brief and to the point. All footnotes, such as content and copyright notes, belong in one of two places: on a separate page following the references, where the title *Footnotes* is centered at the top of the page in upper case and lower case, or at the bottom of the manuscript page where the information is introduced.

Tables

When deciding to use a *table*, keep the following in mind:

- All tables must be in electronic format. Be sure to indicate which tables will appear in the article and which will be available in an online supplemental archive.
- Tables can be either single- or double-spaced, with a 12-point font. Table notes should be double-spaced.
- It is best to prepare tables with standard word-processing programs.
- Each row and column of the table should be labeled.
- Headings used for columns are centered at the top of the column.
- If the purpose of the first column of a table is to define variables, then that column is left justified; the columns that follow (those reporting statistics) are right justified.

Figures

When deciding whether to use a figure (i.e., charts, drawings, graphs, tables, etc.), always remember that figures should be used only to illustrate main points made within the manuscript. Also be careful to achieve a reasonable balance between text and graphics in your manuscript.

Here are the basic formatting rules used with figures (i.e., charts, drawings, graphs, etc.):

- As with the tables, all figures must be in electronic format. Be sure to indicate which figures will appear in the article and which will be available in an online supplemental archive.
- Color figures are expensive to reproduce so use these only when color is necessary for proper interpretation of the figure.
- Figures must not "overshoot" the standard 1-inch margin.
- Figure titles should be brief and to the point.

- All figures must be referred to within the text of the manuscript and should be labeled with Arabic numerals in the order in which they are first mentioned in the text.
- Be consistent!

Appendices and Supplemental Materials

Any appendices to the manuscript should be placed after the tables and figures. The word *Appendix* should be centered at the top of the page and should not be followed by letters or numbers except to distinguish between multiple appendices, if any are present. An outline of the materials presented in the appendix is left-justified under the appendix label. The appendix may include figure captions, figures, tables, printed materials used, computer printouts of data, and so forth. This first page is merely a list of what the appendix section contains.

If there is supplemental material that is not easily presented in print—such as lengthy computer code, audio or video files, oversized tables, color figures, etc.—a web-based archive may be made available. Be sure to submit supplemental archives in file formats that are widely accessible, such as ASCII, Word, PDF, HTML, Excel, AVI, MP3, etc.

4

MISCELLANEOUS RULES OF APA FORMAT

Running Head

The running head of a manuscript is a summary of the title of the manuscript. The running head should not exceed 50 characters, including spaces between words. On the title page only, the running head appears as *Running head:* and is followed by the actual abbreviated title in ALL CAPS. On all subsequent pages, the format should simply be the running head itself in ALL CAPS. The running head is located 1 inch from the top of the page (standard margin) and should appear flush left.

Example (Title Page):
Running head: ABBREVIATED TITLE OF ARTICLE

Example (All Other Pages):
ABBREVIATED TITLE OF ARTICLE

Levels of Heading

APA provides formatting styles for five levels of headings, though the number and level of headings will vary based on the length and complexity of your manuscript.

Level 1 Headings
Should Be Centered, Boldface, Uppercase and Lowercase

Level 2 Headings Are Flush Left, Boldface, Uppercase and Lowercase

Level 3 headings are indented, boldface, and lowercase ending with a period.

Level 4 headings are indented, boldface, italicized, and lowercase ending with a period.

Level 5 headings are indented, italicized, and lowercase ending with a period.

Headings for Tables

Column headings in tables identify the information presented in the table. These headings enable the reader to follow the data in an organized manner. Headings should be brief and identify the data that follows. Capitalize the first letter of the first word in each heading.

APA format uses several levels of column headings:

- Level I: Column heads, cover one column

- Level II: Column spanners, cover two or more columns

- Level III: Decked heads, stacking of heading

Example: Level I

Marriage

Example: Level II

Marriage	
First	Second

Example: Level III

Marriages	Marriages
First	Second

5

ABBREVIATIONS FOR APA FORMAT

The primary reason for using abbreviations is to clarify and simplify writing. When deciding to abbreviate, consider the following:

1. Will the abbreviation reduce repetition?
2. Is there a standard abbreviation for the term?
3. Does the abbreviation lend itself to clarity and simplicity?

When choosing to abbreviate terms, remember that overusing abbreviations can confuse the reader and hinder comprehension. In addition, abbreviations used fewer than three times should be omitted from the manuscript, because they may be hard for the reader to remember.

The How's of Abbreviation

The term that is to be abbreviated must first be identified (spelled out) in the text and then be followed by the abbreviation in parentheses. Once the term has been identified, it is then appropriate to use the abbreviation throughout the remainder of the manuscript without any further spelling-out of the term.

> NOTE: Abbreviations cannot start a sentence. Always spell out the term when beginning a sentence.

Some minor rules apply to the use and placement of the period (.) with abbreviations. Use a period with initials representing names, when abbreviating *the United States,* with Latin abbreviations, and with reference abbreviations. However, do not use periods with state abbreviations, capital letter abbreviations, or with measurement abbreviations.

> NOTE: When abbreviating the word *inch,* it is appropriate to use a period to avoid confusing the abbreviation with the preposition *in.*

Figures and Tables

Abbreviations used in figures must be identified in the legend or caption. Abbreviations used in tables must be identified in the title of the table or in a table note.

Forming the Plural

To form the plural of an abbreviation, add *s* without an apostrophe.

> NOTE: Units of measurements are generally not pluralized. To make the abbreviation for *page* plural, however, use *pp.,* not *pgs.*

Useful Latin Abbreviations

cf.	compare	i.e.	that is
e.g.	for example	viz.	namely
etc.	and so forth	vs.	versus, against

6

GRAMMAR & STYLE

Apostrophes

There are two reasons to use apostrophes:

1. To show possession

2. To form contractions

Possession

The English language is very regular about showing possession. In fact, English has no "exceptional" possessives. In other words, we use *'s* or *'* without fail.

- Use *'s* after a **singular noun:**

    John's boat

    the player's fault

    James's garden

    the dog's bowl

    Mary's coat

    her friend's brother

- Use ' after a **plural noun:**

    the cats' dishes (dishes belonging to more than one cat)

    the Smiths' car (a car owned by more than one Smith)

    the students' assignments (the assignments of the students)

- Use *'s* after irregular plurals:

    the men's suits

    the children's toys

    the women's project

Tricky Points of Possession

Although the plural of brother-in-law is **brothers-in-law**, the possessive is **brother-in law's**. The possessive plural is **brothers-in-law's**.

Names that end in -s:

- Mr. Thomas owns a home. That home is **Mr. Thomas's** home.
- Mr. and Mrs. Williams have a home. That home is the Williamses' home. (The tricky point here is that the proper noun needs to be made plural before the possessive is added. Thus, for instance, the plural of Jones is Joneses, and the plural of Douglass is Douglasses. To make them possessive, simply add ', as in the Joneses' vacation or the Douglasses' cabin.)

Another example:

You are addressing party invitations to the Weaver family and the Jones family. What do you write on the envelope?

- The Weavers
- The Joneses

Thus, you will be mailing the **Weavers'** invitation as well as the **Joneses'** invitation. Or you could say that you are mailing the

Weavers' and the **Joneses'** invitations. If, however, someone named Weaver and someone named Jones share a residence and you are mailing only one invitation, then you are mailing the **Weaver and Jones's** invitation (to show possession of the same item by more than one person).

If Pat Jones and Chris Weaver host a party together, it's **Pat and Chris's party,** but if each one has a party, then it's **Pat's and Chris's parties.**

Contractions

Use an apostrophe where you remove letters to show contraction:

do n<u>ot</u>	→	don't	government → gov't	
could <u>have</u>	→	could've (not could of!)	continued → cont'd	
he <u>will</u>	→	he'll	it <u>is</u> → it's*	
can<u>not</u>	→	can't	who <u>is</u> → who's*	

*It's is the contraction of *it is. Its* shows possession, like *my, your,* and *their. Who's* is the contraction of *who is* while *whose* is a possessive form (as in "Whose socks are on the floor?").

Capitalization

Capitalization is a part of English grammar that dictates the appropriate use of proper nouns (i.e., names, places, and things) and adjectives, as well as the beginning of a new sentence. The following explanations acquaint you with the do's and don'ts of capitalization.

- Capitalize the first letter of the first word in a sentence.

    The sessions for the conferences are to be held inside.

- Capitalize the first letter after a colon if it is used to begin a subtitle in a literary citation.

  Student to student: A new form of communication (book title)

  Anderson, C. E. & Whittfield, J. (1999). Psychological terms: A new form of communication *(1st ed.). Boston: Allyn & Bacon. (book reference)*

- Capitalize the first letter of a proper noun that is hyphenated.

  Ellen Cole-Thomas (proper noun)

- Capitalize other hyphenated words only when they begin a sentence.

  Mothers-in-law are helpful in acquiring family histories.

- Capitalize proper nouns and adjectives, including proper names and derivatives of proper names, abbreviations of names, brand names, holidays, historical events, days of the week, months of the year, street names, cities and states, monuments, drug trade names, and geographical locations.

- Capitalize the first letter of titles of dignitaries, political offices, ethnic groups, and religions when used in specific situations to designate specific individuals.

  The President of the United States during World War II was Franklin Roosevelt.

  The Catholic Congress will meet in Kansas City, Mo.

  The members of the new firm are Latinos.

  Dean Edwards from the Department of Medicine at the University of California will be the guest lecturer for new interns at the Blackburn Eye Clinic.

Commas

Use commas to do the following:

- Separate items in a list
- Separate coordinate adjectives
- Join independent clauses with a coordinate conjunction (*and, but, for, or, so, yet, nor*)
- Set off introductory words, phrases, and clauses
- Set off transitional elements and tag questions
- Set off nonessential information
- Separate quoted words from words of introduction or explanation

In addition, commas have specific uses in addresses, dates, names, numbers, and correspondence.

Items in a List

The items can be individual words, phrases, or clauses, but they must be all the same type, or parallel in structure, and there need not always be a conjunction. (When the items in the list already contain commas, use semicolons to separate the items—see the section on semicolons.)

Words

- red, white, and yellow
- green, orange, blue
- slowly, methodically, and deliberately
- quickly, easily, perfectly
- ran, jumped, and slid
- sat, cried, sniffed
- dog, cat, and fish
- Pat, Terry, Chris

Phrases

- Chris went to *the store, the library, and the pool.*
- Marty took many items: *my book, her pencil, Pat's markers.*
- I have looked *on the table, under the bed, and in the den.*
- Pat believes in *thinking quickly, acting spontaneously, and enjoying completely.*
- While you *watch television, chew gum, and fold laundry,* I will prepare dinner.

Clauses

- Because *it's late, the weather is awful, and I am out of gas,* I'm staying home.

Independent Clauses

Use a comma before a coordinate conjunction (*and, but, for, or, so, yet, nor*) to join independent clauses (complete sentences). If one of the clauses is not independent, then do not use a comma with the conjunction.

Tom caught two fish. He ate one for dinner.
- Tom caught two fish, and he ate one for dinner.
- Tom caught two fish and ate one for dinner.

George was hungry. He ate Tom's other fish.
- George was hungry, so he ate Tom's other fish.

The dog chased the ball. It rolled under the chair.
- The dog chased the ball, and it rolled under the chair.

I am tired. I have work to finish.
- I am tired, but I have work to finish.
- I am tired but have work to finish.

She had a headache. She took a nap.

- She had a headache, so she took a nap.

Jane did not like tonight's movie. She also didn't like the one we saw last week.

- Jane did not like tonight's movie, nor did she like the one we saw last week.
- Jane did not like tonight's movie nor the one we saw last week.

Introductory Words, Phrases, and Clauses

Use a comma after introductory elements.

Words

- *However,* he wanted a new gold fish.
- *Consequently,* his parents bought him a fish.
- *Tomorrow,* he will buy a second fish.
- *Obviously,* he loves fish.

Phrases

- *Early in the novel,* the author introduces the main characters.
- *In the first chapter,* we meet Mitzi.
- *Of all my cats,* Mutsy is my favorite.
- *To let me know she's hungry,* she pushes her bowl to me.
- *Sleeping on my feet,* Mutsy always knows when I awaken.

Clauses

- *When the children went to school,* their parents celebrated.
- *While the dog barked,* the rabbit ran away.
- *Because ice covered the streets,* classes were cancelled.
- *As I was telling you,* the store on the corner is having a sale.
- *Although it is raining,* we will still have the picnic.

Semicolons and Colons

There are two reasons to use **semicolons:**

1. To join closely related independent clauses
2. To separate items containing commas in a list

Joining Independent Clauses

Independent clauses (IC) are complete sentences. A comma does not have enough strength to join independent clauses without the help of a coordinate conjunction (*and, or, for, but, so, yet, nor*), but a semicolon wields enough power to accomplish the task. Thus, on either side of a semicolon must be an independent clause: **IC; IC.**

Examples of joined sentences:

John studied many hours for the test. He had the highest score in the class.

- John studied many hours for the test; he had the highest score in the class.
- John studied many hours for the test, and he had the highest score in the class.
- John studied many hours for the test and had the highest score in the class.

The rains came. The river overflowed its bank.

- The rains came; the river overflowed its bank.
- The rains came, and the river overflowed its bank.
- When the rains came, the river overflowed its bank.

Separating Items in a List

Occasionally, items in a list already contain commas, so it becomes confusing to separate those items with more commas. Semicolons replace the commas that would normally be used to separate the listed items.

Example of separating items in a list:

The guest list included Jane Doe, the club president, Fred Smith, the vice president, Pat Jones, the treasurer, and Chris Wilson, the secretary.

While it is intuitively clear that only four people are actually listed, the punctuation identifies seven: (1) Jane Doe, (2) the club president, (3) Fred Smith, (4) the vice president, (5) Pat Jones, (6) the treasurer, and (7) Chris Wilson, the secretary. To cut the guest list almost in half, use semicolons:

The guest list included Jane Doe, club president; Fred Smith, vice president; Pat Jones, treasurer; and Chris Wilson, secretary.

Colons

Colons have some special uses including separating hours and minutes (2:00 p.m.), separating chapter and verse in Bible references (John 3:16), separating titles from subtitles (*Working Wood: A Guide for the Country Carpenter*), and concluding a salutation in a formal letter (Dear Dr. Whozit:). But if a colon is used in a sentence outside its special uses, often to signal a forthcoming list or a restatement of the point made in an independent clause, it must be preceded by an independent clause: **IC: _____.**

Examples of colons:

The guest list included the following people: Jane Doe, club president; Fred Smith, vice president; Pat Jones, treasurer; and Chris Wilson, secretary. (Compare this example with the previous one. In the previous sentence, *The guest list included* is not an independent clause, so there is no colon after *included*, but in this example, *The guest list included the following people* is a complete sentence and thus requires a colon before the list.)

The child stayed awake all night waiting for one person: Santa Claus. (Compare with "The child stayed awake all night waiting for Santa Claus.")

Her backpack contained all the essential items: books, pencils, and scantrons. (Compare with "Her backpack contained books, pencils, and scantrons.")

Moby-Dick begins with the following words: "Call me Ishmael." (Compare with "Moby-Dick begins with 'Call me Ishmael.' ")

Verbs

All actions take place in the past, the present, or the future, and verbs are the words that express the action within a sentence; they change their form to accommodate tense and number. Most verbs typically change from present to past tense by ending the verb in *-ed*. Many words require helping verbs to clarify action (e.g., forms of *to be* and *to have* "help" the main verbs in sentences).

Examples of verbs:

She jumps on the bed. *(present)*

I jumped on the bed to play with the dog. *(past)*

Andraya will jump on the bed when the dog barks. *(future)*

It is best to write in the active, rather than passive, voice.

Helping Verbs
Helping verbs are used to change verb tense. Some helping verbs are forms of *to be* and *to have* as well as *should, could, would, may, might,* and *must*.

Irregular Verbs
These verbs change their spelling when used in the past tense, and helpers are needed to express the correct meaning within a sentence. Here is a list of some irregular verbs.

Present	*Past*	*Past with Helpers*
begin	began	have begun
break	broke	have broken
choose	chose	have chosen
drive	drove	have driven
eat	ate	have eaten
fall	fallen	have fallen
grow	grew	have grown
know	knew	have known
leave	left	have left
lie	lay	have lain

Present	Past	Past with Helpers
lay	laid	have laid
sit	sat	have sat
speak	spoke	have spoken
take	took	have taken
throw	threw	have thrown
write	wrote	have written

Agreement Extras

- Singular subjects are used with singular forms of verbs; plural subjects are used with plural forms of verbs. The verb *to be* is the exception.
- The pronoun *you* is always considered plural.
- The simple past form of an irregular verb should never be used with a helper.
- The past form of a verb with a helper needs a helper to be considered as a verb.
- A verb must agree with its subject, not with a noun or pronoun that comes between the subject and the verb.

7

QUOTATIONS

All material taken directly from any other document must be enclosed in quotation marks. Keep in mind the following:

- Use double quotation marks when quoting material found in text (see Example 1); use single quotation marks if a quote is included in the original quoted material.
- When referring to a quoted document in the text of the manuscript, provide the author's name, date of publication, and page number(s) all in parentheses.
- Include quotations up to 40 words in the text of the manuscript.
- When the passage being quoted is longer than 40 words, create a *block quotation* on a new line by indenting five spaces and typing material double-spaced within this blocked format. Do not use quotation marks. (See Example 2.)
- When omitting anything from quoted material, use three ellipses points. (See Example 3.)
- If quoting from an online source that is not paginated, provide a paragraph number if one is visible or cite the heading and the number of the paragraph. Cite references immediately following the quotation.
- Include all reference sources on the reference page. All quoted material should be accurate.
- It is the author's responsibility to decide if permission is needed to quote another person. Permission is not needed to quote from APA-copyrighted journals, as long as the quotation does not exceed 500 words.

Chapter Seven

Example 1:

The last experiment that included freshmen in a psychology class failed to support the hypotheses. Marvin Thompson responded to questions concerning this study by saying, "often this is expected when a convenient sample is used." (Thompson, 1979, p. 13)

Example 2:

Teall (1971) wrote,

> One of the most important men in the early exploration of Oklahoma never saw Oklahoma himself. The man was Estevanico—sometimes called Estevan or Stephen. Estevanico was a black man, and while much is known about the last years of his life and his death, little is known about his birth or his early years. (p.7)

Example 3:

Carol's new car has a number of options: seat warmers, special headlights, . . . all included in the 2009 model.

8

REFERENCING IN APA FORMAT

Basic rules of referencing:

- APA style requires that references are cited within the text (using author and date) and also listed alphabetically in a double-spaced reference list at the end of the manuscript.
- With electronic journal articles—which now have become the norm—be sure to include as much electronic retrieval information as possible so that others can locate your sources (see discussion of digital object identifiers below).
- Do not indent the first line of a reference entry, because each entry needs to have a hanging indent. Indent the succeeding line(s) 1/2 inch (five spaces).
- Alphabetize references according to the first author's last name. Use the second author's last name to continue alphabetizing only if the first author's name is listed in the reference section more than once. If no author is listed, alphabetize according to the title of whatever is being referenced.
- Use periods after the author's first and middle initials.
- Space one time after each period in the references to conserve space.

Periodical (Journals, Newsletters, Magazines)

```
Last Name, Initial(s) (Year/Date of

    Publication). Title of article is listed

    here. Name of Periodical, volume

    number(issue number), page numbers. doi:

    xx.xxxxxxxxxx
```

Last Name, Initial(s): List all authors of the publication in the order they are listed on the actual publication. Spell out the last name(s) and follow with the first initial (and middle initial if given). In the case of multiple authors, list all authors using the ampersand symbol (&) to separate the next to last and last author's names. This format for authorship applies to all referencing. The exception to this format is authorship without specific individuals, such as no author.

Year/Date of Publication: Type the year in parentheses. Occasionally, a month or season, depending on the publication, will be given. In the latter case, type the year first followed by a comma and then the month or season.

Title: Type the full title of the article. Capitalize only the first word of the title and any proper nouns. If there is a subtitle, conclude the title with a colon (:), and capitalize the first letter of the first word of the subtitle.

Name of Periodical: Italicize the full name of the journal in which the article appeared. Follow the name of the journal with a comma.

Volume Number and Issue Number: Italicize the journal's volume number. If the journal citation does not list an issue number, follow the volume number with a comma. When an issue number is listed, the volume number should be followed immediately with the issue number in parentheses, *not italicized,* followed by a comma.

Page Numbers: Type the page number(s) separated by an en dash (–), concluding with a period.

DOI: Because uniform resource locators (URLs) tend to change, scholarly publishers now assign a **digital object identifier (DOI)** to journal articles and other documents found online. A DOI is a unique string of numbers (and sometimes letters) assigned by a registration agency and provides a permanent link to the content online. Always provide the DOI in references if it is available. If a DOI has not been assigned, give the URL using the following format: Retrieved from http://www.xxxxxxxx. You do not need to include retrieval dates unless you expect the source material to change over time.

Jones, K., & Kessel, R. (2009). Tracing human

existence. *Evolve, 25*(8), 124-128.

doi:12.3456/78910

Entire/Special Section of a Journal

Brown, A. E. (Ed.). (1996). The rules of play

in Special Olympics [Special issue]. *The*

Journal of Sport Psychology, 300(5).

If the issue has no editor(s), the title moves to the first position in the citation.

Magazine Article

References to articles in magazines are similar to periodicals with only one difference. When typing the year/date of publication, include the year, month, and day (if given).

Monograph with Issue (or Whole) Numbers and Serial Number

Gray, B. T. & Watson, K. (2005). Time

 management with couples with dual careers.

 Monograph in the Studies on Careers in the

 New Millennium, 23(Serial No. 50).

The issue (or Whole) number is in parentheses, followed by the serial number.

Monograph Bound into a Journal with Continuous Pagination

Kappa, A. C., & Booker, R. B., Jr. (2000). The

 life and times of women denied education in

 third world countries [Monograph]. *The*

 International Journal on Women's Studies,

 133, 201-220.

Use brackets to identify the literary form.

second language. *Seniors Today, 12,* 81-85.

Abstract obtained from *PsycNet:*

Developmental Psychology, 2000, *4,* Abstract

No. 501.

Secondary sources are often found within a primary source of reference—books, articles, papers, and so forth.

Book

Last Name, Initial(s). (Year of Publication).

   Title of book goes here (edition). Location

   of Publisher: Name of Publisher.

Year of Publication: List the year that the book was published.

Edition: If the book includes an edition, which is usually a number, enclose it in parentheses immediately following the title of the book. Use the abbreviation of *ed.* when listing the edition's number. Do not italicize the information regarding the edition.

Location of Publisher: Type the city and state (or country if outside the United States), followed by a colon (:).

Name of Publisher: Identify the publishing company that published the book, followed by a period.

Mitchell, J. (1982). *The mythos of*

   homosexuality (2nd ed.). London, England:

   Express Publishers.

Electronic Version of Print Book

Last Name, Initial(s). (Year of Publication).

    Title of book goes here (edition) [Include

    information about digital edition here].

    Retrieved from (DOI or URL here)

Electronic retrieval information replaces publisher location and name for online books.

Electronic-Only Book

Last Name, Initial(s). (Year of Publication).

    Title of book goes here (edition).

    Retrieved from (DOI or URL here)

Article or Chapter in an Edited Book

Last Name, Initial(s). (Year of Publication).

    Title of article or book chapter goes here.

    In Initial(s)., Last Name (Eds.), *Title of*

    book (page numbers). Location of Publisher:

    Name of Publisher.

In *Initials.*, *Last Name:* The name(s) of the book's editor(s) are listed with the initial(s) preceding the last name(s).

Page numbers: Preface the page numbers with *pp.* (or with *p.* if information is found on one page).

Bond, V. (1980). The psychology of life:

    Working with blended families. In J. Wynn,

    Jr., M. White, & M. Boat (Eds.), *Family*

    psychology (pp. 27-36). Boston, MA: Brooks.

In case no author or editor is listed, alphabetize (excluding a, an, *and* the*) the entry according to the title of the book, still italicized, in the place where the author's name would be listed.*

When referencing the Diagnostic and Statistical Manual of Mental Disorders, *use the following basic citation reference, filling in the necessary information:*

American Psychiatric Association. (19xx).

    Diagnostic and statistical manual of mental

    disorders (xx ed.). Washington, DC: Author.

Publication Information:

DSM–III	(1980)	3rd ed.
DSM–III – R	(1987)	3rd ed., revised
DSM–IV	(1994)	4th ed.
DSM–IV–TR	(2000)	text revision

Encyclopedia or Dictionary

Arnold, P., & Loftis, E. (1994). Curriculum. In
The world book encyclopedia (Vol. 4, pp.
301-311). New York, NY: World Book
Encyclopedia.

Chandler, J. (1990). *The dictionary of
pediatric medicine* (9th ed., Vol. 5). San
Francisco, CA: Smith.

Technical or Research Report

Crawford, G. P., & Parks, L. C. (2001).
*Variability in delinquent behavior among
incarcerated juveniles* (Diagnostic and
Evaluation Rep. No. 236). Dallas, TX: Conn
Publishing.

*References to technical or research reports follow the same format as
those for general periodicals with only one difference. The report
number (if available) is included in parentheses directly after the title.
If the report was found online, identify the publisher in the retrieval
statement (i.e., "Retrieved from . . . ").*

Report as an Article or Chapter in an Edited Edition

Tolouse, J. Z., Union, B., & Tion, C. A. (2003,

August). Identification of subconscious

thought pattern in infants with fetal

alcohol disorder. In K. R. Whitter & W. M.

Starr (Eds.), *Cognitive factors related to*

infant development (NIH Publication No. 32-

9311, pp. 24-45). New York, NY: U.S.

Department of Child Welfare.

Proceedings Published Regularly

Nichols, M., & Boyd, G. H. (2006). Using

Functional Magnetic Resonance Imaging

(fMRI) to identify soft tissue mass.

Proceedings of the Regional Radiological

Society, 33, 876-890.

The same format is used for meetings, symposiums, and periodicals.
Add DOI at end of citation if proceedings are published online.

Unpublished Contribution to a Symposium

Constantine, P. A. (1998, April). Use of
assessment measures with children with
PTSD. In J. B. Voyce (Chair), *Cognitive
behavioral assessment of children with
anxiety disorders.* Symposium conducted at
the meeting of the American Pediatric
Organization, Los Angeles, CA.

Include the group providing the symposium.

Dissertation or Thesis Abstract
Dissertations and master's theses are referenced in the same format.

Published Doctoral Dissertation or Master's Thesis

Last Name, Initial(s). (Year of Publication).
Title of dissertation (Doctoral
dissertation). *Dissertation/Master's
Abstracts International, volume number*
(issue number if given), page number.

Eden, D. K. (1971). Cost accounting: The

necessary core in accounting (Master's

thesis). *Dissertations Abstracts*

International, 35(X51007), 1981E.

A doctoral dissertation or master's thesis should be identified as such in parentheses after the title of the work. If the dissertation/thesis was retrieved from the web, provide the note "Retrieved from" followed by the URL or DOI to the end of the citation.

Unpublished Doctoral Dissertation or Master's Thesis

Last Name, Initial(s). (Year Written). *Title of*

dissertation/thesis. (Unpublished doctoral

dissertation/master's thesis, Name of

University, City of University, State).

Cunby, D. (1985). *Dentistry and the stress*

placed on children. (Unpublished doctoral

dissertation/master's thesis). University

of California, Davis.

Title of dissertation/thesis: Note that the title, including the concluding period, should be *italicized*.

If the dissertation/thesis was retrieved from the web, provide the note "Retrieved from" followed by the URL or DOI at the end of the citation.

Review of Book/Film/Video

Last Name, Initial(s). (Year of Publication).

Title of review [Review of the

book/film/video *Title of Book/Film/Video*].

Name of Journal, volume number(issue

number), page numbers.

Ravencroft, A. (2001). NRMs in children's

cartoons [Review of the film *The Witch of

Riverbend*, 2001]. *Journal of Children's

Media, 1*(2), 4-6.

Title of Review: If a title is not given for the actual review, use the information inside the brackets as the title.

If the review was retrieved from the web, provide the DOI or URL at the end of the citation.

Unpublished Paper Presented at a Meeting

Last Name, Initial(s). (Year of Meeting,
Month). *Title of unpublished paper.* Paper
presented at the meeting of Title of
Meeting, City, State.

Title of Meeting: Insert the title of the meeting.

Bowmen, E. (2001, May). *Stress and daily
hassles.* Paper presented at the meeting of
the Association for International Medicine,
Chicago, IL.

Poster Session

Last Name, Initial(s). (Year of session,
Month). *Title of poster.* Poster session
presented at the annual meeting of the Name
of Organization Sponsoring Session, City,
State.

Name of Organization Sponsoring Session: Insert the name of the organization that sponsored the poster session.

Carlos, N. A. (1999, September). *Diversity in the U.S.* Poster session presented at the regional meeting of the Multicultural Society of America, Denver, CO.

Unpublished Manuscript Not Submitted for Publication

Last Name, Initial(s). (Year manuscript was written). *Title of unpublished manuscript.* Unpublished manuscript.

Griggs, Z., & Johnson, V. (1994). *Senior adults: Pedagogical strategies for teaching computer technology.* Unpublished manuscript.

Internet Message Boards and Online Communities

Message Posted to a Newsgroup, Online Forum, Discussion Group, or Electronic Mailing List

Last Name, Initial(s). (Date of Post). Re:

discussion thread name here [Online forum

comment OR Electronic mailing list

message]. Retrieved from URL here

Blog Post

Author Name (could be a nickname or screen

name). (Date of Post). Title of post here

[Web log post]. Retrieved from URL here

Audiovisual Media

Motion Picture

Producer, A. A. (Producer), & Director, B. B.

(Director). (Year). *Title of motion picture*

[Motion picture]. Country of Origin:

Studio.

Television Series

```
Last Name, Initial(s). (Producer). (Year of
    Broadcast). Title of television series
    [Television series]. City, State of
    Distributor: Name of Broadcasting Company.
```

Alphabetize the entry by the last name of the producer.

```
Shelton, W. (Producer). (1997). City in focus
    [Television series]. Los Angeles, CA:
    American Broadcasting Company.
```

Single Episode from a Television Series

```
Whipple, D. R. (Writer), & Mudscone, T. B.
    (Director). (2000). He's going down
    [Television series episode]. In J. J.
    Walker (Producer), Living on the inside.
    Polka, Nebraska: Quads Broadcasting.
```

Music Recording

Livingston, J. C. (2000). Life is but a dream

[Recorded by J. T. Cuervo]. On *My highway*

[Cassette]. Nashville, TN: Freedom Records.

(2002)

The name of the writer is listed with the last name first (e.g. Livingston, J. C.), while the name of the recording artist is listed with the first and middle initials preceding the last name (e.g. J. T. Cuervo). Be sure to identify the medium type on which the recording was done, such as CD, cassette, etc.

Podcast

Name (Producer). (Date of broadcast). *Title*

[Audio podcast]. Retrieved from URL here

9

EXAMPLE APA MANUSCRIPT

To view a sample research paper in APA style, visit http://www.apastyle.org and type "sample paper" into the search box, or type the following direct link into your browser: http://www.apastyle.org/manual/related/sample-experiment-paper-1.pdf

BIBLIOGRAPHY

Anderson, C. E., Carrell, A. T., and Widdifield, J. L., Jr. (2004). *APA and MLA writing formats*. Boston, MA: Pearson Education, Inc.

American Psychological Association. (2010). *Publication manual of the American Psychological Association* (6th ed.). Washington, DC: Author.

American Psychological Association. (2001). *Publication manual of the American Psychological Association* (5th ed.). Washington, DC: Author.

American Psychological Association. (1994). *Publication manual of the American Psychological Association* (4th ed.). Washington, DC: Author.

Blumenthal, J. C., Zahner, L., Frank, R., & Lazarus, A. (1966). *The English language*. New York, NY: Harcourt, Brace.

Gibaldi, J. (1999). *MLA handbook for writers of research papers* (5th ed.). New York, NY: MLA.

Hodges, J. C., and Whitten, M. E. (1967). *Harbrace college handbook*. New York, NY: Harcourt, Brace.

Teall, K. M. (1971). *Black history in Oklahoma: A resource book*. Oklahoma City, OK: Oklahoma City Public School Title III, ESEA.